THE CLAY SANSKRIT LIBRARY

FOUNDED BY JOHN & JENNIFER CLAY

EDITED BY

RICHARD GOMBRICH

WWW.CLAYSANSKRITLIBRARY.ORG
WWW.NYUPRESS.ORG

Artwork by Robert Beer.
Cover design by Isabelle Onians.
Layout & typesetting by Somadeva Vasudeva.
Printed and Bound in Great Britain by
TJ International, Cornwall on acid free paper

MUCH ADO ABOUT RELIGION

BY BHAṬṬA JAYANTA

EDITED AND TRANSLATED BY

CSABA DEZSŐ

NEW YORK UNIVERSITY PRESS
JJC FOUNDATION
2005

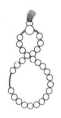

First Edition 2005

The Clay Sanskrit Library is co-published by
New York University Press
and the JJC Foundation.

Further information about this volume
and the rest of the Clay Sanskrit Library
is available on the following websites:
www.claysanskritlibrary.org
www.nyupress.org

ISBN 978-0-8147-1979-4

Library of Congress Cataloging-in-Publication Data
Jayanta Bhaṭṭa, fl. 850–910.
Āgamaḍambara. English
Much ado about religion / by Jayanta Bhatta;
edited and translated by Csaba Dezső.
p. cm. – (The Clay Sanskrit Library)
Translated from Sanskrit.
Includes bibliographical references and index.
ISBN 978-0-8147-1979-4
1. Sanskrit drama. 2. Nyāya–Drama.
I. Dezső, Csaba. II. Title. III. Series.
PK3794.J3472A713 2005
891'.22–dc22 2004026265

CONTENTS

A *sandhi* grid is printed on the inside of the back cover

SANSKRIT ALPHABETICAL ORDER

Vowels:	*a ā i ī u ū ṛ ṝ ḷ ḹ e ai o au ṃ ḥ*
Gutturals:	*k kh g gh ṅ*
Palatals:	*c ch j jh ñ*
Retroflex:	*ṭ ṭh ḍ ḍh ṇ*
Labials:	*p ph b bh m*
Semivowels:	*y r l v*
Spirants:	*ś ṣ s h*

GUIDE TO SANSKRIT PRONUNCIATION

a — b*u*t
ā, â — r*a*ther
i — s*i*t
ī, î — f*ee*
u — p*u*t
ū, û — b*oo*
ṛ — vocalic *r*, American p*ur*dy or English p*re*tty
ṝ — lengthened *ṛ*
ḷ — vocalic *l*, ab*le*
e, ê, ē — m*a*de, esp. in Welsh pronunciation
ai — b*i*te
o, ô, ō — r*o*pe, esp. Welsh pronunciation; Italian s*o*lo
au — s*ou*nd
ṃ — *anusvāra* nasalizes the preceding vowel
ḥ — *visarga*, a voiceless aspiration (resembling English *h*), or like Scottish lo*ch*, or an aspiration with a faint echoing of the preceding vowel so that *taiḥ* is pronounced *taih*^{i}

k — lu*ck*
kh — blo*ckh*ead
g — *g*o
gh — bi*gh*ead
ṅ — a*n*ger
c — *ch*ill
ch — mat*chh*ead
j — *j*og
jh — aspirated *j*, he*dgeh*og
ñ — ca*n*yon
ṭ — retroflex *t*, *t*ry (with the tip of tongue turned up to touch the hard palate)
ṭh — same as the preceding but aspirated
ḍ — retroflex *d* (with the tip of tongue turned up to touch the hard palate)
ḍh — same as the preceding but aspirated
ṇ — retroflex *n* (with the tip of tongue turned up to touch the hard palate)
t — French *t*out
th — ten*t h*ook

d	*d*inner
dh	guil*dh*all
n	*n*ow
p	*p*ill
ph	u*ph*eaval
b	*b*efore
bh	a*bh*orrent
m	*m*ind
y	*y*es
r	trilled, resembling the Italian pronunciation of *r*
l	*l*inger
v	*w*ord
ś	*sh*ore
ṣ	retroflex *sh* (with the tip of the tongue turned up to touch the hard palate)
s	hi*ss*
h	*h*ood

CSL PUNCTUATION OF ENGLISH

The acute accent on Sanskrit words when they occur outside of the Sanskrit text itself, marks stress, e.g. Ramáyana. It is not part of traditional Sanskrit orthography, transliteration or transcription, but we supply it here to guide readers in the pronunciation of these unfamiliar words. Since no Sanskrit word is accented on the last syllable it is not necessary to accent disyllables, e.g. Rama.

The second CSL innovation designed to assist the reader in the pronunciation of lengthy unfamiliar words is to insert an unobtrusive middle dot between semantic word breaks in compound names (provided the word break does not fall on a vowel resulting from the fusion of two vowels), e.g. Maha·bhárata, but Ramáyana (not Rama·áyana). Our dot echoes the punctuating middle dot (·) found in the oldest surviving samples of written Sanskrit, the Ashokan inscriptions of the third century BCE.

The deep layering of Sanskrit narrative has also dictated that we use quotation marks only to announce the beginning and end of every direct speech, and not at the beginning of every paragraph.

CSL PUNCTUATION OF SANSKRIT

The Sanskrit text is also punctuated, in accordance with the punctuation of the English translation. In mid-verse, the punctuation will not alter the *sandhi* or the scansion. Proper names are capitalized, as are the initial words of verses (or paragraphs in prose texts). Most Sanskrit metres have four "feet" *(pāda):* where possible we print the common *śloka* metre on two lines. The capitalization of verse beginnings makes it easy for the reader to recognize longer metres where it is necessary to print the four metrical feet over four or eight lines. In the Sanskrit text, we use French *Guillemets* (e.g. *«kva saṃcicīrṣuḥ?»*) instead of English quotation marks (e.g. "Where are you off to?") to avoid confusion with the apostrophes used for vowel elision in *sandhi*.

Sanskrit presents the learner with a challenge: *sandhi* ("euphonic combination"). *Sandhi* means that when two words are joined in connected speech or writing (which in Sanskrit reflects speech), the last letter (or even letters) of the first word often changes; compare the way we pronounce "the" in "the beginning" and "the end."

In Sanskrit the first letter of the second word may also change; and if both the last letter of the first word and the first letter of the second are vowels, they may fuse. This has a parallel in English: a nasal consonant is inserted between two vowels that would otherwise coalesce: "a pear" and "an apple." Sanskrit vowel fusion may produce ambiguity. The chart at the back of each book gives the full *sandhi* system.

Fortunately it is not necessary to know these changes in order to start reading Sanskrit. For that, what is important is to know the form of the second word without *sandhi* (pre-*sandhi*), so that it can be recognized or looked up in a dictionary. Therefore we are printing Sanskrit with a system of punctuation that will indicate, unambiguously, the original form of the second word, i.e., the form without *sandhi*. Such *sandhi* mostly concerns the fusion of two vowels.

In Sanskrit, vowels may be short or long and are written differently accordingly. We follow the general convention that a vowel with no mark above it is short. Other books mark a long vowel either with a bar called a macron (*ā*) or with a circumflex (*â*). Our system uses the macron, except that for initial vowels in *sandhi* we use a circumflex to indicate that originally the vowel was short, or the shorter of two possibilities (*e* rather than *ai*, *o* rather than *au*).

When we print initial *â*, before *sandhi* that vowel was	*a*
î or *ê*,	*i*
û or *ô*,	*u*
âi,	*e*

âu,	*o*
ā,	*ā* (i.e., the same)
ī,	*ī* (i.e., the same)
ū,	*ū* (i.e., the same)
ē,	*ī*
ō,	*ū*
āi,	*ai*
āu,	*au*

’, before *sandhi* there was a vowel *a*

FURTHER HELP WITH VOWEL SANDHI

When a final short vowel (*a*, *i* or *u*) has merged into a following vowel, we print ’ at the end of the word, and when a final long vowel (*ā*, *ī* or *ū*) has merged into a following vowel we print ” at the end of the word. The vast majority of these cases will concern a final *a* or *ā*.

Examples:

What before *sandhi* was *atra asti* is represented as *atr’ âsti*

atra āste	*atr’ āste*
kanyā asti	*kany” âsti*
kanyā āste	*kany” āste*
atra iti	*atr’ êti*
kanyā iti	*kany” êti*
kanyā īpsitā	*kany” ēpsitā*

Finally, three other points concerning the initial letter of the second word:

(1) A word that before *sandhi* begins with *ṛ* (vowel), after *sandhi* begins with *r* followed by a consonant: *yatha” rtu* represents pre-*sandhi* *yathā ṛtu*.

(2) When before *sandhi* the previous word ends in *t* and the following word begins with *ś*, after *sandhi* the last letter of the previous word is *c* and the following word begins with *ch*: *syāc chāstravit* represents pre-*sandhi* *syāt śāstravit*.

(3) Where a word begins with *h* and the previous word ends with a double consonant, this is our simplified spelling to show the pre-*sandhi*

form: *tad hasati* is commonly written as *tad dhasati*, but we write *tadd hasati* so that the original initial letter is obvious.

COMPOUNDS

We also punctuate the division of compounds (*samāsa*), simply by inserting a thin vertical line between words. There are words where the decision whether to regard them as compounds is arbitrary. Our principle has been to try to guide readers to the correct dictionary entries.

EXAMPLE

Where the Deva·nágari script reads:

कुम्भस्थली रक्षतु वो विकीर्णसिन्दूररेणुर्द्विरदाननस्य।
प्रशान्तये विघ्नतमश्छटानां निष्ठ्यूतबालातपपल्लवेव॥

Others would print:

kumbhasthalī rakṣatu vo vikīrṇasindūrareṇur dviradānanasya /
praśāntaye vighnatamaśchaṭānāṃ niṣṭhyūtabālātapapallaveva //

We print:

Kumbha|sthalī rakṣatu vo vikīrṇa|sindūra|reṇur dvirad'|ānanasya
praśāntaye vighna|tamaś|chaṭānāṃ niṣṭhyūta|bāl'|ātapa|pallav" êva.

And in English:

"May Ganésha's domed forehead protect you! Streaked with vermilion dust, it seems to be emitting the spreading rays of the rising sun to pacify the teeming darkness of obstructions."

"Nava·sáhasanka and the Serpent Princess" I.3 by Padma·gupta

DRAMA

Classical Sanskrit literature is in fact itself bilingual, notably in drama. There women and characters of low rank speak one of several Prakrit dialects, an "unrefined" *(prākṛta)* vernacular as opposed to the "refined" *(saṃskṛta)* language. Editors commonly provide such speeches with a Sanskrit paraphrase, their "shadow" *(chāyā)*. We mark Prakrit speeches with ⌜opening and closing⌟ corner brackets, and supply the Sanskrit *chāyā* in endnotes. Some stage directions are original to the author but we follow the custom that sometimes editors supplement these; we print them in italics (and within brackets, in mid-text).

WORDPLAY

Classical Sanskrit literature can abound in puns *(śleṣa)*. Such paronomasia, or wordplay, is raised to a high art; rarely is it a *cliché*. Multiple meanings merge *(śliṣyanti)* into a single word or phrase. Most common are pairs of meanings, but as many as ten separate meanings are attested. To mark the parallel senses in the English, as well as the punning original in the Sanskrit, we use a *slanted* font (different from *italic*) and a triple colon *(:)* to separate the alternatives. E.g.

> Yuktaṃ Kādambarīṃ śrutvā kavayo maunam āśritāḥ
> *Bāṇa|dhvanāv* an|adhyāyo bhavat' îti smṛtir yataḥ.
>
> It is right that poets should fall silent upon hearing the Kádambari, for the sacred law rules that recitation must be suspended when *the sound of an arrow : the poetry of Bana* is heard.
>
> Soméshvara·deva's "Moonlight of Glory" I.15

INTRODUCTION

"MUCH ADO ABOUT RELIGION" *(Āgama|ḍambara)* is a unique satirical college-drama, in which Bhatta Jayánta presents the contemporary affairs of various religious schools and their relation to the politics of the ruling sovereign of Kashmir, King Shánkara·varman (883–902CE).

Although several details of Bhatta Jayánta's life are lost to us, his personality takes a more distinct shape than that of many classical Indian poets and philosophers. His son Ábhinanda[1] has left us a short genealogy, from which it appears that Jayánta's ancestors were Bengali brahmins who traced their descent back to the sage Bharad·vaja. One of them settled in a territory at the frontiers of Kashmir. His grandson, Shakti·svamin became the minister of King Lalitáditya-Muktápida, of the Kárkota dynasty (c. 724–761CE).[2] This information makes it probable that Jayánta was in his fifties or sixties at the end of the ninth century.[3]

Thus it appears that Jayánta was born into a wealthy and respected orthodox brahmin family. He soon turned out to be a child genius: at a tender age he composed a commentary to Pánini's grammar and earned the name "(New) Commentator" *(Nava-) Vṛttikāra*.[4] Later he made himself master of various doctrines (*śāstras*) and religious scriptures (*āgamas*),[5] distinguished himself in scholarly debates[6] and passed on his knowledge to a circle of students. Jayánta's play was staged by the circle of his students.

Jayánta seems to have written three works on Nyaya philosophy, which emphasizes logic. Two of them are extant:

his magnum opus, the *Nyāya/mañjarī* ("A Cluster of Flowers of the Nyáya-tree"), and the *Nyāya/kalikā* ("A Bud of the Nyáya-tree"). From the opening and closing benedictory verses of the *Nyāya/mañjarī* we can presume that Jayánta was a devotee of Shiva, while the fact that he thinks very highly of the *Atharva/veda*[7] might indicate, as Raghavan pointed out, "that Jayánta belonged to the Atharvaveda."[8]

Only one truly literary work of Jayánta is extant: the *Āgama/ḍambara*, a play in four acts. Since a verse that is quoted in the play (Act Four, verse 53) as Jayánta's wise saying (*sūktam*) is also found in the *Nyāya/mañjarī* (vol. I, p. 640), it seems probable that Jayánta wrote the *Āgama/ḍambara* following his major work on Nyaya.[9]

The *Āgama/ḍambara* provides valuable details about Jayánta's political career. We learn that he was an adviser of the Kashmirian king Shánkara·varman (883–902), and played a great part in banishing the heterodox sect of the "Black-Blankets" (*nīl'/âmbaras*) from Kashmir.[10] The sad fate of the Black-Blankets is also mentioned in the *Nyāya/mañjarī*:[11]

> "Some rakes, as we are told, invented this Black Blanket Observance, in which men and women wrapped together in a single black veil make various movements. King Shánkara·varman, who was conversant with the true nature of Dharma, suppressed this practice, because he knew that it was unprecedented, but he did not suppress the religions of Jains and others in the same way."

Kálhana does not give a favorable account of the king whom Jayánta served as adviser,

> "Poets and kings of these modern times augment their own work by plundering the poems or the property of others. Thus this ruler, who possessed but little character, had whatever was of value at Paribása·pura (the town built by Lalitáditya), carried off in order to raise the fame of his own city."[12]

Later King Shánkara·varman came more and more under the sway of avarice and became a "master in exploiting his people."[13] Since his campaigns had probably emptied the treasury, the king introduced fines, taxes and systematic forced labor, and established two new revenue offices.[14] He also deprived the temples of the profits they had from the sale of various articles of worship; simply "plundered," as Kálhana puts it, sixty-four temples through special "supervising" officers;[15] resumed under direct state management villages held as land grants by the temples; and, by manipulating the weight in the scales, cheated the temple-corporations, reducing the allotment assigned as compensation for the villages.[16]

The villages gradually sank into poverty under the fiscal oppression, while clerks, secretaries and tax collectors ruled.[17]

Unlike his father, Avánti·varman, who showered honors and fortunes on scholars and poets,[18] Shánkara·varman was not a liberal patron of the arts: as Kálhana says, it was because of him that the learned were not respected.[19] The king was so afraid of spending money that he turned his back on the worthy, and as a result such eminent poets as Bhállata had to live in penury. Shánkara·varman himself, giving proof of his boorishness, refused to speak Sanskrit, and used Apabhrámsha instead, a language fit for drunkards, in Kálhana's estimation.[20]

As we shall see, Jayánta gives a more favorable account of King Shánkara·varman. On the basis of the information gathered from his play and Kálhana's *Rāja/taraṅgiṇī* we can sketch the portrait of a king who kept tight central control over both fiscal and religious matters in Kashmir, and preferred his subjects to be dutiful and conformist. He certainly disliked the squandering of money, and a nobleman who organized lavish dinners for mendicants instead of offering his wealth and services to the king could surely expect the confiscation of his property.[21]

In a verse in the *Nyāya/mañjarī*, Jayánta gives curious details about the circumstances under which he wrote his magnum opus:[22]

> "I had been transferred by the king to this forest, a wordless place of confinement. I have spent the years here in the pastime of writing a book."

Chakra·dhara, the commentator of the *Nyāya/mañjarī*, supplements this rather enigmatic verse with the following information:[23]

> "The report runs that he spent a long time by His Majesty King Shánkara·varman's order in the forest, somewhere in Khasa-land in Kashmir."

As Wezler has pointed out,[24] it is unlikely that Jayánta wrote the *Nyāya/mañjarī* as a political prisoner like Gandhi or Nehru. Since Shánkara·varman led his campaign through territories lying to the southwest from Kashmir, it seems possible that Jayánta was sent to this hill region of the

Khashas, not very far from his homeland, with some kind of political commission. The word "confinement," suggests that this may not have been a promotion; but it was not a lifelong exile either, since he seems to have returned to the circle of his students as their professor.

A Champion of Orthodoxy

Sankárshana, the leading character of Jayánta's play, is a young and dynamic follower of the orthodox school of Mimámsa, who has just finished his Vedic studies and so become a "graduate" *(snātaka)*. His ardor knows no bounds: he is eager to find someone who dares to be an "enemy of the Veda", in order to batter him flat with the ram of reasoning.[25]

The *raison d'être* of Nyaya, as delineated by Jayánta in the *Nyāya/mañjarī*, appears to be remarkably similar to the graduate's mission. According to Jayánta, the primary task of Nyaya is to protect the authority of the Veda.[26] However, as Kataoka has pointed out,[27] this mission does not tally with the statements of older Nyaya-scholars.

The rigor with which Jayánta separates Veda-protecting Nyaya from heterodox schools of reasoning contrasts with the works of some earlier Nyaya-scholars, who appear to have composed commentaries on heterodox materialistic (*Cārvāka*) works as well.[28] Jayánta, far from making excursions into the field of heterodox doctrines, takes a strong line against "depraved logicians" and their destructive speculations.[29]

Considering all this, it may seem surprising that the leading character of Jayánta's play, the crusader of Vedic orthodoxy, is not a representative of the Nyaya school but a follower of Mimámsa. In the first act, Sankárshana systematically refutes in front of distinguished and "unbiased" umpires[30] the Buddhist monk's arguments about "universal momentariness" and "consciousness as the only reality". Thus he scores his first victory against the depraved logicians who try to undermine Vedic order,[31] and exhorts the Buddhists to stop deceiving themselves and others with the promise of a better afterlife for those who follow the Buddha's doctrine.

In the second act, the Mimámsaka lets another heterodox teacher, a Jain monk, slip, not considering him a significant threat to the established socio-religious order.[32] The debauched behavior of the Black-Blankets, however, requires instant measures, as do the shady practices of the Shaiva adepts.

Problems start to emerge for our hero in the third act of the play, when he has to refine the circle of those sects whose presence in the kingdom is unwanted. In fact, the Mimámsaka is ready to form an alliance with the Shaiva professor (representing the moderate doctrine of Shaiva Siddhánta) against the irreligious Charváka materialist. The Mimámsaka and the Shaiva professor defeat their Charváka opponent with an exemplary division of labor.

The moral is that, notwithstanding a few doctrinal differences, Mimámsakas and Saiddhántika Shaivas should join forces to defeat the irreligious and thereby prevent the king from ruling in an inordinately materialistic way.

The Prelude preceding the final act makes it clear that Sankárshana has lost the trust of Vedic brahmins. He is in a great dilemma: either he should enter into a debate and prove the falsity of the teachings of the Váishnava Bhágavatas, a religion supported by the queen and another member of the court, just as he did in the case of heretics, or he should defend them, in which case he would completely lose face before the followers of Vedic orthodoxy (*Váidikas*). Sankárshana cannot resolve the tension between his devotion to Vishnu and his duty as a Mimámsaka to reject all non-Vedic scriptures. It is the great Nyaya-scholar, Dhairya·rashi, who smoothes all differences away as the arbitrator appointed by the court in the debate between Váishnavas and Váidikas. Sankárshana's is happy to lend his tacit support.

Dhairya·rashi's mission is not to enter into a controversy or to defeat anybody in debate; on the contrary, he comes to pour oil on troubled waters. Accordingly he delivers a long lecture instead of discussing things, and his overwhelming authority gives even more weight to his words.

He proves to be "one who upholds the validity of all religious scriptures". For him the criterion of validity is not so much the veracity of a proposition in a given scripture but, rather, the degree of its recognition and its inherent possibilities for overthrowing the social order. This probably fitted the broader "Religionspolitik" of the king.

The right person to decide on such delicate issues as "which conduct is wicked enough to be suppressed" and "what are the criteria of this wickedness" is the king himself, and those in his service who enforce his orders. Sankárshana's position in these questions, like his career and livelihood as a married householder, depends on the will of his superiors.

A Note on the Edition and the Translation

The text printed has been based on two medieval Indian manuscripts[33] and the *editio princeps* of V. Raghavan and A. Thakur, two eminent Sanskrit scholars.[34]

I have made numerous emendations. My critical apparatus will be found on the page dedicated to this work on our website, www.claysanskritlibrary.org; so will a fuller version of this introduction, and more detailed notes to my translation.

Acknowledgements

In preparing a critical edition of the play, I owe a debt of gratitude first and foremost to Professor Alexis Sanderson[35] and Dr. Harunaga Isaacson, and I would also like to express my thanks to Dr. James Benson, Dr. Dominic Goodall, Dr. Kei Kataoka, Dr. Somadeva Vasudeva, Dr. Alex Watson, Dr. Judit Törzsök, Dr. Ryugen Tanemura, Dr. Peter Bisschop, Mr. Lance Cousins, Dr. H. N. Bhatt, and scholars and students in various reading groups from Oxford and Hamburg to Philadelphia and Tokyo.

Translating Much Ado About Religion has proved to be a demanding enterprise. On the one hand, the translator is supposed to transmit (at least to a certain extent) the literary qualities of the play, including Jayánta's sense of humor and satire. On the other hand, the reader expects a clear interpretation of the complicated arguments of the philosophical debates. I could only try to produce a readable (and hopefully enjoyable) translation, and to formulate even the more demanding arguments in a lucid way.

NOTES

1 *Kādambarī/kathā/sāra*, pp. 1f, vv. 5–12.

2 On the chronology of the *Kārkoṭa* dynasty see RT(S), vol. I, pp. 66ff. Kálhana does not mention *Śaktisvāmin*. He does, however, mention a minister of Lalitáditya called Mitra·sharman (*Rāja/taraṅgiṇī* 4.137f.).

3 Cf. HACKER 1951, pp. 110ff.

4 See *Āgama/ḍambara*, Prologue, and Act Four, verse 52; also *Kādambarī/kathā/sāra*, verse 11, and *Nyāya/mañjarī*, vol. II, p. 718.

5 See *Kādambarī/kathā/sāra*, verse 11, *Āgama/ḍambara*, Act Two, and Act Four, verse 52.

6 See *Nyāya/mañjarī*, vol. II, p. 718.

7 Cf. *Nyāya/mañjarī*, vol. I, p. 5. Jayánta spares no pains to prove the Veda-status of the *Atharva/veda*, and he even asserts that it is actually the foremost of all the four Vedas (*Nyāya/mañjarī*, vol. II, p. 626).

8 RAGHAVAN and THAKUR, p. iii.

9 Actually, there are many more parallel passages in the two texts (without the indication of the source in the play).

10 See Act Two, Act Three.

11 *Nyāya/mañjarī*, vol. I, p. 649:
Asit'/âika/paṭa/nivīt'/âviyuta*/strī/puṃsa/vihita/bahu/ceṣṭam*
nīl'/âmbara/vratam idaṃ kila kalpitam āsīd viṭaiḥ kaiś cit.
Tad apūrvam iti viditvā nivārayām āsa dharma/tattva/jñaḥ
rājā Śaṅkara/varmā, na punar Jain'/ādi/matam evam.
(**Asitaika*° em. ISAACSON: *amitaika*° ed;
*∪ *âviyuta*∩ *Pāṭhāntaras* and *Śodhanas*, at the end of vol. II.:
°*āniyata*° *ed.* ("unrestrained").)

12 *Rāja/taraṅgiṇī* 5.160–161, tr. Stein in RT(S), vol. I, p. 207.

13 *prajā/pīḍana/paṇḍitaḥ*, *Rāja/taraṅgiṇī* 5.165.

14 *ibid.* 5.167ff.

15 *ibid.* 5.168–169.

16 *ibid.* 5.170–170. See also Stein's notes in RT(S), vol. I, pp. 208f.

17 *ibid.* 5.175ff.

18 *ibid.* 5.33f. Kálhana mentions Mukta·kana, Shiva·svamin (the author of the *Kapphin'/âbhyudaya*), Ánanda·várdhana (the author of the *Dhvany/āloka*), and Ratnákara (who composed the *Hara/vijaya*) as members of Avánti·varmans assembly (*sabhā*).

19 *ibid.* 5.179.

20 *ibid.* 5.204–6.

21 Cf. *Āgama/ḍambara*, Act Two. Shánkara·varman's policy in religious matters was revived by *Yaśaskara* (939–948), who restored order in Kashmir after the chaotic reigns of various debauched kings following the death of Shánkara·varman. *Yaśaskara*, himself a brahmin and elected as king by an assembly of brahmins, was a champion of orthodoxy, and, similar to Shánkara·varman, he was not favorably disposed toward antidharmic religious practices (cf. *Rāja/taraṅgiṇī* 6.108ff).

22 *Nyāya/mañjarī*, vol. II, p. 199: *Rājñā tu gahvare 'sminn aśabdake bandhane vinihito 'ham, grantha/racanā/vinodād iha hi mayā vāsarā gamitāḥ.*

23 *Granthi/bhaṅga*, p. 167: *Kaśmīre kva cit Khasa/deśe cira/kālam aṭavyām asau* śrī/Śaṅkara/varmaṇo rājña ājñayā sthitavān iti vārtā.* (**aṭavyām asau* conj., or possibly *āraṇye 'sau* : *āraṇyā-[nyā]m asau* ed.)

24 Wezler 1976, p. 344.

25 See *Āgama/ḍambara*, Act One, verse 11.

26 Cf. *Nyāya/mañjarī*, vol. I, p. 7.

27 Kataoka, pp. 5ff.

28 Cf. Steinkellner 1961, pp. 153ff.

29 *Nyāya/mañjarī*, vol. I, p. 7.

30 One of them is called *Viśvarūpa*, whose name might echo that of a commentator of the *Nyāya/bhāṣya* (cf. Steinkellner 1961, p. 158; Wezler 1975, pp. 139ff.)

31 The *Bhikṣu* whom the *Mīmāṃsaka* defeats is called Dharmóttara, just as one of Dharma·kirti's most prominent followers, who, according to the *Rāja/taraṅgiṇī* (4.498), settled in Kashmir. His arguments are similar to those of Dharma·kirti on the one hand, and to the views of *vijñāna/vāda* as presented by Kumárila on the other. The *Mīmāṃsaka* in his refutation (just as *Jayánta* in the *Nyāya/mañjarī*) draws upon Kumárila's *Śloka/vārtika*.

32 As Jayánta reports, King Shánkara·varman also gave quarter to the Jains (*Nyāya/mañjarī*, vol. 649). On the other hand, the Jain theory of "many-sidedness" (*anekānta/vāda*) is not far removed from certain ideas expounded by *Kumārila* (cf. Uno).

33 *Pā:* Pāṭan, Hemacandrācārya Jaina Jñānamandira ms 17472, paper, Jaina Nāgarī; *Pu:* Pune, Bhandarkar Oriental Research Institute, MS 437 of 1892–95, Paper, Jaina Nāgarī.

34 *Āgamaḍambara, otherwise called Ṣaṇmatanāṭaka of Jayanta Bhaṭṭa*, edited by Dr. V. Raghavan and Prof. Anantalal Thakur, Mithila Research Institute, Darbhanga, 1964. This edition was based on the same manuscript material (mss Pā and Pu) that was available for myself.

35 The English translation of the title of Jayánta's play does credit to his ingenuity.

DRAMATIS PERSONÆ

In order of appearance:

Sūtradhāraḥ:	Stage Director
Pāripārśvakaḥ:	his Assistant
Bhikṣuḥ:	Buddhist Monk, called Dharmóttara
Upāsakaḥ:	his Disciple
Saṅkarṣaṇaḥ, snātakaḥ:	Mimámsaka Graduate, later King Shánkara·varman's functionary
Baṭuḥ:	Boy, the Graduate's pupil
Prāśnikāḥ:	Arbiters
Ceṭaḥ:	Dogsbody
Kṣapaṇakaḥ:	Jain Mendicant
Kṣapaṇikā:	Jain Nun
Bhikṣuḥ:	Jain Monk, called Jina·rákshita
Śiṣyāḥ:	his Disciples
Tāpasaḥ:	Jain Ascetic
Nīlāṃbarāḥ:	Black-Blankets (a goup of antinomian ascetics)
Prathamaḥ sādhakaḥ:	First Shaiva Adept, called Kankála·ketu (Skeleton-Banner)
Dvitīyaḥ sādhakaḥ:	Second Shaiva Adept, called Shmashána·bhuti (Crematory-Ash)
Puruṣaḥ:	Manservant
Bhaṭṭārakaḥ:	Saiddhántika Shaiva Abbot, called Dharma·shiva
Tāpasāḥ:	Shaiva Ascetics
Vṛddhāmbhiḥ:	Materialist (*Cārvāka*) philosopher
Śiṣyāḥ:	his Pupils
Ṛtvik:	Vedic Officiant
Upādhyāyaḥ:	Vedic Instructor
Mañjīraḥ:	King's functionary
Dhairyarāśiḥ:	alias Bhatta Sáhata, an eminent philosopher of the Nyáya school
Vādinaḥ:	Disputants

PROLOGUE: DISILLUSION

Tad Brahma vaḥ krama|vinaśyad|anādy|avidyam
uddyotatāṃ sphurad|amanda|nav'|âbhinandam
saṃvit|pade 'vataraṇ'|ônmukha eva yatra
śāmyanti kānta|viṣay'|ântara|bhoga|vāñchāḥ.

Nāndy|ante sūtra|dhāraḥ:

Aho aho naṭatvaṃ nāma jaghanyaḥ ko 'pi satat'|âbhyasta|s'|ûtkaṭa|kapaṭa|vyāpāra|ḍambaraḥ kuṭumba|bharaṇ'|ôpāyaḥ!

Haro Viṣṇur Brahmā munir avanipaḥ pāmara|paśur
viṭo bhīruḥ śūraḥ pramudita|matir duḥkhita iti:
spṛśan sarv'|ākārān viharati jane nistrapatayā
naṭo vastu|sthityā jaṭhara|bharaṇe śilpa|śaraṇaḥ.

1.5 Tad varam imaṃ kuśilpam alpa|phalam alaghu|kleśam atitrapā|karam upasaṃhṛtya kva cid āśrame kim api guru|kulam upāsīnaḥ sakala|duḥkh'|ôparamaṃ paramaṃ puruṣ'|ârtham abhigantuṃ yatiṣye. *(vimṛśya)* tat kv' êmaṃ kṛpaṇakaṃ kṛpā|pātra|prāyaṃ kuṭumba|bharam arpayitvā gamyatām? *(agrato 'valokya)* bhavatu, amuṣya tāvad āśayaṃ vijñāsye.

Praviśya pāripārśvakaḥ, sūtra|dhāram *avalokya:*

Kim ayam adya nirveda|parimlāna|vadana iva dṛśyate? pṛcchāmy enam. *(upasṛtya)* bhāva, kim idaṃ viṣaṇṇa|vadanam āsyate? nanu kva cana viniyukto 'si Vṛtti|kāra|śiṣyaiḥ?

MAY BRAHMAN, THE GRADUAL DESTROYER of beginningless ignorance, in which intense, fresh joy coruscates, and at the very start of whose "descent" to the level of consciousness desires for the enjoyment of other pleasing objects cease, shine forth for you.

At the end of the benediction the DIRECTOR *says:*

Shame, for shame! An actor's is truly an extremely vile livelihood, a ceaseless tumult of utter deception.

Shiva, Vishnu, Brahma, a sage, a king, a brutish fool, a rake, a coward, a hero, a happy man, a sad one: the actor assumes all roles, feeling no shame before the people—in reality he is just resorting to craft to fill his belly.

Better, then, that I should wind up this vile craft, which 1.5
bears small fruit but causes great trouble and yet more shame, attach myself to the household of a guru in some ashram, and strive to reach the highest goal of man: the cessation of all sufferings. *(reflecting)* So to whom should I consign this wretched burden of my family, a mere object of pity, before I leave? *(looking ahead)* Well, let me first find out what he thinks.

Enters the ASSISTANT, *looks at the* DIRECTOR, *and says:*

Why does his face seem haggard with disillusion today? I'll ask him. *(approaching)* Sir, why so sorrowful a face? Surely you haven't been engaged by the pupils of that Writer of the Commentary for some task?

SŪTRA° *Pūrvoktaṃ yatiṣya ity|antaṃ paṭhati.*

PĀRI°: Alam asthāne nirvedena. ko nu khalu deveṣu manuṣyeṣu tiryakṣu vā kapaṭa|caryām uttīrya param'|ârthe paryavasitaḥ? sarva ev' âyaṃ Brahm'|ādis tiryak|paryanto jantu|grāmaḥ saṃsāre māyay" âiva parivartate. bhavataḥ kim adhikaṃ jātam?

1.10 Māyā|viḍambyamānasya viśvasya jagato yathā
vyavahāro na saty'|ârthas tath" âsmākaṃ bhaviṣyati.

SŪTRA°: Māriṣa, yath" āha bhavān. kiṃ tv ayam īdṛśo 'py aśakya|nirvāha āsmākīno vyavahāraḥ.

PĀRI°: Bhāva, katham iva?

SŪTRA°: Māriṣa, Bharata|munin" ôpadiṣṭe daśa|rūpaka|prayoge kila kṛta|śramā vayam? adya c' âtrabhavataḥ śaiśava eva vyākaraṇa|vivaraṇa|karaṇād Vṛtti|kāra iti prathit'|âpara|nāmno Bhaṭṭa|Jayantasya śiṣya|pariṣad" âham ājñaptaḥ, yath" âsmad|guroḥ kṛtir abhinavam Āgama|ḍambaraṃ nāma kim api rūpakaṃ prayoktavyam iti. tad idam alaukikam aśāstrīyam aprayukta|pūrvaṃ kathaṃ prayuñjmahe? tad asyāḥ ku|jīvikāyā upekṣaṇam eva śreyaḥ.

The DIRECTOR *repeats what he said above up to "sufferings."*

ASSISTANT: Don't be disillusioned, there's no need. Who among gods, humans or animals has ever escaped from deceit and then reached the supreme goal? This whole multitude of creatures, from god Brahma down to the animals, revolves in worldly existence through illusion alone. Is your lot any worse?

> Our conduct cannot be different from that of the whole world that is fooled by illusion: ultimately unreal. 1.10

DIRECTOR: My friend, as you say. But even though our conduct is no worse than theirs, still I find it impossible to carry on with it.

ASSISTANT: Why, sir?

DIRECTOR: My friend, have I not exerted myself in the staging of the ten dramatic styles as taught by sage Bhárata? Yet now comes the honorable Bhatta Jayánta, also well known as the Writer of the Commentary because he wrote an exegetical work on grammar when he was just a child. His circle of pupils has ordered me to put on a new work of their teacher, an extraordinary play called *Much Ado About Religion*. So how shall I stage it, since it is neither worldly nor does it follow the dramatic rules, and has never before been performed? Therefore it is better for me just to give up this wretched livelihood.

PĀRI°: Bhāva, m" âivam. anatikramaṇīya|śāsanāḥ khalv atra|bhavanto Vṛtti|kārasya śiṣyāḥ. yat punar aśāstrīyam iti śaṅkase, tatra kaḥ prayoktur aparādhaḥ?

1.15 Kāvyaṃ karoti sa kavir Bharat'|ôpadeśam
ullaṅghya, tasya ca tathā prathayanti śiṣyāḥ,
sāmājikās tava ta eva: bhavān prayuṅktām.
pārśva|sthitaḥ parivadiṣyati kiṃ jano 'nyaḥ?

SŪTRA°: Kṛtaṃ jan'|âpavādena.

PĀRI°: Tat kiṃ rāja|bhayam āśaṅkase?

SŪTRA°: *(sasmitam)* Tad api n' âsti.

PĀRI°: Tat kiṃ vilambase? nanu niyujyantāṃ tāsu tāsu Saugat'|Ārhat'|ādi|bhūmikāsu kuśīlavāḥ.

1.20 SŪTRA°: Māriṣa, na śaknomy eva durvaham idam udvoḍhum indra|jāla|māyā|prāyaṃ naṭa|vṛttam.

Aśāstrakaṃ v" âstu tad|anvitaṃ vā
kāvyaṃ, janaḥ kupyatu rajyatāṃ vā,
ahaṃ tu nirviṇṇa|manāḥ svavṛttim
utsṛjya tīrthāni cinomi tāvat.

Bhavān punaḥ kṛpaṇakam asmat|kuṭumbakaṃ vā saṃvāhayatu, mām eva v" ânugacchatu.

ASSISTANT: Sir, say not so. Surely there is no point putting up a fight against the commands of these honorable pupils of the Writer of the Commentary. As for your worry that it does not follow the rules, is this the fault of the director?

> This poet composes a poem paying no heed to the 1.15
> teachings of Bhárata, and despite this his pupils propagate it, and what's more they are also your audience. So just put it on. Why would someone else, a bystander, bother to find fault with it?

DIRECTOR: I'm not bothered about people's abuse.

ASSISTANT: So are you afraid of some threat from the king?

DIRECTOR: *(smiling)* It's not that, either.

ASSISTANT: Then why procrastinate? Assign the actors their various parts—the Buddhist, the Jain and so forth.

DIRECTOR: My friend, I simply cannot carry on with this 1.20
intolerable thespian career, so full of trickery and illusion.

> Let the poem flout the rules or obey them, let people be angry or pleased—as for me, I am weary of it all: I shall quit my career now and make pilgrimage to the sacred places.

As for you, either please support my indigent family or follow me.

Mayā tv idānīm ev' âsmin mahati vihāre vīta|rāga|bhikṣu|śata|parigṛhīte n'|âtidūre nirvāṇa|mārga|deśini tattva|bubhutsunā praveṣṭavyam.

Iti niṣkrāntau.

1.25 *Prastāvanā.*

I myself am eager to know the truth. I will enter this great monastery nearby, where hundreds of monks, who have transcended passion, live, and which shows the path to final release.

Exeunt ambo.
End of the prologue. 1.25

PRELUDE TO ACT ONE: THE BUDDHA'S TEACHING

*(Tataḥ praviśati āsana|sthaḥ rakta|paṭa|saṃvītaḥ śākya|*BHIKṢUR UPĀSAKAŚ *c' âgrataḥ.)*

BHIKṢUḤ: *(savairāgyam)*

Anādau saṃsāre sthitam idam aho mūḍha|manasāṃ
janitvā jantūnāṃ maraṇam atha mṛtv" âpi jananam.
iyaṃ sā duḥkhānāṃ saraṇir iti saṃcintya kṛtinā
nidhātavyaṃ ceto janana|maraṇ'|ôcchedini pade.

UPĀ°: ⌜Bho bhadaṃta, kiṃ khu edaṃ jaṇaṇa|maraṇa|vavahāra|bāhiraṃ ṭhāṇaṃ? keṇa vā uvāeṇa edaṃ pāvīyadi?⌟

1.30 BHIKṢUḤ: Dhīman, yadi śuśrūṣur asi tad iha catur|ārya|satya|parijñāne yatnam ādhehi.

UPĀ°: ⌜Bho bhadaṃta, kāïṃ uṇa tāïṃ cattāri ayya|saccāïṃ?⌟

BHIKṢUḤ: Dhīman, duḥkhaṃ samudayo nirodho mārga iti catvāry ārya|satyāni.

UPĀ°: ⌜Bho bhadaṃta, ittiya|metteṇa ṇa me pavoho uppaṇṇo. savittharena uvadisadu bhavaṃ.⌟

BHIKṢUḤ: Āyuṣman, bodhyase.

1.35 Sva|saṃvedyaṃ tāvat
sukha|visadṛśaṃ duḥkham akhilaṃ;
yatas tasy' ôdbhūtiḥ
sa tu samudayo moha|mahimā;
nirodho nirvāṇaṃ
sakala|paritāpa|vyuparama;
upāyas tat|prāptau
kuśala|matibhir mārga uditaḥ.

(Then enter the Buddhist MONK, *seated on a stool and dressed in a red robe, and his lay* DISCIPLE *in front of him.)**

MONK: *(with dispassion)*

> In this beginningless existence this is the way things are, alas: deluded creatures are born and then die, and dying they are born again. A wise man, seeing that this is the path of sorrow, should direct his thoughts toward the state in which birth and death come to a close.

DISCIPLE: O Reverend, what is this place which is outside the transactions of birth and death? And by what means is it reached?

MONK: My intelligent friend, if you are eager to learn, then 1.30
strive to comprehend now the Four Noble Truths.

DISCIPLE: O Reverend, what are those Four Noble Truths?

MONK: My intelligent friend, Suffering, the Cause of Suffering, the Cessation of Suffering, and the Path: these are the Four Noble Truths.

DISCIPLE: O Reverend, that much isn't enough to enlighten me. Please teach me the details.

MONK: Sir, I'll make you understand.

> *Pro primo*, everything is Suffering, personally expe- 1.35
> rienced as contrary to happiness. That from which it arises is the Cause, the power of delusion. Cessation is Nirvana, the end of all afflictions. The Path is taught by the right-thinking to be the means to attain Nirvana.

UPĀ°: ⌜Bho bhadaṃta, keṇa dāṇi uvāeṇa appā ṇaṃ dīhara|pabaṃdha|paüttaṃ mottūṇa duttaraṃ dukkha|gahaṇaṃ ṇivvāṇe ṇivasadi?⌟

BHIKṢUḤ: Sādho, na sādhu budhyase. na khalu ātmā nāma kaś cid yo duḥkha|saṅkaṭam uttīrya nirvāṇam adhigacchati. nanu,

Saṃsāra|kār"|âgārasya
dāruṇ'|āyāsa|kāriṇaḥ
ayam eva dṛḍhaḥ stambho
yaḥ sthir'|ātma|graho nṛṇām.

Tathā hi:

1.40 Ayam aham iti paśyato hi jantor
bhavati mam' êdam iti dhruvaṃ pratītiḥ.
aham iti ca mam' êti c' âvagacchan
na hi vijahāti jaḍ'|āśayaḥ kutṛṣṇām.

Avipralupta|tṛṣṇasya dūre vairāgya|bhāvanā,
anabhyaste ca vairāgye saṃsāra|taraṇaṃ kutaḥ?

UPĀ°: ⌜Bho bhadaṃta, jadā dāva ṇatthi yyeva ko vi appā, ko dāṇi saṃsāra|dukkhaṃ aṇubhavadi? ko vā edaṃ uttaria ṇivvāṇ'|âgāraaṃ paḍivajjadi?⌟

BHIKṢUḤ: *(sasmitam)* Vatsa, nirodho nirvāṇam apavargaḥ samāptir iti nitye 'pi sati ātmani sutarām aghaṭamānam. na hi nityasya nirodha upapadyate. tasmād vijñāna|mātram ev' êdaṃ harṣa|viṣād'|ādy|aneka|rūpa|rūṣitam anādi|prabandha|pravṛtta|vicitra|vāsan"|ânusāra|samāsādita|

DISCIPLE: O Reverend, by what means does the Self leave behind these deep waters of suffering, which have been flowing continuously for a long time and are difficult to cross, to then settle in Nirvana?

MONK: Good fellow, you don't really get it. In fact, there is no such thing as a Self to escape the straits of suffering and arrive at Nirvana. Surely,

> This alone is the firm pillar propping up the jailhouse of existence, where cruel torment is suffered —one's obsession with a permanent Self.*

To explain:

> A creature who believes "this is me" will inevitably 1.40
> be convinced that "this is mine"; and, thinking in terms of "me" and "mine," the dull-minded will surely not give up his harmful desires.
>
> For someone whose craving has not ceased, the cultivation of dispassion is remote; and how could one cross over the ocean of existence without cultivating dispassion?

DISCIPLE: O Reverend, if there is in fact no permanent self, then who experiences the suffering of existence? Or who rises out of it and arrives at the house of Nirvana?

MONK: *(smiling)* My child, cessation, Nirvana, final beatitude or completion would be all the more impossible if there were a permanent self. For what is permanent cannot possibly cease. Therefore this world is just consciousness contaminated by the various forms of joy, sorrow, etc., having a broad variety of aspects in accordance with

vitat'|ākāra|bhedam amunā nairātmy'|ādi|bhāvanā|mārgeṇa vyapanīta|vividh'|ôpādhi|paṭal'|ôpahita|nān"|ākāra|kāluṣyam amala|saṃvin|mātra|niṣṭham avatiṣṭhatāṃ vā santān'|ātmanā, santatir eva vā vicchidyatām ity ayam eva nirvāṇa|mārgo nedīyān.

UPĀ°: ⌜Bho bhadaṃta, jadi ṇatthi thiro appā, paraloe kassa kamma|bhoo? iṇhiṃ pi kassa sumaraṇa|ṇibaṃdhaṇā hoṃti vavahārā?⌟

1.45 BHIKṢUḤ: Kuśalaṃ bodhyase.

Artha|kriyā|sādhanatāṃ na nityāḥ
 kram'|âkramābhyām upayānti bhāvāḥ.
n' ârtha|kriyāṃ kāṃ cid asādhayanto
 bhavanti c' âite param'|ârtha|santaḥ.

Evaṃ hi vadanti nīti|vidaḥ—«yad ev' ârtha|kriyā|kāri tad eva param'|ârtha|sat» iti. api ca,

N' âyaṃ kumbho naśvar'|ātma" ânyathā vā
 hetor nāśaṃ mudgar'|āder upaiti.
vyartho vā syād akṣamo vā sa hetuḥ,
 kalpe 'py asy' ânāgamād vā na naśyet.

Ten' ātma|lābha|samanantaram eva bhāvā
 naśyanti, bhānti tu tathā sama|santatitvāt.
santāna|vṛttim avalambya ca kartṛ|bhoktṛ|-
 smṛty|ādi|kārya|ghaṭan" âpi na duḥ|samarthā.

the various latent impressions that have been operating in a beginningless continuum. When this path of the cultivation of there being no self, etc., has grounded this in pure consciousness alone, having removed its many kinds of defilements caused by the mass of various adventitious properties, then let it remain in a stream, or let the stream itself be cut off: this is indeed the fast track to Nirvana.

DISCIPLE: O Reverend, if there is no permanent self, who enjoys the fruit of his actions in the next world? And in the present, too, whose are these activities which are memory-based?*

MONK: I'll skillfully make you understand. 1.45

> Permanent entities cannot have causal efficacy either gradually or instantaneously; and since they cannot have efficacy, they are not ultimately real.*

For so say the wise: "Only that which has causal efficacy can be ultimately real."* Furthermore:

> This pot,* whether perishable by nature or not, cannot be destroyed by a hammer or other cause. Such a cause would be either useless or incapable;* or because this cause might not occur for an aeon, the pot might not perish.

> Therefore entities perish as soon as they come into existence, but they appear real because they are in the same continuum.* Also, because they exist in a continuum, it is easy to account for the fabrication of effects, such as a stable agent who is also the

1.50 UPĀ°: ⌈Jadi saalo khaṇa|bhaṃguro bhāva|sattho, ṇatthi yyeva edassa biie khaṇe avatthidī, tā kahaṃ eso viṇṇāṇeṇa visaī|kāduṃ pārīadi? attho khu viṇṇāṇeṇa saha aṇu vā teṇa pakāsijjade, viṇṇāṇaṃ vā jaṇeṃto vi ṇo ṇiaṃtaṇaṃ āāraṃ vā appatteṇa teṇa visaī|karīadi. aṇṇahā edaṃ paccakkhaṃ khaṇa|bhāïṇo dullahaṃ.⌋

BHIKṢUḤ: Āyuṣman, yadi sphuṭaṃ paśyasi tad artho 'pi nāma na kaś cid vijñānasya yo viṣaya|bhāvam upayāti. jñānam ev' êdaṃ nīla|pīt'|ādy|ākāra|khacitam avabhāti. kutaḥ?

Ākāra|dvitay'|āśritaṃ na yugapaj
jñān'|ârthayor vedanaṃ
loke, 'rthaś ca jaḍaḥ prakāśa|vapuṣā
jñānena ced gṛhyate,
syād ādau grahaṇaṃ pradīpavad, anākāraṃ ca no gṛhyate
jñānaṃ. tena tad eva bhāti vividh'|ākāraṃ. kuto 'rtho 'paraḥ?

Tasmāt sarvaṃ śūnyaṃ
sarvaṃ kṣaṇikaṃ nirātmakaṃ sarvam
sarvaṃ duḥkham it' îtthaṃ
dhyāyan nirvāṇam āpnoti.

enjoyer of the fruits of the deeds of that agent, and memory, etc.

DISCIPLE: If all entities are momentary, i.e., do not remain 1.50
for a second moment, then how can consciousness make them its object? It is quite clear that an object must be revealed either together with consciousness or afterward, and by it. Or, even if it produces cognition, it cannot be made its object without that cognition being confined or taking on some form. Otherwise we cannot account for the perception of something momentary.*

MONK: Sir, if you see clearly then there isn't really such a thing as an entity to become the object of consciousness. It is consciousness itself that appears, inlaid with blue, yellow and other forms. If you ask why?

> People do not have a simultaneous, biform perception of the cognition and its object. And if the object, which is devoid of consciousness, is grasped by intrinsically radiant cognition, then grasping would be grasped first, just as the light of a lamp is perceived first. But a cognition without a form cannot be grasped. Therefore this cognition itself shines with various forms. How could there be any other objective entity?

> Therefore everything is empty, everything is momentary, everything lacks an enduring essence, everything is suffering. Meditating in this way one reaches Nirvana.

Nepathye gaṇḍikā|dhvaniḥ

1.55 UPĀ°: *(śrutvā)* ⌜Bho bhadaṃta, eso khu saala|bhikkhu|saṃgha|saṃghaḍaṇa|velā|pisuṇo gaṃḍi|saddo samucchalio, tā ettha bhavaṃ pamāṇaṃ!⌟

BHIKṢUḤ: Yady evaṃ tad yathā velā n' âtikrāmati tathā samācarāmaḥ. *(utthāya parikramya diśo 'valokya)* eṣa khalu mṛṇāla|tantu|dhavala|yajñ'|ôpavīta|lāñchita|śyāma|vakṣaḥ|sthalo veṇu|yaṣṭi|hastaḥ ko 'pi brāhmaṇa|yuvā ito 'bhivartate. tad yāvad eṣa na velā|vighnam utpādayet tāvad yathā|prāptam anutiṣṭhāmaḥ.

UPĀ°: ⌜Bho bhadaṃta, ko vi a kālo edassa bamhaṇa|juvāṇassa iha ṭṭhidassa vaṭṭadi. jassiṃ yyeva khaṇe imassiṃ rukkha|mūle bhadaṃto uvaviṭṭho tassiṃ yyeva khaṇe eso iha paviṭṭho bhadaṃteṇa ṇa lakkhido. ladā|jāl'|aṃtarideṇa ediṇā sayalo yyeva āyaṇṇido bhadaṃta|vaṇṇido uvaeso.⌟

BHIKṢUḤ: Yady evaṃ tataḥ kiṃ tathā|vidhen' âiva vayam idānīṃ velāṃ laṅghayāmaḥ?

Iti sah' ôpāsakena niṣkrāntaḥ

A wooden gong sounds offstage.

DISCIPLE: *(listening)* O Reverend, that must be the wooden gong that marks the time for the whole community of monks to come together. So it is for your Reverend to decide what we ought to do! 1.55

MONK: In that case let's make sure we are not late.* *(They stand up, walk about and look around.)* Here comes a young brahmin, his dark chest marked by a sacred thread white as a lotus fiber, and with a bamboo staff in his hand. Let us take appropriate action lest he should make us miss the appointed time.

DISCIPLE: O Reverend, this young brahmin has been standing here for quite a long time. He came here at the very moment you sat down under this tree, though Your Reverend did not notice him. Hidden by the net of vines, he overheard the whole teaching Your Reverend gave.

MONK: Be that as it may, why should I be late now on account of a person like this?

Exits together with the DISCIPLE.

ACT ONE: THE BUDDHISTS DEFEATED

1.60 *Tataḥ praviśati yathā|nirdiṣṭaḥ* SNĀTAKO BAṬUŚ *ca.*

SNĀTA°:

> Sv'|âdhyāyaḥ paṭhito yathā|vidhi, parā-
> mṛṣṭāni c' âṅgāni ṣaṇ,
> mīmāṃs" âpi nirūpit" êti vihitaṃ
> karma dvi|janm'|ôcitam.
> nity'|ādhūta|kutarka|dhūsara|girāṃ
> yāvat tu Veda|dviṣāṃ
> nyakkāro na kṛtaḥ kṛtārtha iva me
> tāvan na vidyā|śramaḥ.

Agryāś c' âite Veda|viplava|kṛtāṃ ku|buddhayaḥ Śauddhodani|śiṣyakāḥ. tad enān eva stenān iva tāvan nigṛhṇīmaḥ. *(parikrāmati.)*

BAṬUḤ: ⌜Ayya, uvaṇīdaṃ mae edaṃ ṇhāṇ'|ôvaaraṇaṃ. ṇhāduṃ patthido ayyo.⌟

1.65 SNĀTA°: Kiṃ c' âtaḥ?

BAṬUḤ: ⌜Ṇa khu aṇuūlaṃ uvaciṭṭhadi. vihāra|gāmī khu esa magga|jaṇo sayalo saṃcaradi.⌟

SNĀTA°: Nanv atra vihāre bhikṣūn avalokya tataḥ snāsyāmaḥ.

BAṬUḤ: ⌜Jaṃ ayyo āṇavedi.⌟

Ubhau parikrāmataḥ.

Then enters the GRADUATE *as described above, and the* BOY. 1.60

GRADUATE:

> I have duly studied the Veda, mastered the six auxiliary sciences,* and examined *Mīmāṃsā** as well. Thus I have performed the duties appropriate for a twice-born person. But until I humiliate the enemies of the Veda, who dirty their speech with incessantly brandished pernicious argumentation, the efforts I made in my studies will seem frustrated.*

And these stupid disciples of Shuddhódana's son* are foremost among those who vandalize the Veda. Thus they will be the first for me to punish like thieves. *(He walks about.)*

BOY: Sir, I have brought along the bathing paraphernalia. You were going to bathe, sir.

GRADUATE: So what? 1.65

BOY: The circumstances are clearly not favorable.* All these people on the road must be going to the monastery.

GRADUATE: Then let's take a look at the monks in this monastery first, and bathe afterward.

BOY: As you command, sir.

Both walk about.

1.70 SNĀTA°: *(agrato 'valokya)* Aho vihārasya rāmaṇīyakam! iha hi

Prāsādāḥ śaśi|raśmi|śubhra|himavad|
śṛṅga|pratisparddhinaḥ,
snigdhāny āmra|vaṇāni, śādvala|citā
hṛdyā latā|maṇḍapāḥ,
unmīlad|bisa|kanda|dantura|śarad|
vyom'|ânukār'|ôdakāḥ
padminyo viharat|saro|ruha|rajo|
rakt'|âṅga|bhṛṅg'|âṅganāḥ.

Padminīṃ nirvarṇayan

Adhaḥ|śākhair ūrdhva|
sthita|vitata|mūlaiḥ kamalinī|
jalaṃ dhatte lakṣmīṃ
pulina|taru|ṣaṇḍaiḥ pratimitaiḥ.
ih' ântar dṛśyante
viṭapa|viniviṣṭāḥ kṣiti|ruhāṃ
vihaṅgāḥ khādantaḥ
phala|śakalam uttāna|vadanāḥ.

BAṬUḤ: ⌜Ayya, pekkha eyāṇaṃ maüa|pavaṇ'|aṃdolia|vicitta|dhaya|vaḍa|maṃḍia|meru|gaṃḍiā|ṇivvisesa|pāsād'|abbhaṃtara|viṇivesidāṇaṃ kaṇaa|maïāṇaṃ pajjharaṃta|ṇiraṃtara|pahā|vitthāraga|suṃdara|vaṇṇ'|ābharaṇa|bhūsiāṇaṃ Buddha|paḍimāṇaṃ caṃdaṇa|ghaṇasāra|ghusiṇa|maaṇāhi|vilevaṇa|kusuma|dhūv'|ôvahāra|sāmiddhī. aho acchariaṃ!⌟

1.75 SNĀTA°: *(nirvarṇya)* Na khalu tapasvi|jana|maṭhikā|sthānam idam, rāj'|ôdyānam etat. kaṣṭaṃ bhoḥ kaṣṭam!

GRADUATE: *(looking ahead)* O what a charming monastery!* 1.70
For here

> There are temple-towers rivalling Himalayan peaks gleaming with moonbeams; dense mango groves; delightful vine bowers full of grass; and female bees, their bodies reddened with lotus pollen, are roaming above the lotus ponds, whose water bristles with emerging lotus shoots, and imitates the autumn sky.

He looks at the lotus pond.

> The water of the lotus pond is beautiful with the groups of trees on the bank reflected branches downward and their extensive roots upward. Here on the water I can see birds sitting on the tree boughs, eating pieces of fruit with open beaks.

BOY: Sir, behold the abundance of offerings: flowers, incense, and anointments of sandal, camphor, saffron and musk, offered to golden Buddha-images radiating dense, great effulgence, nicely colored and adorned with decoration. These images are housed within high temples similar to Mount Meru and decorated with colorful flags trembling in the gentle breeze. How wonderful!

GRADUATE: *(looking)* Clearly this is not a seminary for as- 1.75
cetics, this is a royal garden! *O tempora o mores!*

Viṭa|pathika|luṇṭhyamānair
vandhye pathi jāta|gahana|diṅ|mohaiḥ
asthāne kṣipyante
vividhāni dhanāni dhanavadbhiḥ.

Kil' âpramāṇe 'py asminn āgame viṣaya|sukha|parāṅmukha|manasāṃ samādhi|bhāvan"|âbhyāsa|saktānāṃ yathā tathā kalpita|prāṇa|vṛttīnāṃ kim evaṃ|vidhair anupaśānta|jan'|ôcitair bhoga|sādhana|vibhavaiḥ?

BAṬUḤ: ⌜Ayya, pekkha pekkha, edassiṃ dhavala|hara|sihare surahi|kusuma|dhūva|gaṃdha|pabbhāra|ṇibbhara|bharida|dasa|disā|muhe ede vaṃdaā bhoaṇ'|ômmuha vva dīsaṃti.⌟

SNĀTA°: Sādhu lakṣitam. tat kadā cid āvāṃ dṛṣṭvā sva|vyāpāra|yantraṇām anubhaveyur ete bhikṣavaḥ. tad ih' âiva latā|maṇḍape tāvad ebhir anupalakṣyamāṇau kṣaṇaṃ paśyāva eṣāṃ vyavahāram.

1.80 *Tathā kurutaḥ.*

SNĀTA°: *(sakautukam avalokya)* Aye! kena cid api bhikṣu|saṅgha|bhojan'|ônmukhena nāpi snātam.

BAṬUḤ: ⌜Ciṭṭhadu ṇhāṇaṃ, aṃbara|parivattaṇa|mettaṃ pi ṇa kadaṃ!⌟

SNĀTA°: *(nipuṇaṃ nirvarṇya)* Ācamana|kalpo 'py eṣāṃ śūdra|nirviśeṣaḥ. katham! catvāro varṇā varṇa|saṅkarā api vā sarva ev' âikasyāṃ paṅktau bhuñjate! aho ramyam āśrama|vratam!

Robbed by their rakish guides, the rich have completely lost their way on a futile path, and throw away their manifold riches on unsuitable things.

Even if this religion is a sham, this abundance of forms of entertainment fit for those who are not at peace is useless for people who have allegedly turned their mind away from sensual pleasures, devoted to the repeated cultivation of meditation and sustaining themselves in whatever way.

BOY: Sir, look, look, these Buddhist devotees seem to be ready for the meal in the tower of this whitewashed mansion, which completely fills the ten quarters with masses of fragrance of perfume, flowers and incense.

GRADUATE: Well observed. Perhaps these monks would feel inhibited in their habits if they noticed us.* So now we shall observe their practice for a second right here in this bower of creepers, unnoticed by them.

They do so. 1.80

GRADUATE: *(looking full of expectation)* Goodness! None of them has even performed his ablutions in his haste to eat the monastic meal.

BOY: Let alone bathing, they haven't even changed their clothes!

GRADUATE: *(looking carefully)* Even their procedure for purification by sipping water is the same as that of Shudras! Golly! People from the four estates and even those from the mixed estates are all eating in one and the same row! How pleasant is this ashram's observance!

BAṬUḤ: ⌜Ayya, ṇa ittiaṃ yyeva edaṃ! pekkha edāṇa parivisaṃtīṇa bhakkha|dāṇ'|ômmuhāṇa thora|thaṇa|maṃḍalāṇa dāsīṇa viviha|vibbhamā kaḍakkhā bhikkhu|vayaṇesu ṇivaḍaṃti. edaṃ ca kiṃ pi ṇimmala|kalasa|ṇikkhittaṃ pāṇayaṃ uvaṇīdaṃ.⌟

1.85 SNĀTA°:

Pakva|rasa|śabda|nihnutam
anya|vyapadeśam atra madhu|pānam,
māṃs'|âśanaṃ ca koṭi|
traya|rahitam. Aho tapaḥ kṛcchram!

BAṬUḤ: ⌜Ayya, pekkha pekkha, eso bhikkhū.⌟

⌜Tisio vi piaï ṇa tahā jīhāï bhamaṃta|kuvalaaṃ pāṇaṃ,
diṭṭhīhi jahā dāsīṇa viāsia|loaṇaṃ vaaṇaṃ.⌟

SNĀTA°: Bhavatu, dṛṣṭo vīta|rāgāṇām āśrama|samācāraḥ.

1.90 BAṬUḤ:

⌜Ujyāṇesu ṇivāso,
sulahaṃ pāṇaṃ ca sulaham aṇṇaṃ pi,
ṇa ya kiṃ pi ṇiyama|dukkhaṃ:
dhaṇṇo vaṃdattaṇaṃ lahaï.⌟

SNĀTA°: Alam idānīṃ parihāsena. eṣa sa mahā|paṇḍitaḥ prasiddho Dharmottara|nāmā bhikṣuḥ kṛt'|āhāraḥ prāsādād avatīrya taror adhaś chāyāyām śādvala|bhuvam adhyāste. tad upasarpāva enam.

Tataḥ praviśati yathā|nirdiṣṭo BHIKṢUR UPĀSAKAŚ *ca.*

BOY: Sir, there is more! Look, here are buxom maidservants ready to serve the food, and catching the eyes of the monks with their flirtatious glances! And here some drink is being served in a spotless jar.

GRADUATE: 1.85

> There is wine here masquerading as "fruit juice",*
> and there is meat allegedly fit for vegetarians.* Oh,
> what cruel asceticism!

BOY: Sir, look, look, this monk*

> Although thirsty, is not so much drinking the beverage, in which a water lily is whirling, with his tongue as he is drinking with his eyes the candid faces of the maidservants.

GRADUATE: That will do, we have seen the monastic discipline of the passion-free.

BOY: 1.90

> Living in pleasure gardens, with drink and food
> both easy to obtain, untroubled by restrictions:
> lucky are those who become Buddhists.

GRADUATE: That's enough jeering now. Here comes the famous great scholar Dharmóttara, the Buddhist monk. Having finished his meal, he is descending from the palatial building to sit down on a grassy spot, in the shade under a tree. So let's approach him.

Then enters the Buddhist MONK *as described above, and his* DISCIPLE.

BHIKṢUḤ: Āyuṣman, api gṛhītaṃ tad bhavatā hṛdaye dayā|nidher bhagavato Bodhi|sattvasy' ôpadeśa|jātam?

1.95 UPĀ°: ⌜Puṇo vi bhadaṃto aṇuggahaṃ karissadi.⌟

BHIKṢUḤ: *(agrato 'valokya)* Ayam asāv ady' âpi brāhmaṇa|yuvā sthita eva. vivakṣor iv' âsya mukhaṃ paśyāmi.

SNĀTA°: *(upasṛtya)* Bhikṣo, kuśalino bhavantaḥ? kaccid avighnam upapadyata iyam āśrama|caryā?

BHIKṢUḤ: Svāgatam. anupahat" êyam śādvala|bhūmiḥ. upaviśyatām.

SNĀTA°: *(upaviśya)* Kiṃ punar asy' ôpadiṣṭam ācāryeṇa yatr' âivaṃ grahaṇam pṛcchyate?

1.100 BHIKṢUḤ: *(upāsakam uddiśya)* Brūhi, yad eṣa pṛcchati.

SNĀTA°: K" êyam avajñā, «upāsaka brūhi!» iti? baṭo, śṛṇv asya yad ayam ācaṣṭe.

BHIKṢUḤ: Brāhmaṇa, «sṛṇv asmāt» iti nanu vaktuṃ yuktam.

SNĀTA°: Bho rakta|paṭa! na khalu «ākhyāt" ôpayoge» ity asya viṣaya evaṃ|vidhāḥ pralāpāḥ. hanta, «naṭasya śṛṇoti» ity ayam ev' âtra nyāyo yuktaḥ.

BHIKṢUḤ: Aho maukharyaṃ dvijanmano yasya tri|bhuvan'|âika|guroḥ parama|kāruṇikasya bhagavato Buddhasya <śāsanaṃ>* pralāpaḥ!

MONK: Sir, have you treasured up in your heart the teachings of the most compassionate Lord Bodhi·sattva?

DISCIPLE: Please, Reverend, favor me again. 1.95

MONK: This young brahmin whom we saw before is still there. His face looks like he is eager to speak.

GRADUATE: *(approaching)* Monk, how are you? I trust that your religious observance continues unimpeded.

MONK: Welcome. This grassy spot is not impure. Please sit down.

GRADUATE: *(sitting down)* But what is it that you, as mentor, have taught him, that you were just asking if he had grasped?

MONK: *(to his* DISCIPLE*)* Reply to his question. 1.100

GRADUATE: What an insult: "Disciple, reply"! Boy, listen to what he says.

MONK: Brahmin, surely the proper usage is "Learn from him."

GRADUATE: My dear red-robe! Ravings like this are not governed by the grammatical rule "The noun denoting the teacher is in the ablative case if there is a formal instruction." Look, the only appropriate usage here is "He hears from the actor in the genitive case."*

MONK: O what an abusive twice-born, for whom the <teaching> of the supremely compassionate Lord Buddha, the only master of the three worlds, is raving!

1.105 SNĀTA°: *(*UPĀSAKAM *uddiśya)* Tvam api kathaya tāvat, kim anena pāṭhito 'si.

UPĀ°: ⌈Ṇaṃ cattāri me ayya|saccāï guruṇā uvadiṭṭhāï dukkhaṃ samudao ṇiroho maggo tti.⌋

SNĀTA°: *(sasmitam)* Idaṃ tat parama|kāruṇika|śāsanam? ayaṃ ca na pralāpo yatra nairātmya|darśanaṃ śreyo|mārga iti gīyate?

BHIKṢUḤ: Dvijāte, agnīṣomīy'|ādi|paśu|viśasanaṃ śreyaḥ|sādhanaṃ sādhv ity etad|dṛṣṭi|bhāvanā|kaluṣit'|ântaḥ|karaṇānāṃ bhavad|vidhānāṃ pralāpa iv' âyam ābhāti param'|ârth'|ôpadeśaḥ.

SNĀTA°: Katham? ayaṃ durācāraḥ śākyo Veda|vākyeṣv api vivadate! kim kurmaḥ? kasy' âgrato brūmaḥ? patita|saṅgha|sambādha ev' âyaṃ vihāro vartate. *(diśo 'valokya, saharṣam)* aho bat' âmī vihār'|ôdyāna|darśana|dohadino 'tibahavaḥ puṇyair atra|bhavanto Viśvarūpa|prabhṛtayo mahā|vidvāṃsaḥ prāśnikā upasthitāḥ. bhavatu, labdho 'vasaraḥ pāpānāṃ nigrahasya.

1.110 *Tataḥ praviśanti yathā|vibhavaṃ* PRĀŚNIKĀḤ.

PRĀŚNIKĀḤ: Eṣa snātaka|Saṅkarṣaṇa eṣa ca bhikṣu|Dharmottaro vivadamānāv iva vadana|lakṣmy" âiva lakṣyete. hanta, paśyāmas tāvat. *(goṣṭhīṃ parikrāmanti.)*

GRADUATE: *(to the* DISCIPLE*)* As for you, tell me now what he taught you. I.105

DISCIPLE: Why, the master has taught me the Four Noble Truths: Suffering, the Cause of Suffering, the Cessation of Suffering, and the Way.

GRADUATE: *(smiling)* That's the teaching of the supremely compassionate one? And this is not raving where the realization of having no Self is celebrated as the path leading to salvation?

MONK: Brahmin! The teaching of Ultimate Reality seems to be raving for the likes of you, your mind muddied by cultivating the doctrine that the slaughter of animals like the one sacrificed for Agni and Soma is a means to attain salvation!

GRADUATE: What? This depraved Buddhist finds fault even with Vedic ordinances! What shall I do? In whose presence shall I speak? This monastery is crowded only with the community of renegades. *(He looks around and says delightedly)* Great! As a reward of my good works, Vishvarupa and these other many honorable professors have come eager to see the garden of the monastery, handy arbiters for me. All right, I've got the opportunity to punish these criminals.

Then enter as many ARBITERS *as can be afforded.* I.110

ARBITERS: To judge just by the luster of their faces, this graduate, Sankárshana, and this Buddhist monk, Dharmóttara, appear to be quarrelling. Come, let's have a look. *(They make a few steps around the gathering.)*

BHIKṢUḤ: Svāgatam āryāḥ, ih' ôpaviśyatām. *(iti śādvala|bhūmiṃ nirdiśati.)*

PRĀŚNIKĀḤ: *(upaviśya)* Kim iha prastutam? *(iti* BHIKṢUṂ *pṛcchanti.)*

BHIKṢUḤ: Amuṣya yajñ'|ôpavītino Bodhi|sattv'|ôpadeśaḥ pralāpa iv' ābhāti.

I.115 SNĀTA°:

Ayam aham, eṣa ca bhikṣuḥ,
parīkṣakāḥ kṛtadhiyo bhavanta iti
sār'|âsāra|vicāre
kuto 'nya evaṃ|vidho 'vasaraḥ?

PRĀŚNI°:

Nyāyyaṃ ced abhidhīyate parimitaṃ
siddh'|ânta|bījaṃ vacaḥ,
heyaṃ cec chala|jāti|nigraha|pada|
prāyaṃ kathā|ḍambaram,
n' âiv' ērṣyā hṛdi, vāci no paruṣatā,
na bhrū|vibhedo mukhe,
sādhūnāṃ yadi vāda eṣa tad ime
sarvatra sabhyā vayam.

BHIKṢU|SNĀTAKAU: Evam etad yath" āryāḥ samādiśanti.

I.120 PRĀŚNI°: Tat ko 'tra|bhavatoḥ prathama|pakṣavādī?

SNĀTA°: Kṛta eva bhikṣuṇā pūrva|pakṣ'|ôpanyāsa upāsakaṃ prabodhayatā.

MONK: Welcome, gentlemen, please take a seat here. *(Saying this, he points at the grassy spot.)*

ARBITERS: *(sit down and ask the* MONK*)* What are you discussing?

MONK: That person invested with the sacred thread calls the Bodhi·sattva's teaching raving.

GRADUATE: 1.115

> Here am I, and here is the monk, you are prudent arbiters: what an incomparable opportunity to consider the strong and weak points of the argument!

ARBITERS:

> If your talk is correct, moderate, and springs from the established truth; if you avoid discourse full of quibbles, futile rejoinders, and vulnerable points, with a noisy mass of bad disputation; if there is no envy at all in your heart, no roughness in your words, no frowning on your face; if this is a discussion among virtuous persons, then we are always ready to serve as assessors.

MONK & GRADUATE: It will be as you command, gentlemen.

ARBITERS: So which one of you has put forward his thesis 1.120
first?

GRADUATE: The monk has indeed set forth the prima-facie view while teaching the disciple.

BHIKṢUḤ: *(snātakam uddiśya)* Api śrutaṃ tad bhavatā?

SNĀTA°: Śrutam.

BHIKṢUḤ: Yady evaṃ tad anubhāṣyatām.

I.125 SNĀTA°: Bāḍham. saṅkṣepata ev' ânubhāṣyate tāvat.

Duḥkhaṃ, tasya nimittaṃ,
tad|uparamas, tad|upapattaye mārgaḥ
nairātmya|darśan'|ākhyas,
tat|siddhiḥ kṣaṇikatā|siddheḥ.

Tat kṣaṇikatvaṃ sattvān,
nāśaṃ prati kāraṇ'|ânapekṣatvāt.
smṛty|ādi|vyavahāraḥ
santāne hetu|phala|bhāvāt.

Kṣaṇiko 'pi na bāhyo 'rthaḥ
kaś cit saṃvitti|viṣayatāṃ yāti.
ākāra|nicaya|khacitaṃ
cakāsti vijñānam ev' êdam.

Tasmāt sarvaṃ śūnyaṃ,
sarvaṃ kṣaṇikaṃ, nirātmakaṃ sarvam,
sarvaṃ duḥkham it' îtthaṃ
dhyāyan nirvāṇam āpnoti.

I.130 *(BHIKṢUM Uddiśya)* api bhavaty evam?

BHIKṢUḤ: *(sāvajñam)* Āṃ, bhavati saṅkṣiptam.

SNĀTA°: Tad atr' êdānīṃ śrūyatām.

PRĀŚNI°: Avahitāḥ smaḥ.

MONK: *(to the* GRADUATE*)* Did you hear it?

GRADUATE: I did.

MONK: If so, then repeat it.

GRADUATE: Of course. I'll be brief:

> Suffering; its cause and its cessation; the path to attain that, called "the realization of having no Self"; this is established through the establishing of momentariness.
>
> Things are momentary because they exist, and since their destruction requires no cause. Activities such as memory are possible because of causal relations in the continuum.
>
> But no external thing, even if it were momentary, can become the object of cognition. This consciousness alone shines forth, studded with a multitude of forms.
>
> Therefore everything is empty, everything is momentary, everything lacks an enduring essence, everything is suffering. Meditating thus one reaches Nirvana.

(To the MONK*)* Is it O.K. like that?

MONK: *(contemptuously)* Yes, as a summary.

GRADUATE: Now it is my turn.

ARBITERS: We are all ears.

SNĀTA°:

I.135 Ayaṃ yath"|ôktaḥ kṣaṇa|bhaṅga|siddhau
satyāṃ bhaved apy apavarga|mārgaḥ,
vicāryamāṇās tu na naipuṇena
spṛśanti bhāvāḥ kṣaṇa|bhaṅguratvam.

BHIKṢUḤ: Kutaḥ?

SNĀTA°: Hetv|abhāvād eva.

BHIKṢUḤ: Nan' ûkto hetuḥ: «sattvāt» iti.

SNĀTA°:

I.140 Sattv'|ākhyaṃ yad avādi mānam alasad|
dṛṣṭānta|vandhy'|ātmanaḥ
sambandha|grahaṇaṃ na śakyam ṛjunā
mārgeṇa dhūm'|âgnivat.

BHIKṢUḤ: Yady evaṃ tataḥ kim? vyatireka|mukhen' âpi vyāpti|graho vyāptigraha eva.

Nityebhyaḥ krama|yaugapadya|virahād
vyāvartamānaṃ punas
tat sattvaṃ nidadhīta bhaṅgiṣu padaṃ
gaty|antar'|âsambhavāt.

GRADUATE:

> Even if this aforementioned path to final beatitude 1.135
> does exist, provided that momentariness is established, nevertheless, when one thoroughly examines entities, they do not come in contact with momentariness.

MONK: Why not?

GRADUATE: Simply because there is no logical reason for that to be so.

MONK: But surely the logical reason has been put forth: "because of existence."

GRADUATE:

> The concomitance with the probandum, i.e., "mo- 1.140
> mentariness," of the proof of "existence," which you Buddhists teach cannot be ascertained in a straight way, as can be in the case of smoke and fire, since no example appears to support it, and since therefore it is useless.*

MONK: If so, then what of it? Ascertaining the concomitance even by means of logical discontinuance is still an ascertainment of the concomitance.*

> But that existence,* being excluded from permanent things because of the absence of both gradual and instantaneous efficacy, will have a foothold in momentary entities, because it has nowhere else to go.*

SNĀTA°:

Nityebhya iva ten' âiva vyāpak'|âsambhavena te
kṣaṇikebhyo 'pi bhāvebhyaḥ sattvaṃ vyāvartatetarām.

1.145 Paśya:

Utpadya kāṃ cid api yady ayam ārabheta
bhāvaḥ kriyāṃ kṣaṇikatāṃ na tathā sat' îyāt.
tasy' ātma|lābha|samanantaram eva mṛtyu|
kroḍī|kṛtasya karaṇ'|âvasaraḥ kuto 'nyaḥ?

BHIKṢUḤ: Kṣaṇa|bhaṅgiṣu bhāveṣu nanv iyān eva kārya|kāraṇa|bhāvaḥ: «idaṃ pratīty' êdaṃ pratīyate» iti pratītya|samutpāda|mātram.

SNĀTA°: Asty atra' ânyad api vaktavyam. tad āstām. idaṃ tu brūmaḥ: asmin mate kāraṇatvam eva na tāttvikaṃ, bhāvānāṃ viśeṣa upādāna|kāraṇatvāt.

Tatra sva|karma|phala|bhoga|samarthan'|ādi
jñāneṣu hetu|phala|bhāva|kṛtaṃ samagram
hīyeta. hetu|phala|bhāva ih' âstu ko 'pi:
jñān'|ântareṣu para|santati|jeṣu tulyaḥ.

GRADUATE:

> Existence is all the more excluded even from your momentary things, just as from permanent things, because they, too, cannot have the invariably concomitant property.*

Look: 1.145

> If this entity performed an action after it had arisen, in that case it could not be momentary. Or, if it is embraced by death immediately after coming into being, how could it have another opportunity to act?

MONK: But, surely, causal relationship among momentary things is only this much: "after cognising A, B is cognised," that is, merely "arising of a cognition after getting a former cognition."*

GRADUATE: There is more to be said in this matter, but let it be for now. Instead, I put forth the following: on the basis of this view, the condition of being a cause is not real itself, since entities are material causes with regard to a particular thing.

> In that state of affairs* all operations, which are brought about by causality, such as the capability of every awareness in a stream to experience the results of its past actions, would fail. Or let there be some kind of causal relation here:* it would be the same with regard to other cognition-phases that have arisen in other streams.

I.150 BHIKṢUR *Adho|mukho bhūmim ālikhati.*

SNĀTA°:

Kārya|kāraṇa|bhāve vā siddhe 'pi param'|ârthataḥ
jñān'|ânyatv'|ânapāyāt kā sva|karma|phala|bhoktṛtā?

Api ca, «kṣaṇikā bhāvāḥ sattvāt» iti sādhya|viparyaya|sādhanād viruddho 'yaṃ hetuḥ.

BHIKṢUḤ: Katham iva?

I.155 SNĀTA°: Uktaṃ kṣaṇikānāṃ n' ârtha|kriyā|kāritvam iti. sthāsnavas tu bhāvāḥ sahakāri|sannidhāne krameṇa yugapad vā nirvartayitum utsahanta ev' êty artha|kriyā|kāritvam iti tat|sthairya|siddhiḥ.

BHIKṢUS *tūṣṇīm āste.*

SNĀTA°:

Ātma|hāniś ca bhāvānāṃ hetv|adhīn" ātma|lābhavat,
anvaya|vyatirekau hi sadṛśāv ubhayor api.

BHIKṢUḤ: Nanv anyathā|siddhau vināśa|hetāv anvaya|vyatirekau, tasya visabhāga|santati|nimittatvāt. utpattihetāv anvaya|vyatirekau kāry'|ântar'|âbhāvān na tathā bhavitum arhataḥ.

The MONK *draws on the ground with eyes downcast.* I.150

GRADUATE:

> Or even if the causal relation is established as really true, because the otherness of the awarenesses remains, how could anyone enjoy the fruits of his own actions?

Moreover, in the argument "Things are momentary because of their existence," the logical reason is contradictory, since it proves the opposite of the property to be established.*

MONK: How so?

GRADUATE: It has been stated that momentary entities cannot be efficacious. Permanent things, however, together with the assisting factors, are indeed able to act either gradually or instantaneously: this is causal efficacy, and in this way their stability is proved. I.155

The MONK *remains silent.*

GRADUATE:

> The destruction of things also depends on some cause, just as their coming into being, for the agreement in presence and in absence of cause and effect is similar for both.*

MONK: But surely, as for the cause of destruction, the agreement in presence and in absence of cause and effect is established in another way, since it* is the cause of a different continuum.* As for the cause of arising, the

1.160 SNĀTA°: *(sasmitam)* Kim icchayā dveṣeṇa vā? kāry'|ântar'|âbhāvo 'pi keṣāṃ cin mate durbhaṇo 'bhivyakty|ādeḥ sambhavāt.

BHIKṢUḤ:

N' ôtpatti|hetūn virahayya dṛṣṭam
utpadyamānaṃ kva cid eva kāryam.

SNĀTA°:

Vināśa|hetūn virahayya dṛṣṭam
kiṃ vā vinaśyat kva cid eva kāryam?

1.165 BHIKṢUḤ: Nanu vināśa|hetv|asannidhānān manv|antareṣv api kaś cin na vinaśyed ghaṭa iti niryāso bhavet.

SNĀTA°: *(sopahāsam)* Kaṣṭaṃ bhoḥ kaṣṭam, nityatve ghaṭasya sati samāptā loka|yātrā, utsannāḥ prajāḥ, upasthito jagatām ghata eva nitya|mṛtyuḥ. yasya hi n' âsti vināśa|kāraṇam ākāś'|āder iva bhavatv asau nityaḥ, kiṃ jātam? na ca n'|âsti vināśa|kāraṇam, avayavinām avayava|vibhāg'|ādeḥ avaśyaṃ|bhāvitvāt. api ca re mūḍha, bhavat|pakṣe 'pi ghaṭa|kṣaṇa|santatir anucchinnā tath" âiva kiṃ na dṛśyate? āgataṃ ced asyāṃ visabhāga|santati|kāraṇaṃ, hanta tarhi vināśa|kāraṇam api mat|pakṣe tath" âiva āgamiṣyat' îti sa samānaḥ panthāḥ. tad ayam īdṛśaḥ kṣaṇa|bhaṅga|pakṣaḥ.

agreement in presence and in absence of cause and effect cannot be thus,* because there is no other kind of effect.

GRADUATE: *(smiling)* Out of desire or aversion? Some people hold that we can hardly say that there is no other kind of effect, since manifestation and the like can take place.*

MONK:

> No effect has ever been seen arising without the causes of arising.

GRADUATE:

> Have you ever seen an effect being destroyed, without the causes of destruction?

MONK: Surely that would mean that no pot could be destroyed, even with the passage of aeons, if there was no cause of destruction present.

GRADUATE: *(with a sneer)* Mercy on us! If the pot is eternal then worldly affairs are finished, people are ruined, the eternal death of the world, which is nothing but a pot, is breathing down our neck! For let that thing be eternal which has no cause to destroy it, like space, for example: what's the problem with that? But composite entities do have a cause of destruction, because the separation of their constituents, etc., must inevitably take place. Moreover, you imbecile, do you not realize that, even accepting your position, the stream of pot-moments is likewise not destroyed?* If a cause of a different stream has appeared in it, well, then, according to my position, the cause of destruction will also appear in the same

BHIKṢUḤ *Salajjam āste.*

UPĀ°: ⌜Are re duṭṭha|bamhaṇa, kadhaṃ bhadaṃtaṃ adhikkhivasi?⌟

BAṬUḤ: ⌜Are re vaṇṇa|saṃkarā, uvajjhāassa evaṃ vāharasi?⌟

1.170 UPĀ°: ⌜Kassa eso uvajjhāo? ṇavaraṃ eassa uṭṭa|muhassa.⌟

BAṬUḤ *Sakrodham uttiṣṭhann* UPĀSAKA/*mukhe capeṭāṃ pātayitum icchati.*

SNĀTAKA|BHIKṢU|PRĀŚNIKĀḤ: Alam alam aticāpalena! *(iti nivārayanti.)*

SNĀTA°: Api ca sthairya|grāhiṇyā «sa ev' âyam» iti pratyabhijñayā bādhito 'yaṃ hetuḥ. tiṣṭhatu vā pratyabhijñā, yad idam animeṣa|dṛṣṭer atruṭita|sattāka|padārtha|grāhi pratyakṣaṃ tad api bādhakam eva. tasmiṃś ca tādṛśi pratyakṣe sati, yat ke cid avicakṣaṇāḥ kṣaṇa|grāhi pratyakṣam ācakṣate tad api pratikṣiptam eva, kṣaṇasya dīrgha|kālat''|ânupapatter, iha ca tathā grahaṇāt.

PRĀŚNI°: Kṛtaṃ vistareṇa.

way: the course of reasoning is the same. So such is this position of momentariness.

The MONK *sits embarrassed.*

DISCIPLE: Hey, you damned brahmin, how dare you insult the Reverend?

BOY: Hey, you cross-breed, that's how you speak to the professor?

DISCIPLE: Whose professor is he? Only this camel-faced 1.170
feller's.

The BOY *jumps up angrily and wants to slap the face of the* DISCIPLE.

GRADUATE, MONK, ARBITERS: Keep your hair on! *(They separate them.)*

GRADUATE: What's more, this logical reason is contradicted by recognition that grasps stable things, when we think "This is that same thing." Or let us leave aside recognition. The perception of someone who does not wink, which grasps objects as having unbroken existence, that perception, too, undoubtedly contradicts the logical reason. And although there *is* such a perception, some ignoramuses claim that "perception grasps object-phases": clearly this claim is also refuted, since a moment cannot last for long, and in this case* grasping happens in that way.

ARBITERS: Don't go into further details.

I.175 Ākarṇitaḥ karṇa|sukha|prado 'yaṃ
tvad|varṇitaḥ snātaka nīti|mārgaḥ.
tena vyudastaḥ kṣaṇa|bhaṅga|vādo.
vijñāna|vāde tv abhidhatsva kiṃ cit.

SNĀTA°: Bhikṣo, śrūyatām.

Grāhya|grāhakayor dvayor avagatir
mā bhūn. nan' ûddyotatāṃ
jñān'|ātmā: sa kim ātmanaḥ prakaṭayaty
ākāram anyasya vā?
n' âhaṃ nīlam iti pratītir, idam ity
eṣā tu saṅgacchate
vicched'|âvagatiḥ paratra. tad ayaṃ
grāhyo 'sti bāhyo dhruvam.

BHIKṢUḤ: Yady asti kiṃ na saṃvedyate?

SNĀTA°: Ka eva āha na saṃvedyata iti? nanu saṃvedyata eva «nīlam idam» iti.

I.180 BHIKṢUḤ: Sādho, jñān'|âvabhāso 'yaṃ, jñānasya prakāś'|ātmakatvāt; n' ârthasy' âvabhāso 'yaṃ, tasya jaḍ'|ātmakatvāt; ubhay'|âvabhāsaś ca n' âst' îti tvay" âpy uktam.

SNĀTA°: Jñānam api prakāśamānam anya|prakāś'|ātmakam eva prakāśate, n' ātma|prakāś'|ātmakam. prakāśya|prakāśo hy asau prakāśo, na prakāśa|prakāśa eva. ayam eva hi prakāra uddyotānām. tad uktaṃ, «trayaḥ prakāśāḥ sva|para|prakāśāḥ» iti. na tu tadānīṃ tattvato jñānaṃ

> Our ears have delighted to hear this course of argumentation you expounded, graduate. It has refuted the doctrine of momentariness. Now say something about the doctrine of consciousness. 1.175

GRADUATE: Listen, monk.

> Let there be no simultaneous perception of both the object and of the cognition that grasps it. If you say, "Let the nature of cognition shine forth," then does it make manifest its own form, or the form of something else? There is no cognition in the form of "I am blue"; rather, this cognition of the other thing as different, namely "that,"* agrees with the facts. Therefore this external object of cognition must exist.

MONK: If it exists, then why is it not experienced?

GRADUATE: Who ever said that it is not experienced? Surely it *is* experienced in the form of "This is blue."

MONK: Good fellow, this is the appearance of cognition, 1.180 since cognition is of the nature of light; this is not the appearance of an object, since it has an insentient nature; and even you said that there can be no simultaneous appearance of both.

GRADUATE: Cognition, too, inasmuch as it shines forth, shines as the shining forth of something else, not as the shining forth of its own self, since this shining is the shining forth of what is to be shone on, and not just the shining forth of shining. For this is the way lights are. It has been said: "The three lights* illuminate themselves

prakāśate, nīl'|ādy|ākāro hi prakāśate. na tu jñānaṃ nīl'|ādy|ākāram, anvaya|vyatirekābhyāṃ tasya gotv'|ādivad bodha|rūpatv'|ânavadhāraṇād iti.

BHIKṢUS *tūṣṇīm adho|mukho mahīm ālikhati.*

SNĀTA°: Bho atra|bhavantaḥ prāśnikāḥ, kathayata kataraḥ pakṣaḥ virājate?

PRĀŚNI°: Kim asmān pṛcchasi? bhikṣuṇ" âiva maunam avalambamānena samarthito bhavat|pakṣaḥ.

1.185 SNĀTA°: Tad vayam idānīṃ snānāya gacchāmaḥ. anujñātum arhatha. bhavadbhir api dṛṣṭaṃ prekṣaṇakam. idānīṃ yath"|âbhimatam anuṣṭhīyatām. (BHIKṢUM *uddiśya*)

Yady eṣa para|lokāya bhikṣavo bhavatāṃ śramaḥ,
sthīyatāṃ, kṛtam etena tad|viparyaya|kāriṇā.

Atha kaurukucī|kūrca|ḍambar'|ālamban'|ātmakaḥ
jīvik"|ârthaḥ prayatno 'yaṃ, tad yath"|êṣṭaṃ vidhīyatām.

Iti niṣkrāntāḥ sarve.

Prathamo 'ṅkaḥ.

and other things."* But it is not really cognition that shines forth then,* for it is forms such as blue that shine forth. And forms such as blue are not "cognitions," because they are not established by positive and negative concomitance to have the nature of cognition in the way cowness is.*

The MONK *draws on the ground in silence, with eyes downcast.*

GRADUATE: Honorable arbiters, tell us which one of the two positions is superior?

ARBITERS: Why are you asking us? The monk himself supports your position by keeping silence.

GRADUATE: Then I am going to have a bath now.* Please excuse me. As for you, you have seen the spectacle, now do as you please. *(to the* MONK*)* 1.185

> Monks, if this effort of yours is for the sake of a better afterlife, then stop, enough of it, since it brings about the opposite result.
>
> If this exertion of yours, namely resorting to masses of hypocrisy and humbug, is in order to make a living, then go on with it as you wish.

Exeunt omnes.

End of the first act.

PRELUDE TO ACT TWO: LUSTFUL ASCETICS

Tataḥ praviśati CEṬAḤ.

CEṬAḤ:

⌜Ṇa pivīyadi śīyalā śulā
    ṇa a dāśīi śamaṃ lamīadi,
śulahaṃ ca ṇa maṃśa|bhoyaṇaṃ
    viśame bamhaṇa|vāśae ido.⌟

⌜Tā kiṃ kalīadi? ṇasti yyeva ṇiya|bhaṣṭake palihalia appaṇo gabbha|dāśāṇa gadī. āṇaṃ pi tāriśaṃ bhaṣṭake aveṣkadi yeśu ṇa khajjadi ṇa pijyadi. jado ajya āṇatte bhaṣṭakeṇa hage: «ale kajjalaā, gaśca pekkha khavaṇaya|vaśadīe kiṃ Jiṇa|raṣkida|bhikkhū asti ṇa va» tti. ṇa a jāṇāmi kahiṃ śā khavaṇaa|vaśadī.⌟ *(parikramya vīthīm avalokayan savitarkam)* ⌜eśu vistiṇṇa|luṃcida|loma|kiṃśālu|viśala|śavalidā ede paṃśu|kaṇā laṣkīaṃti. tā eśu yyeva luṣka|gahaṇe khavaṇaa|vaśadīe hodavvaṃ.⌟ *(kati cit padāni gatv" âgrato vilokya saharṣam)* ⌜iaṃ yyeva śā khavaṇaa|vaśadī, jado eśu ṇilaṃtala|ladā|paṃjal'|aṃdhayāle luṣka|mūle kuvidaṃ khavaṇiaṃ paśādeṃte eśe khavaṇae dīśadi.⌟ *(kṣaṇaṃ nirūpya)* ⌜adi|kovaṇā khu eśā duṭṭhā khavaṇiā yā calaṇa|paḍidaṃ pi edaṃ khavaṇaya|yuāṇaṃ palihalia dūlaṃ gadā. eśe vi tavaśśī paluśa|vaaṇe khavaṇae dīśadi.⌟

2.5 *Tataḥ praviśati picchikā|hastaḥ* KṢAPAṆAKAḤ.

Then enters the DOGSBODY.*

DOGSBODY:*

> One cannot drink chilled booze, nor make love to
> the servant girls, nor is it easy to get a meat dish,
> in this comfortless brahmin household.

So what to do? A born slave has no recourse if he turns his back on his own masters, that's for sure. Even the errands my master thinks up are such that one cannot eat or drink while running them. For just now my master has ordered me: "Hey, Sooty, go and see if the monk Jina·rákshita is in the abode of the Jain mendicants or not." And I've no idea where that abode of the Jain mendicants can be. *(He walks about, looks at the road, and muses:)* These specks of dust here seem to be speckled by scattered tufts of plucked-out, awn-like hair.* So the abode of the Jain mendicants must be right here in this forest. *(He takes a few steps, looks ahead and says joyfully:)* This must be the abode of the Jain mendicants, since here, under a tree, in the darkness of the dense net of vines, a monk seems to be appeasing an angry nun. *(He looks for a second.)* This harpy nun must be furious indeed: she's shaken off the young mendicant and gone away, even though he threw himself at her feet. And the poor monk seems to have a grim visage.

Then enters a Jain MENDICANT, *holding a broom made of peacock tail feathers.* 2.5

KṢAPAṆAKAḤ: *(sāsram)* ⌜Haddhī, para|loe durāsāe paḍhamaṃ khavaṇattaṇaṃ mae gahiaṃ. khalidassa tattha iṇhiṃ diṭṭh'|âdiṭṭhā khu me ṇaṭṭhā, jado esā vi duṭṭhā tāvasī calaṇa|paḍidassa vi me ṇa pasīdadi.⌟ *(akṣiṇī pramṛjya)* ⌜aï duṭṭhā baṃdhaï, gaccha tuvaṃ! kiṃ tae visarisaṃ kaṃ vi khavaṇiaṃ ṇa pāvissaṃ?⌟

CEṬAḤ: *(vicintya)* ⌜Jāva eśe khavaṇae maṃ ṇa pekkhadi tāva hage khavaṇiā|veśaṃ kaduya edaṃ khavaṇaaṃ uvahaśiśśaṃ.⌟ *(ātmānaṃ nirūpya)* ⌜laṃba|kaṇṇe khu hage. ṇa āṇaṇe maśśu|lomā me ubbhiṇṇā. ṇa ya khavaṇiyāṇa veṇi|baṃdhe śīśe śaṃbhāvīyadi. tā śuale me khavaṇiā|veśe.⌟ *(tathā karoti. nirūpya)* ⌜picchiā|metta|śuṇṇe śaṃpadaṃ me khavaṇiā|lūe vaṭṭadi.⌟ *(agrato 'valokya saharṣam)* ⌜śāhu! khavaṇiāe śaṃdhālida|paliccaïaṃ picchiaṃ geṇhia uvaśappiśśaṃ.⌟ *(tathā kṛtvā)* ⌜ayya, paṇamāmi. paliśśaṃta mhi śaṃpadaṃ. tā ācakkhaśu maṃ ajja kahiṃ bhaṣṭake Jiṇa|rakkhida|bhikkhū vaṭṭadi.⌟

KṢAPA°: *(sāśvāsam ātma/gatam)* ⌜Ṇa esa atta|paraṃmuho vva me devvo lakkhīyadi. aṇṇā khu esā taruṇa|khavaṇiā uvaṇadā.⌟ *(prakāśam)* ⌜aï bāla|tavassiṇi, kiṃ tujjha Jiṇa|rakkhida|bhikkhuṇā? parissaṃtā khu dīsasi. tā iha yyeva ṇijjaṇe sisira|ladā|gahaṇe uvavisia vīsama muhuttaaṃ.⌟

CEṬAḤ: ⌜Kudo me ṇicca|dukkhidāe maṃda|bhaggāe vīśāme?⌟

MENDICANT: *(weeping)* Poor me! Because of the vain hope of a better afterlife, first I became a Jain monk. I have deviated from that, and now both the present and the future* have come to nothing for me, for this harpy nun, too, is not appeased even if I throw myself at her feet. *(He wipes his eyes.)* Hey, you harpy bitch, get you gone! Can't I find another nun who is not like you?

DOGSBODY: *(pondering)* Before this monk notices me I'll dress up as a Jain nun, and make fun of him. *(He looks at himself.)* To be sure, I have long ears, there are no beginnings of a beard on my face, and no one would expect a Jain nun to wear a ponytail on her head. So I can easily assume the appearance of a Jain nun. *(He does so and looks about.)* Now all I need is a broom of peacock feathers to look like a Jain nun. *(Looking ahead, he says joyfully:)* Splendid! I'll take the nun's broom that she had been holding and then left behind,* and go closer. *(He does so.)* Sir, I bow to you. I am very tired now, so please tell me, where is the reverend monk Jina·rákshita now?

MENDICANT: *(cheering up, to himself)* It seems my luck will not turn its back on me now. Here we have another young nun showing up. *(openly)* O my mendicant girl, what business do you have with the monk Jina·rákshita? You look very tired indeed. So sit down right here in this lonely, cool thicket of vines, and rest for a spell.

DOGSBODY: I've always been unhappy and I'm ill-fated. How could I have a rest?

2.10 KṢAPA°: *(sa|sneham)* ⌜Kiṃ imassiṃ bāla|bhāve vi te dukkha|kāraṇaṃ?⌟

CEṬAḤ: *(niḥśvasya)* ⌜Ayya, ciṭṭhadu eśe maha ḍaḍḍha|vuttaṃte. Jiṇa|rakkhida|bhikkhu|paüttiṃ me ācakkhadu bhavaṃ.⌟

KṢAPA°: ⌜Bālie, eso khu Jiṇa|rakkhida|bhikkhū abbhaṃtare atta|sissāṇa majjhe vakkhāṇaaṃ kareṃto ṇiaggoha|rukkha|mūle ciṭṭhadi. tuvaṃ puṇa khaṇaṃ uvavisia vaṇṇehi dāva attaṇo ṇivvea|kāraṇaṃ.⌟

CEṬAḤ: *(upaviśya niḥśvasya)* ⌜Ayya, kiṃ eśu śaṃśāla|hadāe lajjā|ṇihāṇe vaṇṇīyadi?⌟ *(roditi.)*

KṢAPA°: *(akṣiṇī ceṭasy' ôtpuṃsayan)* ⌜Bālie, vaṇṇehi. hiaa|nivviseso khu eso jaṇo bāliāe.⌟

2.15 CEṬAḤ: ⌜Bāla|kumālika yyeva pavvajida mhi maṃda|bhāïṇī.⌟

KṢAPA°: ⌜Tado uṇa?⌟

CEṬAḤ: ⌜Tado īś'|īśi|ubbhijjyaṃta|vilala|juvvaṇa|lakkhaṇāe aṇicchaṃtīe yyeva me aśikkhida|maaṇa|laśāe keṇa vi taluṇa|khavaṇaeṇa śīla|khaṃḍaṇā kadā.⌟

KṢAPA°: *(saharṣam ātma|gatam)* ⌜Amaa|ṇaï yyeva me uvaṇadā.⌟ *(prakāśam)* ⌜bālie, īrisa yyeva saṃsāra|ṭṭhidī. tado uṇa?⌟

CEṬAḤ: ⌜Ayya, tado kāl'|aṃtale śaṇiaṃ śaṇiaṃ muṇia|maaṇa|laśaṃ maṃ palihalia śe khavaṇae aṇṇaśśiṃ ḍaḍḍha|muṭṭhīe vuḍḍha|khavaṇiāe paśatte.⌟

MENDICANT: *(with affection)* You are just a child, but you 2.10
already have a reason to be unhappy?

DOGSBODY: *(with a sigh)* Sir, let us not waste our breath for my execrable story. Please tell me the whereabouts of the monk Jina·rákshita.

MENDICANT: Little girl, this monk Jina·rákshita is inside, delivering a lecture to his disciples, under the *nyag·rodha*-tree. But sit down for a second and tell me now the cause of your disillusion.

DOGSBODY: *(sits down and sighs)* Sir, what point is there in relating now the piled-up shame of a girl whom life has crushed? *(He cries.)*

MENDICANT: *(wiping the* DOGSBODY*'s eyes)* Tell me, my moppet. I am no different from your heart, sweetie.

DOGSBODY: Ill-fated that I am, I turned a recluse when I 2.15
was just a little girl.

MENDICANT: And then?

DOGSBODY: Then, as the delicate signs of my youth were becoming slightly visible, but I was still not familiar with the savor of passion, some young monk offended my decency, entirely against my will.

MENDICANT: *(joyfully to himself)* I've chanced upon a river of nectar! *(openly)* C'est la vie, sweetie. And then?

DOGSBODY: Sir, then later on, as I had gradually become conversant with the savor of passion, that monk dumped me and got stuck on another firm-fisted* old nun.

2.20 KṢAPA°: ⌜Teṇa hi saṃmuhādo †śīo†. paṃgula|aṃdha|ṇāaṃ karemha.⌟

Iti CEṬAṂ *kaṇṭhe gṛhītvā balāc cumbati.* CEṬAḤ *kṛtaka/lajjam adho/mukham āste.*

KṢAPA°: ⌜Bālie, kiṃ maṃ ṇa pekkhasi?⌟

CEṬAḤ: ⌜Kahaṃ ṇu pekkhiśśaṃ? tae vi maṃ palihalia aṇṇado gaṃtavvaṃ.⌟

KṢAPA°: ⌜Bālie, mā evaṃ bhaṇa. dāsa|vattaṇiaṃ te karaïssaṃ.⌟ *(ceṭasya vakṣasi hastaṃ nikṣipya)* ⌜kiṃ ajja vi te thaṇaā ṇa ubbhiṇṇā?⌟

2.25 CEṬAḤ: *(sa/lajjam)* ⌜Kiṃ had'|āśā kaliśśaṃ?⌟

KṢAPA°: *(nābhi/mūle ceṭasya hastaṃ niveśya puruṣa/lakṣaṇam asy' ôpalakṣya, sa/vilakṣaṃ sa/kopaṃ ca)* ⌜Haddhī had'|āsa, daḍhaṃ tae khalī|kado mhi.⌟ *(prahartum icchati.)*

CEṬAḤ: ⌜Ale le tāvaśa|kāmuā, jadi kiṃ pi ācaṣkaśi tā Jiṇa|rakkhida|bhikkhuṇo phukkalaïśśaṃ.⌟

KṢAPA°: *(kṣaṇaṃ vimṛśya ceṭasya pādayoḥ patitvā)* ⌜Ṇa tae eso parihāso kassa vi pagāsidavvo.⌟

CEṬAḤ: ⌜Kiṃ me ukkocaaṃ?⌟

2.30 KṢAPA° *piṃchikā/mūlād uddhṛtya kim api dadāti.*

MENDICANT: †. . . †* Let's do as the lame and the blind in the proverb. 2.20

He puts his arms around the DOGSBODY*'s neck and kisses him forcibly. The* DOGSBODY *feigns bashfulness and sits with eyes downcast.*

MENDICANT: Sweetie, why don't you look at me?

DOGSBODY: How could I look? You too will dump me and go to another.

MENDICANT: Sweetie, don't say such thing. I shall be your slave! *(He puts his hand on the* DOGSBODY*'s chest.)* Your titties haven't even come out yet?

DOGSBODY: *(bashfully)* Poor me, what should I do? 2.25

The MENDICANT *slides down his hand under the navel of the* DOGSBODY, *discovers his genitals, and says with shame and anger:* Dammit, you wretch, you've taken me in badly! *(He is about to slap the* DOGSBODY.*)*

DOGSBODY: Hey, you ascetic lecher, if you say anything I'll squeal on you to the monk Jina·rákshita!

MENDICANT: *(reflects for a second and throws himself at the* DOGSBODY*'s feet)* You mustn't tell anyone about our little joke!

DOGSBODY: What about my hush money?

The MENDICANT *pulls something out from the handle of his broom of peacock feathers, and gives it to the* DOGSBODY. 2.30

CEṬAḤ: ⌜Kade palihāśe. pāvide kahāvaṇae. adhigayā bhiṣkuṇo paüttī. tā śaṃpadaṃ gadua bhaṣṭake viṇṇavemi.⌟ *(parikramy' âgrato 'valokya ca)* ⌜ajya diṭṭhiā vaḍḍhaśi! āgadā de hiaa|vallahā.⌟

*Tataḥ praviśati yath"|ârtha|*KṢAPAṆIKĀ. *kṣapaṇikā|veṣaṃ* CEṬAṂ *nirīkṣya serṣyā|kopam:*

KṢAPAṆIKĀ: ⌜Aï duṭṭha|tāvasi, edaṃ pārakkaṃ piṃchiaṃ geṇhia kahiṃ gamīadi?⌟

CEṬAḤ: ⌜Ayye, geṇha edaṃ piṃchiyaṃ. hage uṇa aṇicchaṃti yyeva edaśśiṃ ladā|gahaṇe ediṇā khavaṇaeṇa khalī|kadā. ṇa me dośe.⌟ *(iti niṣkrāntaḥ.)*

2.35 KṢAPAṆIKĀ: *(kṣapaṇaka|nikaṭam upasṛtya)* ⌜Are duṭṭha|kāmua tāvasī|laṃpaṭa! piṃchiā me visumarida tti jāva paḍiṇivaḍia āgada mhi tāva edassiṃ aṃtare khaṇa|mettaeṇa yyeva edassiṃ ladā|gahaṇe <aṇṇā khavaṇiā ā>liṃgidā. tā saṃpadaṃ aṇuhavasu attaṇo viṇaassa phalaṃ.⌟ *(iti piṃchikā|daṇḍena praharati.)*

KṢAPA°: ⌜Mā evaṃ saṃbhāvedu bhodī. ceḍao khu eso itthiā|vesaṃ kadua maṃ uvahasiduṃ āgado. teṇa had'|āseṇa kovidā bhodī. jaṃ saccaṃ, kosaṃ te pivāmi.⌟ *(iti kṣapaṇikāyāḥ pādayoḥ patati.)*

KṢAPAṆIKĀ: ⌜Kudo de muhe saccaṃ, jassa eso uvasamo?⌟

DOGSBODY: I've made my jest, I've got a coin, I've learned the whereabouts of the monk. So I go now and report to my master. *(He walks about and looks ahead.)* You've hit the jackpot today! Your sweetheart has arrived.

Then enters the real NUN. *She perceives* DOGSBODY, *disguised as a Jain nun, and says full of jealousy and anger:*

NUN: Hey, you ascetic wench, where are you going with someone else's broom in your hand?

DOGSBODY: Take it, ma'am. As for me, I've been deceived by the mendicant in this thicket of vines, entirely against my will. It's not my fault. *(He exits.)*

NUN: *(goes close to the* MENDICANT*)* Hey, you wretched 2.35
lecher, who leers after ascetic women! While I was on my way back, because I'd left behind my broom, in the meantime, in a matter of seconds, you were embracing <another nun>. So now reap the fruit of your discipline! *(She hits him with the stick of the broom.)*

MENDICANT: Do not think so, milady. Can't you see that he was a servant who came here disguised as a woman to make fun of me? That wretch has made you angry. This is the sober truth, I swear it. *(He throws himself at the* NUN*'s feet.)*

NUN: How could the truth come from your mouth, when such is your self-restraint?

KṢAPA°: ⌜Aṇṇaṃ pi kheḍḍaaṃ duṭṭha|ceḍao eso karedi. tā edu bhodī aṇṇato gacchamha.⌟ *(sasambhramam)* ⌜eso khu bamhaṇo ko vi ido āgacchaṃto dīsadi. tā tuvaradu bhodī.⌟

Niṣkrāntau.

MENDICANT: This wretched servant will make yet another jest, so come, my lady, let's go somewhere else. *(with bewilderment)* I see a brahmin coming in our direction, so hurry up, my lady.

Exeunt ambo.

ACT TWO:
THE FEAST OF DISPASSION

2.40 *Tataḥ praviśati* SNĀTAKO BAṬUŚ *ca.*

SNĀTA°:

Kṛtā tāvad goṣṭhī
sapadi nipuṇaṃ|manya|manasāṃ
mad'|ôṣmāṇaṃ teṣām
aruṇa|vasanānām śamayitum.
idānīm icchāmaḥ
kṛpaṇa|matibhiḥ krīḍitum ime
kṛpā|pātra|prāyair
api hi saha nagna|kṣapaṇakaiḥ.

BAṬUḤ: ⌜Ayyassa sā kīḍā. tāṇa uṇa tavassīṇa savvassa|ṇāso.⌟

SNĀTA°: *(sasmitam)* Yath" āha bhavān. gāvaḥ putra|dāraṃ gṛhaṃ kṣetraṃ kṛṣi|vaṇijye sarvam eṣāṃ vinaśyati. kiṃ hi dig|ambarāṇāṃ bhikṣā|bhujāṃ vṛkṣa|mūla|vāsināṃ sarvasvam?

2.45 BAṬUḤ: ⌜Ṇaṃ bhaṇemi. paraloyassa kade dāruṇaṃ dukkha|pabbhāraṃ te tavassiṇo aṇuhavaṃti. tā ayyassa sarassaī|pavāhe ṇivaḍaṃti. tā assiṃ āgama|rukkhae ṇipphalo yyeva edāṇaṃ so paāso.⌟

SNĀTA°: Aho kāruṇiko bhavān! bhavatu, bhavad|anurodhān mṛdu teṣu prabhaviṣyāmaḥ. tad ehi. prāptā vayam eṣām āśrama|padam. praviśāmas tāvat.

Parikrāmataḥ.

SNĀTA°: *(agrato 'valokya)* Ayaṃ sa nyagrodha|taru|chāyāyām aneka|śiṣya|gaṇ'|ôpāsyamānaḥ kim api vyācakṣāṇa iva Jinarakṣita|bhikṣur āste.

Then enters the GRADUATE *and the* BOY. 2.40

GRADUATE:

First I had a quick debate in order to damp the arrogant ardor of those red-robed fellows who fancy themselves clever. This time I want to toy with the feeble-minded naked mendicants, too, who are little more than objects of pity.

BOY: It is fun for you, sir, but for those poor devils it means the demolition of everything they have.

GRADUATE: *(smiling)* As you say, sir. Cattle, family, house, estate, farming and trade: they lose all they have. What then is the "everything" of sky-clad Jain monks who eat alms and live at the foot of trees?

BOY: Why, I'll tell you. Those poor devils undergo loads of 2.45
severe austerities for the sake of a better afterlife. Then they fall into the stream of Your Honor's eloquence. So their efforts will reap no fruit at all from this religion-scrub.

GRADUATE: Well, well! Aren't you compassionate! All right, to do you a favor I'll test my strength lightly on them. So come. We've arrived at their hermitage. Let's enter now.

They walk about.

GRADUATE: *(looking ahead)* The Jain monk Jina·rákshita is sitting here in the shade of a *nyag·rodha*-tree, perhaps lecturing about something, while a group of several disciples sits at his feet.

*Tataḥ praviśati yathā|nirdiṣṭaḥ kṣapaṇaka|*BHIKṢUḤ.

2.50 BHIKṢUḤ: *(svagatam)* Aho! duratikramaḥ saṃsāra|cakra|parivṛtti|kramaḥ.

Niṣiddhaṃ yatnen' âpy
anusarati tān eva viṣayān,
na teṣāṃ vaiṣamyaṃ
vimṛśati vipāke bahu|vidham,
na vidmaḥ kiṃ kurmo:
viśati na śive vartmani manaḥ,
na śāmyaty ev' âiṣā
niravadhir Avidyā bhagavatī.

(vicintya) Tath" âpi yathā|śakti tapasvino divā|niśam anuśāsyā ev' âmī bhikṣavaḥ. *(prakāśam)* ⌜bho bhikkhavā,⌟

⌜Paharaï kayaṃta|vāho,
visamā saṃsāra|vāürā|pāsā.
kaha taraü jīa|hariṇo
pajjaliyaṃ dukkh'|araṇṇam iṇaṃ?⌟

⌜Ahavā,⌟

2.55 ⌜Jiṇa|caraṇa|sumaraṇ'|ôggaya|
ṇisagga|sui|puṇṇa|puggala|balāṇaṃ
kuvido vi kiṃ karissidi
asaraṇa|sūro haya|kayaṃto?⌟

⌜Tā saṃpadaṃ,⌟

⌜Jhāïjjadi Jiṇa|vaaṇaṃ,
tava|ṇiyamehiṃ khavijjaï sarīraṃ:
ittiya|mettaṃ giṇhaha
uvaesa|rahassa|savvassaṃ.⌟

Then enters the Jain MONK *as described above.*

MONK: *(to himself)* Alas! It's extremely difficult to escape the turning of transmigration's wheel.* 2.50

> Even if you hold it back by force, it hankers after the same sense-objects, without considering their various drawbacks in karmic retribution—I don't know what to do: the mind does not take the auspicious path. This goddess of unending Ignorance simply does not give up.

(reflecting) Be that as it may, one just has to discipline these miserable monks day and night, to the best of one's ability. *(openly)* O monks:

> Fate, the hunter keeps shooting, the nooses of the transmigration-trap are dangerous. How can the deer that is the soul get through this burning forest of suffering?

Or, rather:

> What can wretched Fate, even if enraged, do to those in whom the power of the naturally pure "perfect" soul has arisen through meditation on the blessed Jina's teaching? It bullies only those who are defenseless. 2.55

So now:

> Contemplating the words of the Jina and mortifying the body with austerities and observances—that much is the entire secret of the teaching: plant it deep in your minds.

ŚIṢYĀḤ: ⌜Jaṃ bhaṣṭake āṇavedi.⌟

SNĀTA°: *(upasṛtya savinayam)* Api kuśalinaḥ śiṣya|pariṣadā saha bhavantaḥ?

2.60 BHIKṢUḤ: *(savitarkaṃ sva/gatam)* Ayam asau snātakaḥ Saṅkarṣaṇaḥ Saugatān abhibhūya sāmpratam asmān paribubhūṣur ih' āgataḥ. tad apasaraṇam ev' âtra śreyaḥ. dur|viṣaham asya pauruṣam, apūrv" âiṣā vaktṛ|śaktiḥ prajñā ca. *(prakāśam)* svāgatam āryasya. ita upaviśyatām. kuśalam.

SNĀTA°: Kim atra prastutam?

BHIKṢUḤ: Kim atra saṃsāra|gahane prastūyate? yadi santaraṇ'|ôpāyaḥ ko 'pi prāpyate.

SNĀTA°: Nanu gṛhīta ev' âtra|bhavadbhir upāyaḥ. tathā hi,

Na hiṃsā, n' âsatyaṃ,
na gṛha|dhana|vāsa|vyasanitā,
na saktir vyāpāre
kva cid api bhav'|ânantara|phale,
tapaś c' êdaṃ tīvraṃ
vrata|niyama|sambādham anaghaṃ:
grahītavyā k" ânyā
saraṇir iha saṃsāra|taraṇe?

2.65 BHIKṢUḤ: Anukūl'|ālāpa|peśal" âiva bhavādṛśāṃ nirmitā Prajā|patinā rasanā.

SNĀTA°: Bhikṣo, tath" âpy ucyatāṃ kaḥ pradeśo vyākhyātum upakrānta iti.

DISCIPLES: As Your Reverend commands.

GRADUATE: *(comes closer and says politely)* Is Your Honor and the circle of your disciples well?

MONK: *(reflecting, to himself)* That graduate Sankárshana has come here, eager to humiliate us this time, after defeating the Buddhists. It's better to back away on this occasion. His valor is irresistible, his oratorical power and his intellect are unique. *(openly)* Welcome, sir. Please take a seat here. Are you well? 2.60

GRADUATE: What is the chosen topic today?

MONK: What is worth choosing* here, in the jungle of transmigration? If one could only find some means to escape it.

GRADUATE: Why, you've certainly found the means. To explain:

> No violence, no lies, no attachment to house, property or clothes, no absorption in any activity that has its immediate result in worldly existence, and this severe asceticism, faultless and full of vows and observances: what other path could one find here to escape the world of transmigration?

MONK: The Lord of Creatures has fashioned a tongue for your ilk, sir, which is very clever at speaking pleasing words. 2.65

GRADUATE: Monk, tell me nonetheless what subject you have started to lecture on.

BHIKṢUḤ: Mahad atra kautukam? Ārhatānām anek'|ânta|vāda eva gṛha|kṛtyam. sa eva c' êha prastutaḥ.

SNĀTA°: Bhikṣo, yad ucyate,

Eko bhāvaḥ sarva|bhāva|svabhāvaḥ,
sarve bhāvā eka|bhāva|svabhāvāḥ.
eko bhāvas tattvato yena dṛṣṭaḥ,
sarve bhāvās tattvatas tena dṛṣṭāḥ.

2.70 Iti, tatr' êdam iha bhavantaṃ pṛcchāmaḥ:

Eko bhāvaś cet sarva|bhāva|svabhāvaḥ,
lokaḥ kāry'|ârthī kutra kaṃ vā niyuṅktām?
sve sve kārye ced asti bhāva|vyavasthā,
n' âiko bhāvaḥ syāt sarva|bhāva|svabhāvaḥ.

Rūpaṃ yady api bhāvānāṃ tulyaṃ kim api dṛśyate,
tath" âpy ananya|gāmy eṣām asti prātisvikaṃ vapuḥ.

Evaṃ tv aniṣyamāṇe 'smin padārtha|niyame janaḥ
n' âdṛṣṭ'|ârthāṃ na dṛṣṭ'|ârthām ārabheta kva cit kriyām.

BHIKṢUḤ *saṃjñayā* ŚIṢYAṂ *nirdiśati.*

2.75 ŚIṢYAḤ: *(sākūtam)* ⌜Bhaṣṭakā, bhikkhavā viṇṇavaṃti cilāyadi bhaṣṭake, tā saṃpadaṃ amha patthuda|kajja|velā adikkamadi tti.⌟

MONK: Are you dying of curiosity? The Jains' doctrine of many-sidedness is the speciality of our house, and is precisely the present topic under discussion.*

GRADUATE: Monk, there is a quote, namely:

> "One thing has as its nature the nature of all things. All things have as their nature the nature of one thing. That person who sees one thing as it really is has seen all things as they really are."

In that case tell me this: 2.70

> If one thing has as its nature the nature of all things, what would people who have some objective employ, and with respect to what? If things are arranged with regard to their respective effects, then one thing cannot have as its nature the nature of all things.
>
> Even if we see some similar form that is shared among entities, nevertheless each of them does have its own, unique essence.
>
> But if the scheme of things were in the way you say, which we do not accept, people would never embark on any work, whether to affect the afterlife or this life.

The MONK *makes a sign to a* DISCIPLE.

DISCIPLE: *(deliberately)* Reverend, the monks beg to inform 2.75
you: "The Reverend is late, so the time of our present duty is running out now."

BHIKṢUḤ: *(SNĀTAKAṂ prati)* Ārya, bhikṣu|kāryam avasīdati. tad bhavantaḥ pramāṇam.

SNĀTA°: Bhikṣo, yathā|matam anuṣṭhīyatām.

BHIKṢUḤ: *(śiṣyam uddiśya)* ⌜Are re turida|turidaṃ gaḍuya bhikkhūṇaṃ bhaṇa jahā appamattā khaṇaṃ tattha yyeva vilaṃbadha, esa āgado mhi tti!⌟

Niṣkrāntaḥ saśiṣyo BHIKṢUḤ.

2.80 SNĀTA°: Baṭo, dṛṣṭam asya bhavatā dig|ambarasya vaidagdhyam.

BAṬUḤ: ⌜Ayya, ko tujjha vāda|samare saṃmuho ṭṭhāduṃ sakkuṇodi? tā imiṇā vavaesa|palāyaṇeṇa rakkhido ṇeṇa appā.⌟

SNĀTA°: Kim asmābhir asya laguḍaiḥ prahartavyam? vastu jñātavyaṃ, tac ca jñātam eva. asmābhis tu tvad|anurodhād eva n' âtra kārkaśyena vyavahṛtam.

BAṬUḤ:

⌜Maüo vi haḍaï hiaaṃ
  vādabbhiḍiāṇa ayya|vāhāro.
mīṇāṇa thala|gayāṇa
  †ebhāvo sisire vistarassa†⌟

2.85 SNĀTA°: Baṭo, tat kv' êdānīṃ gamyatām?

BAṬUḤ: ⌜Ṇaṃ ṇhāduṃ kīsa ṇa gamīyadi?⌟

MONK: *(to the* GRADUATE*)* Sir, the duty of the monks is being neglected. So please decide as you think proper.

GRADUATE: Monk, do as you please.

MONK: *(to the* DISCIPLE*)* Hey, you, run along and tell the monks that they should stay vigilant where they are for a second: I am on my way!

Exits the MONK *with his* DISCIPLES.

GRADUATE: Boy, you have seen the sky-clad Jain monk's cunning. 2.80

BOY: Sir, who could stand his ground against you in the battle of debate? So he saved himself by escaping under this pretext.

GRADUATE: Should I have given him the stick? One has to learn the facts, and we did learn them. But purely out of regard for you I did not take a strong line in this matter.

BOY:

> Gentle though they may be, your words, sir, hurt
> the heart of your disputants; the fish that have been
> washed ashore †. . . †*

GRADUATE: So where shall we go now, boy? 2.85

BOY: Why don't we go to bathe?

SNĀTA°: *(sasmitam)* Kiṃ bubhukṣito vartase? *(ūrdhvam avalokya)* kaḥ khalv adhun" âiva snānasya kālaḥ? tad varam ih' âiv' Ārhata|vasati|vana|gahane muhur viharāmaḥ.

BAṬUḤ: ⌜Evaṃ karīyadu.⌟

Utthāya parikrāmataḥ.

2.90 SNĀTA°: *(agrato 'valokya savismayam)* Aho ramyaḥ praśama|samucito 'yam uddeśaḥ. tathā hi:

Ghana|snigdha|chāyaṃ
vanam idam, imāḥ śādvala|bhuvaḥ,
payaś c' êdaṃ, puṣp'|ôt-
kara|surabhayo vāyava ime,
mṛgāṇām atr' âmī
viharaṇa|vilāsā bahuvidhāḥ,
khagānāṃ c' âneka|
svara|visara|bhinnā virutayaḥ.

(vicintya)

Ih' âraṇye puṇye
yadi bhavati Ved'|ânta|nirato
nivṛtt'|āśīr|ātmā
niyamita|manovṛtti|nivahaḥ,
dinair alpair eva
vyapagata|bhav'|âdhva|śrama|javaṃ
dhruvaṃ nity'|ānandaṃ
kim api paramaṃ dhāma labhate.

GRADUATE: *(smiling)* Why, are you hungry? *(looking upward)* How could it be bathing time right now? We should rather stay a little while right here, in the thicket of the Jain mendicants' abode.

BOY: Fine.

They stand up and walk about.

GRADUATE: *(looks ahead and says with astonishment)* O, this 2.90
place is so delightful and suitable for relaxation! For:

> This wood gives thick and cooling shade; there are grassy spots and there is also water here; these winds are fragrant from bunches of flowers; the deer playfully gambol here every way; and the trill of the birds is blended with thc swing of many tunes.

(reflecting)

> If someone devoted to Vedanta were to live here in the holy forest, his soul's wishes ceased and the legion of his mental activities curbed, within just a few days he would surely reach an extraordinary, supreme, splendid state, eternally blissful and void of the haste and toils of the mundane path.

Nepathye:

2.95 ⌜Veyaṃtā duttaraṃtā,
taï|kahiya|kahā vittharā saṃkulatthā.
ayyehiṃ tattha ciṃtī-
yadi gahaṇa|gadī atthi ṇatthi tti appā?
dūre ciṭṭhaṃtu te me!
pariharidum idaṃ ghora|saṃsāra|dukkhaṃ
saṃkkhittaṃ ṇimmalatthaṃ
Jiṇa|muṇi|bhaṇidaṃ āgamaṃ āharamhā.⌟

BAṬUḤ: ⌜Ayya, eso khu kāsāa|vasaṇo tāvaso īrisaṃ kiṃ pi maṃtaṃto turida|turidaṃ parikkāmadi. . .⌟ *tataḥ praviśati* TĀPASAḤ.

TĀPASO *« Veyaṃtā. . . » iti paṭhan parikrāmati.*

BAṬUḤ: ⌜Ajja vi Jiṇa|sāsaṇe yyeva eyāṇa ahiṇiveso?⌟

SNĀTA°: Baṭo, tiṣṭhatv etat. kim anena? anyad ev' âinaṃ pṛcchāmaḥ. (TĀPASAM *uddiśya)* bhos tapo|dhana, kv' êdam ākul'|ākulam iva gamyate bhavatā?

2.100 TĀPA°: ⌜Bamhaṇo khu tuvaṃ. tā kiṃ attaṇo bhukkhā|veaṇaṃ ṇa āṇāsi?⌟

SNĀTA°: Kiṃ bhavān bhoktuṃ prasthitaḥ?

TĀPA°: ⌜Adha iṃ?⌟

SNĀTA°: Ka uddeśo gantavyaḥ?

TĀPA°: ⌜Ṇaṃ iha yyeva Jiṇa|rakkhida|bhikkhu|tavo|vaṇe ajja mahā|bhoaṇaṃ vaṭṭadi.⌟

2.105 SNĀTA°: Mahā|bhojane ko hetuḥ?

From offstage:

One can hardly get to the bottom of Vedantic teachings. The stories told in the three Vedas are confusing with verbose details. The highborn speculate on the profound issue therein: "Is there a Self, or isn't there?" Keep them away from me! In order to cast off the excruciating pain of existence, let's stick to the concise, lucid scriptures that the sage Jina taught.* 2.95

BOY: Sir, here comes in hot haste a red-robed mendicant, jabbering something like this... *Then enters an* ASCETIC.

The ASCETIC *walks about reciting "One can hardly get to..."*

BOY: Of all things, these folks still adhere to the Jina's teachings?

GRADUATE: Never mind, boy. What of it? I am going to ask him something else. *(to the* ASCETIC*)* Good day to you, ascetic. Where are you going in such a frantic flurry?

ASCETIC: You are clearly a brahmin, so how come you don't know how it feels to be hungry? 2.100

GRADUATE: Have you set out to dine, sir?

ASCETIC: What else?

GRADUATE: Where will you go?

ASCETIC: Why, just here, in the penance grove of the monk Jina·rákshita there is a great feast today.

GRADUATE: What's the reason for the great feast? 2.105

TĀPA°: ⌜Keṇa vi bhayavado Jiṇa|guruṇo sāsaṇa|gadeṇa ṭhakkureṇa ajja tahiṃ mahā|bhoaṇaṃ uvavādidaṃ, jattha pavvaïya|sahassāïṃ saṃghaḍidāïṃ. tāṇa a sattūṇa rāsīo, tella|ghaḍiā, kaṃcia|kuṃbhīo, guḍa|kūḍayā, tella|pakkāṇa bhakkhāṇa pavvayā uvaṇīā.⌟

SNĀTA°: Bhos tapo|dhana, ath' âtra madhye dadhi|kṣīra|ghṛt'|ādi nāma na kiṃ cid gṛhṇāsi?

TĀPA°: ⌜Ahaha, tumhāṇaṃ bamhaṇāṇa ede samāārā. amha uṇa tavo|haṇā pāṇi|saṃbhavaṃ kiṃ pi ṇa asaṇe ṇa pāṇe ṇa vasaṇe ṇa saaṇe ṇa āsaṇe ṇa aṇṇattha kattha vi sarīr'|ôvaaraṇe viṇivesemha. ṇaṃ mama yyeva ime rukkha|vidala|ṇimmide uvāṇahie kiṃ ṇa pekkhasi? tā bhodu imiṇā kahā|vittharena. bhoaṇa|samao me adikkamadi.⌟

SNĀTA°: Mam' âpi ādeśaya panthānam. vayam api tapo|dhana|vibhūtiṃ paśyāmaḥ.

2.110 TĀPA°: ⌜Evaṃ karīadu, evaṃ karīadu. tā edu bhavaṃ.⌟

Sarve parikrāmanti.

SNĀTA°: Bhos tapo|dhana, Jina|śāsanaṃ pratipanno bhavān katham kāṣāya|vāsāḥ? api Sugata eva Jino bhavatām?

TĀPA°: *(sasmitam)* ⌜Amhāṇaṃ a Sugado bhaavaṃ Jiṇa|gurū. kiṃ ca Jiṇagurū Sugado hodi. aho bhaddā amhe ārahadā, ke vi diyaṃbarā, ke vi rukkha|vidala|metta|vasaṇā, ke vi ratta|vāsā, ke vi sea|vaḍā. pekkha dāva. ido ime ṇiddaya|luṃcaṇa|pasaṃga|lakkhijjaṃta|loma|mūla|viyalaṃta|pavirala|taṇua|soṇia|kaṇā diyaṃbarā. ido khu ime

ASCETIC: A certain nobleman who has embraced the Master Jina's teachings gives there a dinner party today, where thousands of ascetics have gathered together. They are offered piles of groats, jars of sesame oil, vessels of sour gruel, small jugs of molasses and mountains of edibles cooked in sesame oil.

GRADUATE: Tell me, ascetic, among all these dishes won't you get any curd, milk, ghee and the like at all?*

ASCETIC: Ah! No! These customs are proper to you, brahmins. We ascetics, however, do not use anything coming from animals either for eating, or for drinking, or for clothing, or for lying or sitting on, or in any other way of grooming the body. Can't you see these sandals of mine, made of bark? So enough of this chatter! I am late for the dinner.

GRADUATE: Show me, too, the way. I'll also have a look at the riches of the ascetics.

ASCETIC: Do so, do so. Please come, then. 2.110

All walk about.

GRADUATE: Tell me, ascetic, you follow the Jina's teaching, so why do you wear red robes? Is your Jina the Súgata*?

ASCETIC: *(smiling)* For us, too, the blessed Master Jina is Súgata*. Moreover, the Súgata is also called Master Jina.* How fortunate are we, Arhatas,* some of us clad only in sky, some wearing only bark robes, others dressed in red clothes,* others in white robes. Observe! Here come the sky-clad ones, the roots of their hair—visible due to their devotion to merciless plucking—dripping

†cattulavasūra†caccijjaṃta|komala|vakkal'|aṃcalā cīra|vasaṇā. ido ime takkhaṇa|pakka|kaṃdu|uddharia|sarāva|sarisa|vaṇṇa|vasaṇā a bamha|āriṇo tavo|haṇā. ido ime haṃsa|pakkha|paṃḍura|pavaṇa|lulida|paḍa|pallavā sea|vaḍā. tā aho puṇṇa|bhāaṇo so ṭhakkuro jassa ime ajja aṇuggahaṃ karissaṃti!⌟

SNĀTA°: *(sasmitam ātma|gatam)* Puṇya|bhājanam ucyate, n' ânarthakār" îti.

2.115 Na cintayati dantinaṃ,
na turagaṃ, na naukṣeyakaṃ,
na vartma, na kara|grahaṃ,
na kaṭak'|âṅgam uṣṭr'|ādi vā.
iha kṣapita|vitta|sāram avalupta|sevā|vidhiṃ
vidhāsyati nar'|âdhipo
dhruvam imaṃ vibhūti|cyutam.

(prakāśam) Aho tapo|vanasya praśānta|ramaṇīyatā!

Śama|mayam iva dṛśyate jagan,
niyama|may" îva cakāsti medinī,
iha khalu bhava|pāśa|paṅktayo
viśakalitā iva bhānti dehinām.

BAṬUḤ: ⌜Diṭṭhā diaṃbarā cīra|vasaṇā kāsāya|vāsā sea|vaḍā. tā saṃpadaṃ ido ime ṇīl'|aṃbarā dīsaṃtu.⌟

scanty and small blood-drops.* Here come those who wear bark rags, the borders of their soft bark garment smeared with † . . . †.* Here come the ascetic brahmin students, their robes the color of baked earthenware just at this moment taken out of the kiln.* Here come the white-robed ones, the lappets of their garments white as goose wings, fluttering in the zephyr. How meritorious is the nobleman whom they will favor today!*

GRADUATE: *(smiling, to himself)* He is called "meritorious," and not "noxious."

> He does not care about elephants, or horses, or swords, or the roads, or levying taxes, or the division of an army, or camels and the like. Since he squanders the cream of his wealth for such a cause and shirks the performance of his services, I'm sure the sovereign will confiscate his property. 2.115

(openly) How peaceful and charming is this penance grove!

> The world seems to me full of tranquility, the earth appears to be practicing observances. Here it truly looks to me as if the series of snares of existence that bind the embodied souls were broken into pieces.

BOY: We've seen mendicants dressed in thin air, in bark, in red garments and in white robes. And now look at these black-blankets coming this way.

SNĀTA°: *(agrato 'valokya savismayam)* Aho bat' âpūrvam idaṃ tapaḥ! eka|nīla|vasan'|āvṛtāv imau strī|puṃsau kim apy atipeśalaṃ gāyantau saha viharataḥ. *(nipuṇaṃ nirvarṇya)* katham? aneka|saṅkhyāny etāni dṛśyante. bhavatu, ativiplutā pṛthivī, utsannā trayī. (TĀPASAM *uddiśya)* bhos tapo|dhana, vidito 'yaṃ tava navaḥ ko 'pi tapasāṃ prakāraḥ?

2.120 TĀPA°: ⌜Ahaṃ edaṃ ṇa āṇāmi ko eso caüra|ṇiyama|maggo. edaṃ khu takkemi idha mahā|bhoaṇa|kiṃvaaṃtiṃ suṇia bhoyaṇa|metta|lālasā ke vi ede paribbhamaṃti. tā bhodu edāṇaṃ vuttaṃteṇa. samāṇa|cariāṇaṃ yyeva majjhaṃ vaccāmi.⌟ *(iti niṣkrāntaḥ.)*

Tataḥ praviśata eka/nīla/paṭa/prāvṛtau gāyantau strī/puṃsau, vibhav'/ânusāreṇa vā bahūni tathā/vidhāni mithunāni gāyanti.

⌜Jayaï muṇī Ṇīl'|aṃbara|ṇāho,
jeṇa samiŏ bhava|saṃvara|gāho.⌟

⌜Jasu bhaavaṃ tuha sāsaṇa ṇokkhaṃ,
pijjaï kiṃ pi rasāaṇa|sokkhaṃ.⌟

⌜Bhave bhuṃjijjaï itthia|sukkhaṃ,
para|loe pāvijjaï mokkhaṃ.⌟

2.125 ⌜So sijjhaï sarīradā,
laṃghijjaï saṃsāradā.⌟

⌜To aṇṇe je puṇa āsamā,
tāṇa ṇibaṃdhahu āsa mā:
parisosijjaï dehaḍā,
mokkhahi puṇa saṃdehaḍā.⌟

GRADUATE: *(looks ahead and says with astonishment)* God bless my soul, this is a novel kind of asceticism! A woman and a man, wrapped up in a single black garment, amuse themselves singing some uncommonly charming song. *(looking carefully)* What? There seem to be legions of them! Sure enough: the earth is swamped, the three Vedas are uprooted. *(to the* MENDICANT*)* Tell me, ascetic, are you familiar with this new, extraordinary method of asceticism?

ASCETIC: I don't know what is this lovely* method of re- 2.120
ligious observance. I am indeed inclined to think that some people have heard rumors about the dinner party and are hovering about simply because they are eager to get some food. So enough said about their story! I'll join my co-religionists. *(Exits.)*

*Then enter a woman and a man, wrapped up in a single black robe and singing, or, if it can be afforded, many such couples singing as follows:**

Victory to the sage Black-Blanket Lord, who has relieved the obsession of living life within bounds.

One who follows your novel teaching, O Blessed Lord, drinks the unique bliss of the *elixir vitæ*.

In this life he revels in making love to women, in the next world achieves deliverance.

The body bears fruit,* transmigration is escaped. 2.125

Have no faith in other schools where the body is completely emaciated, and liberation remains uncertain.

⌜Sikkhā|joe kāï viḍhappaï?
purusu para|vvasu parisammappaï.⌟

⌜Guṇa pariajjia jaï visara,
so vi u purusaha bhoa|hara.⌟

⌜Pamaḍhiu saṃgamu jeṇa i eso,
† tāṃhasoṇivvalusahajasahāüṇira . . . †⌟

2.130 ⌜Idi jaï jua jua vijāṇi . . . puṇu bhoa.⌟

⌜Sarīrehi kaṃ paesa bhamaṃtā
kaṃ paaṃ ajjaṃti aṇiṭṭhiajammā?⌟

⌜Jaï paramappa|vivattu iṃu,
jaï vā sadda|vivattu iṃu,⌟

⌜To vi avijjā|pasame viṇu
kaha iṃu saalu . . . ?⌟

⌜†satattu† ema je aṇṇe vi
āgama, vihalā saala muṇevi.⌟

2.135 ⌜Ettha parattha vi suhu lahahu
muṇi|Ṇīl'|aṃbara levi . . .⌟

SNĀTA°: *(ciraṃ gītam ākarṇya)* Baṭo, gīta|vyapadeśam aśeṣa|darśan'|ākṣepakaṃ ken' âpi kalpitaṃ vāda|sthānakam idam. ahaṃ tu prāyaścitta|bhīrur na śaknomy eva kaśmalair ebhir vācaṃ miśrayitum.

Strī|puṃsau punas tad eva gāyataḥ.

SNĀTA°: Baṭo, paśya,

What is procured in the pursuit of training? Man ends up a slave!*

If plenty of merits are gathered, they, too, are bound to deprive men of their pleasures.

One who wraps up this union †. . . † . . . *

If every single couple knows thus <. . . >
. . . pleasure again (?)

Without consummating one's birth, where will one roam in one's body and where will one reach?*

If this world is a transformation of the Supreme Self, or if it is a transformation of the Word,

Still, without the cessation of ignorance how could all this . . . ?*

†. . . † having thus learned that all other religions are fruitless.

Obtain happiness both here and in the world beyond, following the sage Black-Blanket . . . *

GRADUATE: *(listening to the song at some length)* Boy, this is a cheap matter of disputation, invented by somebody to abuse all the philosophical systems under the pretext of a song. But I dare not even strike up a conversation with these rotters, for I am loath to suffer the expiatory purification this would require.

The woman and man sing the same song again.

GRADUATE: Look, boy,

Vācaḥ kā cana n' âsti śuddhir, avamaḥ
kāyo 'pi śauc'|ôjjhitaś,
ceto nirvicikitsa|kutsita|tara|
vyāpāra|nityotsavam.
no jāne paraloka|nirbhaya|dhiyaḥ
kasy' âvadātaṃ tapaś|
cary"|āścaryam idaṃ. <na> kaś cid atha vā
puṃsām avadyo vidhiḥ?

2.140 api ca:

Svacchandaṃ carcyamān" ôc-
carati ciram iyaṃ carcarī|gīta|goṣṭhī.
pīyante kānta|vaktr'|ā-
sava|śavala|rasāny astaśaṅkaṃ madhūni.
tanyante tantra|vastu|
vyavahita|niyata|prastut'|ânyonya|śṛṅgair
aṅgaiś ceṣṭā yath"|êṣṭā.
vratam atisubhagaṃ sevyate kena n' âitat?

BAṬUḤ: ⌜Evaṃ ṇedaṃ jadhā ayyo maṃtedi.⌟

SNĀTA°: Mama c' êyaṃ sambhāvanā yan nūtanam adya|pravṛttam idaṃ Mahā|vratam. atiprasṛte gāyamāne 'sminn atimātraṃ viplavate varṇ'|āśrama|samācāro. bhavatu, bhagnam iva trayī|vartma paśyāmi.

Idaṃ tapas taruṇa|mano|bhinandanaṃ
vilokya hi vyapagata|sarva|yantraṇam
pati|vratā api kula|yoṣitaś ciraṃ
sthiraṃ padaṃ dadhati na bhartṛ|veśmasu.

There is no purity in their words, their vile bodies also lack cleanness, their minds always delight in inconsiderate, utterly despicable behavior. I do not know whose heart is so unafraid of the afterlife to engage in this meritorious, wonderful penitential practice. Or is there <no> human behavior disreputable?

Moreover: 2.140

This singing of rhythmic songs, repeated ad libitum, rings as the day is long. Shaking off all scruples, they drink sweet wine, its sap mixed with the lover's saliva. Bodies make licentious movements, their steadily continued mutual arousal concealed by the product of the loom. Who would not observe this extremely sensual vow?

BOY: It is just as you say, sir.

GRADUATE: And I am inclined to think that this is a new, modern Great Vow.* If what they are singing about becomes too widespread, the established conduct of social estates and life-periods will be ruined beyond measure. Sure enough: the path of the three Vedas appears to me to have gone to shivers.

For as soon as they see this "penance," applauded by the greenhorn, in which all restraints are abolished, even faithful housewives will not sojourn long in their husbands' houses.

2.145 BAṬUḤ: *(sasmitam)* ⌜Ayyassa kiṃ jādaṃ? ṇa hu ayyeṇa ajja vi dāra|saṃgaho kado. amhe uṇa dūre dāva esā kadhā.⌟

SNĀTA°: Nanu āryā janayitrī te jīvaty eva.

BAṬUḤ: ⌜Sā khu saṃpadaṃ ado aṇatthādo uttiṇṇā, jā jīvaṃta|mudiā vuḍḍhikā vaṭṭadi.⌟

SNĀTA°: Kṛtaṃ parihāsena. mahān eṣo viplava upasthitaḥ. tad baṭo, cintaya, kim atra pratisamādhānam.

BAṬUḤ: ⌜Ayya, ṇa me paḍibhādi. tumaṃ yyeva jāṇāsi. iṇhiṃ puṇa pavaḍḍhaṃto eso kali|juo. tā kudo ittha īdisāṇa aṇatthāṇa paḍīāro?⌟

2.150 SNĀTA°: Tath" âpi n' ânadhyavasāya|stimitam āsituṃ yuktam. *(vicintya)* bhavatu, labdho 'vakāśaḥ.

BAṬUḤ: ⌜Ko uṇa eso bhavissadi?⌟

SNĀTA°: Nanv asau rājā śrī|Śaṅkara|devaḥ. sa hi varṇ'|āśrama|dharma|maryād"|ācāryas tri|bhuvana|rakṣā|dīkṣito devaḥ svata eva pratikriyām atra jānāti, viśeṣato 'śeṣa|bhav'|āgama|pārage pārśva|vartini tatra|bhavati Bhaṭṭa|Jayante. bhavatu! tam eva śrāvayāmaḥ. na kāla|paripālana|yogyo hy anarthaḥ. baṭo, tadā tvam apy etau bhojan'|âjir'|ôddeśaṃ prasthāpaya gāyantau strī|puṃsau.

BOY: *(smiling)* Why does it bother you, sir? You haven't married yet. As for me, that story is still far away. 2.145

GRADUATE: But your venerable mother is still alive, isn't she?

BOY: She is definitely immune to this disaster by now, since she is a poor old woman, as good as dead.

GRADUATE: Stop joking. A great evil has arisen here. So think, boy, what is the remedy for this.

BOY: Sir, I have no idea. You must know it. But the Iron Age is taking over these days, so how could one counteract such disasters?

GRADUATE: Nevertheless, it is not proper to sit paralyzed, without making some attempt. *(reflecting)* Right, there is a way out. 2.150

BOY: And what will that be?

GRADUATE: Surely the king himself, His Majesty Shánkara·varman. For he, as the sovereign who is the preceptor of the lawful bounds prescribed for the social estates and life-periods, anointed to protect the three worlds, will naturally know the remedy for this case, especially since he has the honorable Bhatta Jayánta by his side, who has mastered all the scriptures of Shiva. That's right! He is the one I shall inform. For a disaster permits no delay. Boy, as for you, push on this singing woman and man toward the dining arena.

BAṬUḤ: ⌜Bho tavassiṇo, ṇaṃ ettha tavo|vaṇe bhoaṇa|kālo tumhāṇaṃ vaṭṭadi. tā kīsa atikkamīyadi?⌟

Iti niṣkrāntāḥ sarve.

2.155 *Dvitīyo 'ṅkaḥ*

BOY: Hallo, mendicants, I say, it is dinnertime for you in this penance grove, so why should you be late?

Exeunt omnes.

End of the second act. 2.155

PRELUDE TO ACT THREE: PANIC AMONG THE FEARLESS

Tataḥ praviśati SĀDHAKAḤ.

SĀDHAKAḤ: *(sodvegaṃ diśo 'valokya)* ⌜Astaṃ|gade khu iṇhiṃ śamae Mah"|ēśa|lāṇaṇaṃ ṇava|śaśaṃke. śuṇṇe aṃdha|āle gaaṇe hiae vva amhāṇaṃ. śaṃpadaṃ bhodi eśe palāaṇ'|âvaśale. tā kahiṃ me pia|vaaśśe Maśāṇa|bhūdī gade jeṇa śamaṃ palāïśśaṃ?⌟ *(parikramy' âgrato 'valokya ca)* ⌜eśe Maśāṇa|bhūdī idha yyeva āgaścaṃte lakkhīyadi.⌟

Tataḥ praviśati dvitīyaḥ SĀDHAKAḤ.

DVITĪYAḤ SĀDHAKAḤ: ⌜Eśe śe vaaśśa|Kaṃkāla|keduṇo maḍhiā. mae śe imaśśiṃ aṃdha|yāle vi īś'|īśi dīśadi. tā uppekkhia uppekkhia padāï gamiśśaṃ.⌟ *(parikrāmati. karṇaṃ dattvā)* ⌜pada|śadde via. bhaavaṃ, maṇṇāmi ṇaala|laṣkaā ido hiṃḍaṃti! ye śaṃpāvia collaṃ ti śaṃkāe baṃdhaṇ'|āālaṃ ṇeṃti, śūle vā ṇiṣkivaṃti, luṣke vā pāśena ullaṃbeṃti. bhodu! bhayavaṃ Bhaïlava|ṇādhe śalaṇaṃ.⌟ *(nipuṇaṃ nirūpya)* ⌜vaaśśa|Kaṃkāla|keduṇo vva vāhāle śuṇīadi.⌟ *(samāśvasy' ôpasṛtya)* ⌜vaaśśa Kaṃkāla|kedū, tava yyeva śayāśaṃ upaśaṃpatte. ṇaala|laṣkaāṇa śaṃkide mhi.⌟

3.5 PRATHAMAḤ: ⌜Ale Maśāṇa|bhūdī tumaṃ? śohaṇaṃ tae kadaṃ yaṃ eśu tuvaṃ āgade. tā tulidaṃ hiṃḍāma. ime aṃdha|āle ṇa vilamadi yāva, śamaṃ yyeva palāamha.⌟

DVITĪYAḤ: ⌜Kiṃ cola|śaṃkāe ṇaala|laṣkaā maṃ māleṃti tti śaṃbhāveśi?⌟

PRATHAMAḤ: ⌜Ṇa eśā me śaṃkā. hoṃtī avi uvaśamadi. aṇṇe uṇa aṇaste uvastide.⌟

Then enters an ADEPT. *

ADEPT: *(looks around nervously)* The horned moon—the Great Lord's mark has set by now. The sky is empty and dark, like my heart. No time like this to slip away. So where is my bosom friend, Crematory-Ash, with whom I shall run off? *(He walks about and looks ahead.)* Here is Crematory-Ash, he seems to be coming right this way.

Then enters the SECOND ADEPT.

2ND ADEPT: Here is comrade Skeleton-Banner's shelter. I can see it dimly even in this darkness. So I'll go watching my steps. *(He walks about and listens.)* I thought I heard footsteps. Good Lord, I think the city guards are walking this way! If they come upon me they'll believe that I have robbed someone and they'll throw me into prison, or put me on the spit, or hang me on a tree. Not to worry! Lord Bháirava is my refuge. *(He looks carefully.)* I thought I heard comrade Skeleton-Banner talking. *(He takes heart and goes closer.)* Comrade Skeleton-Banner, it's you I've stumbled upon! I was afraid it was the city guards.

1ST ADEPT: Hey, Crematory-Ash, is that you? Well done for 3.5
coming here. So let's move on quickly. Let's slip away together while it is still dark.

2ND ADEPT: Are you afraid that the city guards will take you for a thief and put you to death?

1ST ADEPT: I have no such fear. Even if I have, it dissipates. But another evil has arisen.

DVITĪYAḤ: *(sasambhramam)* ⌜Kīśa?⌟

PRATHAMAḤ: ⌜Ayi, asti dāva, kiṃ tae ṇa śudā eśā kiṃ|vadaṃtī? aṇṇe yyeva śaṃpadaṃ eśe duṣṭa|laṣṭe vaṭṭadi.⌟

3.10 DVITĪYAḤ: ⌜Uttammadi me hiaaṃ! tā tulidaṃ āviṣkaledu vaaśśe!⌟

PRATHAMAḤ: ⌜Dāluṇe khu lāe Śaṃkala|vamme. tado vi viśame śe bamhaṇe taśśa amacce dul|āāla|Jayaṃte, jehiṃ te tavaśśiṇo ṇīl'|ambalā vaḍia piṭṭiya Veda|vāhila tti laṭṭhādo ṇivvāśidā. aṇṇe ya je Veda|vāhile tavaśśī labbhadi, śe piṭṭīyadi mālīadi baṃdhīadi ghallīadi. tā amhe vi tāṇa yyeva majjhe gaṇaṇīa mha. śulaṃ piyamha, maṃśaṃ bhakkhamha itthiyaṃ gaścamha. ṇaṃ amhe vi śa|vvamhayāliṇo ṇīl'|aṃbalāṇaṃ. tā śaṃpadaṃ edaṃ śādhaka|veśaṃ ācchādia tulida|hiṃḍaṇena imaśśiṃ aṃdha|yāle alaṣkidā gaścamha.⌟

DVITĪYAḤ: *(sabhayam)* ⌜Evaṃ kalemha!⌟

Parikrāmataḥ.

DVITĪYAḤ: ⌜Vaaśśa Kaṃkāla|kedū, kahaṃ puṇa eśe aṇaste uvaṇade?⌟

3.15 PRATHAMAḤ: ⌜Śuṇa, asti dāva śe śaṇādaka|bamhaṇe Śaṃkaliśaṇa|ṇāme jeṇa Jiṇa|lakkhida|bhikkhu|vaśadi|kāṇaṇe vihalaṃtā gāaṃtā aśaṃkhā ṇīlaṃbala|mihuṇā diṣṭā.⌟

2nd Adept: *(agitated)* How come?

1st Adept: Why, certainly, there is this rumor, haven't you heard it? Nowadays this damned kingdom has completely changed.

2nd Adept: My heart is going pit-a-pat! Come on, comrade, 3.10
spill it quick!

1st Adept: King Shánkara·varman's cruelty is public knowledge. That brahmin, his adviser, the wicked Jayánta is even rougher than he. They nabbed the mendicant black-blankets, beat them to jelly, and expelled them from the kingdom, on the ground that they were outside Vedic religion. And if any other mendicant is caught who is outside Vedic religion, he'll be beaten up, killed, thrown in jail, or slain. Are we not one of them? We drink booze, eat meat, have women. Don't we observe the same religious discipline as the black-blankets? So now let's hide our adept-dress, and move on with rapid steps, unnoticed in this darkness.

2nd Adept: *(alarmed)* Let's do so!

They walk about.

2nd Adept: Comrade Skeleton-Banner, how did this evil crop up?

1st Adept: Listen. To begin with, there is that graduate 3.15
brahmin called Sankárshana. He saw countless black-blanket couples singing and having fun in the grove where resides the monk Jina·rákshita.

DVITĪYAḤ: ⌜Tado?⌟

PRATHAMAḤ: ⌜Tado teṇa śe Jaaṃte jāṇāvide. teṇa a lāe pavohide.⌟

DVITĪYAḤ: ⌜Tado?⌟

PRATHAMAḤ: ⌜Tado lāeṇa śe śaṇādaka|bamhaṇe Śaṃkaliśaṇe āṇāvia vivāhāvia māṇehi paṭṭa|vaṃdheṇa śili|śaddeṇa a śakkalia śaalāe yyeva vaśuṃdhalāe dhamma|laṣk”|âdhiāle ṇiutte. teṇa eśe pajjālide aggī.⌟

3.20 DVITĪYAḤ: ⌜Ṇaṃ dul|āāla|Jayaṃteṇa pajjālide tti ācaṣka.⌟

PRATHAMAḤ: ⌜Asti yyeva edaṃ. tā śaṃpadaṃ kahiṃ gaścamha?⌟

DVITĪYAḤ: ⌜Ṇaṃ yog'|ēśalīe Kālaggi|śihāe aggado vaccamha. teśu eśe uvaśagge kadā vi ṇa bādhadi.⌟

PRATHAMAḤ: ⌜Śā vi eśu kāle pālīyadi?⌟

DVITĪYAḤ: ⌜Evaṃ śaṃkāmi lāaśśa palama|vallabhāe śaala|śuddhaṃta|śāmiṇīe śā istia tti kadā vi laññīe Śuyaṃdhā|devīe laṣkīyadi.⌟

3.25 PRATHAMAḤ: ⌜Śā vi laṣkijjaṃtī kiṃ amha laṣkiduṃ pāledi? bhodu, kaśśiṃ pi gabbhala|pelaṃte dūle di|aṃtale gaścamha.⌟

DVITĪYAḤ: ⌜Yaṃ ācaṣkadi vaaśśe. tā yāva pabhāde ṇa payaṭṭadi tāva tulidaṃ hiṃḍamha.⌟

2nd Adept: And then?

1st Adept: Then he informed Jayánta. He in his turn briefed the king.

2nd Adept: And then?

1st Adept: Then the king sent for that graduate brahmin Sankárshana, got him married, granted him privileges, the right of wearing a turban and using the title Right Honorable, and appointed him to the position of superintendent over the religious matters of the whole country. He started this fire.

2nd Adept: You should rather say that the wicked Jayánta 3.20
started it.

1st Adept: Anyway, that's how things are. So where shall we go now?

2nd Adept: We must present ourselves before Doomsday-Fire's-Flame, the sorceress. These bad times will hopefully not trouble us there.

1st Adept: Is she protected these days?

2nd Adept: I suppose that Queen Sugándha·devi, the chief wife of the king, mistress of the whole harem, will perhaps take her under her shelter, because she is a woman.

1st Adept: Even if she is protected, can she protect us? 3.25
I know! Let's go to some faraway region bounded by forests.

2nd Adept: You're right, comrade. So let's move on quickly before the day begins to break.

Tathā kurutaḥ.

PRATHAMAḤ: ⌜Ale Maśāṇa|bhūdī, yadhā maṃteśi. pabhāde uṇa hiṃḍiduṃ yyeva eśu kulaṣṭe ṇa pālīadi.⌟

DVITĪYAḤ: ⌜Kīśa?⌟

3.30 PRATHAMAḤ: ⌜Viśae viśae ṇaale ṇaale gāme gāme thale thale Ved'|ajjhayaṇa|śaddeṇa tuṭṭaṃti kaṇṇā, ajja|gaṃdheṇa tuṭṭadi ghāṇe, jaṇṇa|dhūmeṇa galaṃti aṣkīi. tā eśe kulaṣṭe laaṇīhiṃ yyeva laṃghīyadu. diaśā uṇa keśu ci vaṇa|gahaṇeśu adivāhīaṃtu.⌟

DVITĪYAḤ: ⌜Evaṃ ṇedaṃ. Śaṃkaliśaṇa|bhaeṇa vi laaṇīśu yyeva amhehiṃ hiṃḍidavvaṃ. diaśā uṇa alaṇṇeśu alaṣkidehiṃ ṇedavvā.⌟

Parikrāmataḥ.

PRATHAMAḤ: ⌜Ale Maśāṇa|bhūdī pavibhatta vva diśāo śaalā. śaṇiaṃ galaṃti ṇaṣkattā. tāva oṇade pabhāde. amhāṇam kiṃ ṇu kādavvaṃ?⌟

Nepathye paṭaha|śabd'|ânantaram: bho bhoḥ paura|jāna|padā, eṣa khalu mahā|rāja|Śaṅka|ravarma|deva|rāj'|ājñayā Bhaṭṭa|Śrī|Saṃkarṣaṇaḥ sarvān eva yuṣmān bodhayati:

3.35 Ye 'tr' ânādi|jagat|pravāha|patitā
nān"|āgamāḥ sādhavas,
te tiṣṭhantu yathā|sthitāḥ sva|samay'|ā-
diṣṭāś carantaḥ kriyāḥ.
ye tu prastuta|dharma|viplava|kṛtaḥ

They do so.

1st Adept: Hey, Crematory-Ash, you're right. But after daybreak one cannot even walk a step in this damned kingdom.

2nd Adept: Why?

1st Adept: In every region, every single town, every vil- 3.30
lage, everywhere the sound of Veda-recitation grates on the ear, the smell of ghee stings the nose, the smoke of sacrifice brings tears to the eyes. So we must cross this damned kingdom strictly by night. The days, however, must be tided over in the depths of some forest.

2nd Adept: Quite right. Also for fear of Sankárshana we must move strictly by night. The days, however, must be spent unnoticed in the woods.

They walk about.

1st Adept: Hey, Crematory-Ash, the quarters all seem to have parted, the stars are slowly waning. Now dawn has arrived. What shall we do?

From offstage, after the sound of drums: Listen here, citizens and villagers! By the royal order of His Majesty King Shánkara·varman, the Right Honorable Bhatta Sankárshana notifies all of you:

> Those virtuous people who have fallen into the be- 3.35
> ginningless stream of the world and belong to various religions—they should remain as they are, performing practices prescribed by their own religious discipline. Those criminal false ascetics, however, who devastate the established social and religious

pāpās tap'|ôpāyinas,
te ced āśu na yānti ghātayati tān
dasyūn iva kṣmā|patiḥ.

UBHAU: *(śrutvā sabhayam)* ⌜Āgade yyeva Śaṃkaliśaṇa|vava-deśeṇa jaṃgame amhāṇa maccū. tā aṇṇado tulida|tuli-daṃ gacchamha.⌟

Niṣkrāntau.

order—if they don't leave immediately, the king will strike them like thieves.

BOTH: *(listening, alarmed)* Our walking death by the name of Sankárshana has truly arrived. So let's move on quickly somewhere else.

Exeunt ambo.

ACT THREE:
RELIGION DENIED AND DEFENDED

Pataḥ praviśati parityakta|snātaka|veśo gṛhīta|gṛhastha|rāja|puruṣ'|ôcita|veśaḥ Śrī|SAṄKARṢAṆO, BAṬUR, *vibhavataś ca parivāraḥ.*

SNĀTA°: Baṭo, api nīl'|âmbar'|ôtsāraṇena parivadaty asmān janaḥ?

3.40 BAṬUḤ: ⌜Ayya, mā evaṃ saṃkadu bhavaṃ! durāārehi alīya| tāvasehi abhibhavijjaṃto paṇaṭṭho yyeva puṇo ayyeṇa païṭṭhido taï|dhammo.⌟

SNĀTA°: Nanu devena Śrī|Śaṅkara|varmaṇā pratiṣṭhāpita iti brūhi. tat kim anye na nīl'|âmbara|chāy"|ânukāriṇa utsāraṇa|yogyāḥ pracaranti pṛthivyām alīka|tāpasāḥ?

BAṬUḤ: ⌜Ayya, Seva|vavaesena jaṃ kiṃ pi āyaraṃtā ittia| kālaṃ diṭṭhā duṭṭhā tāvasā. saṃpadaṃ puṇa agaṇidā ayya|padāveṇa te vi paviralā hoṃti.⌟

SNĀTA°: Sādh' ûktam. may" âpi te na na dṛṣṭāḥ. pātraṃ te nirvāsanasya. tathā hi:

Apeyaṃ kiṃ teṣāṃ?
    nanu virahitaṃ yad dravatayā.
  abhakṣyaṃ yat tiktaṃ
    dalayitum aśakyaṃ ca daśanaiḥ.
ajātā pretā vā
    yadi param agamyā stanavatī.
  tapaḥ|sthānaṃ yogyaṃ
    kim iva? yadi vā śauṇḍika|gṛham.

Then enters the Right Honorable SANKÁRSHANA, *who has divested himself of his graduate-garments and is dressed in garments becoming a married functionary of the king, and the* BOY, *and as many attendants as can be afforded.*

GRADUATE: Boy, do people speak ill of us because we have driven away the black-blankets?

BOY: Have no such fear, sir! You have reestablished the 3.40
religious order of the Three Vedas, which had been truly ruined, vanquished by depraved false ascetics.

GRADUATE: You should rather say that King Shánkara·varman saw to it that it was established. So aren't there other false ascetics roaming at large in the country, imitating the style of the black-blankets, who deserve being driven away?

BOY: Sir, some depraved ascetics who fool around calling themselves Shaivas were seen until this time. But now, having fallen into disrepute because of your ardor, they are scarce.

GRADUATE: Well spoken! Indeed, I have also noticed them. They are eligible for exile. For:

> What do they not think fit to drink? Surely only that which is not liquid. They cannot eat only what is bitter or cannot be cracked by teeth. If there is any being with breasts at all which is not suitable to have sex with, then it must be unborn or dead. What in the world could be an appropriate place for asceticism? Perhaps a pub.

BAṬUḤ: ⌜Jadhā ayyo maṃtedi.⌟

SNĀTA°: Baṭo, so 'pi n' âlpo viplavo varṇ'|āśramāṇām.

BAṬUḤ: ⌜Tāṇaṃ pi so kalaṃko yyeva māhesarāṇaṃ jāṇa vavaeseṇa te vavaharaṃti.⌟

SNĀTA°: Baṭo, samyag abhihitam. tad|udvāsane 'pi devasya yukta ev' âvadhāna|parigrahaḥ. tathā ca:

«Śaivaṃ śāsanam āśritā vayam» iti
prakhyāpya nāma Prabhoḥ
śuddh'|ârtheṣu tad|āgameṣu kudhiyaḥ
kurvanti te viplavam.
tān devo viniyamya samyag amale
mārge yadi sthāpayet,
tad vandye kṣiti|pālane yaśasi vā
kā nāma tasya kṣatiḥ?

BAṬUḤ: ⌜Juttaṃ ṇimaṃ.⌟

SNĀTA°: Nanu gṛhīta ev' âtra mayā rāj'|ādeśaḥ. tan niyujyantām ete mārga|pālās tad|anveṣaṇāya.

BAṬUḤ: ⌜Jaṃ ayyo āṇavedi.⌟ *(iti niṣkramya punaḥ praviśya ca)* ⌜ayya, paṇaṭṭhā raṭṭhādo. aṇṇo puṇa ko vi paṇihī saṃbhaṃto ayyaṃ aṇṇesaṃto āgado. tā ettha ayyo pamāṇaṃ.⌟

SNĀTA°: Ānīyatām asau.

BAṬUḤ *saṃjñayā tam āhvayati. praviśya saṃbhrāntaḥ*

PURUṢAḤ: ⌜Jayadu bhaṣṭake! je ṇāma maheśalā maṃśa|śīdhu|dāśī|vavahāla|śīlā ṇīl'|aṃbala|kiṃ|vadaṃtīṃ yyeva śuṇia te śaalā laṣṭādo paṇaṣṭā. aṇṇe uṇa śuddha|tavaśśiṇo pi śaṃkidā calidum paüttāo. eśu bhaṣṭake pamāṇaṃ.⌟

BOY: It is as you say, sir. 3.45

GRADUATE: Boy, this is also a significant attack on the social estates and life-periods.

BOY: It is certainly a disgrace for those followers of Shiva, too, abusing whose name they do their business.

GRADUATE: You're quite right, boy. The king is certainly doing the right thing when he gives heed to their expulsion, too. Furthermore:

> When they proclaim the Lord's name, saying "We follow Shiva's teaching," these wicked people are doing damage to His chaste religions. If the king subdued them in the right way and established them on the spotless path, why should his laudable protection of the earth or his fame suffer any loss?

BOY: Exactly. 3.50

GRADUATE: Be sure, I've got the king's decree in this matter. So order these patrolmen to search for them.

BOY: As you command, sir. *(He exits and enters again.)* Sir, they have fled from the kingdom. But another excited courier has come looking for you. What do you command, sir?

GRADUATE: Lead him in.

The BOY *calls him in with a sign.*

MANSERVANT: *(enters, says excitedly)* Glory to the master! 3.55
Those followers of Shiva, who are addicted to eating meat, drinking booze and having sex with maidservants, disappeared from the kingdom to a man as soon as the rumor about the black-blankets reached them. But other,

SNĀTA°: Baṭo, sādhūn vyāvartayitum śīghraṃ niyujyantāṃ pradhāna|puruṣāḥ satkāra|pūrvam. *(*PURUṢAṂ *prati)* tvam api re mārgam ādeśayaṃs tair eva saha gaccha.

PURUṢAḤ: ⌜Yaṃ bhaṣṭake āṇavedi.⌟ *(iti niṣkrāntaḥ.)*

BAṬUḤ: ⌜Aho ayyassa pahāvo ucchalido.⌟

SNĀTA°: Baṭo, na yuktam etad yad anādi|prabandha|pravṛtta|sad|āgam'|ânugāminaḥ śaṅkitam āsate. parama|māheśvaro hi rājā Śaṅkara|varma|devaḥ, sarv'|āśrameṣu ca dayāluḥ. tad ehi vayam api ku|śaṅk"|ôpaśamāya Śrī|Dharma|śiv'|āśramam ev' âdya gacchāmaḥ.

3.60 BAṬUḤ: ⌜Jaṃ ayyo āṇavedi.⌟

Parikrāmataḥ.

Nepathye:

Kim śaṅkitāḥ sabhayam āśramiṇaḥ sthitāḥ stha?
devo 'khil'|āśrama|gurur na parāṅ|mukho vaḥ.
yuṣmāsu viplavam iv' ādadhato nirastās
te kṛtrima|vrata|vṛtāḥ Param'|ēśvareṇa.

BAṬUḤ: ⌜Ede khu ayyeṇa ṇiuttā pahāṇa|purisā ugghosaṃtā gadā.⌟

3.65 SNĀTA°: Baṭo, samyag upalakṣitaṃ bhavatā. vayam api satvaraṃ vrajāmaḥ. *(parikramya)* baṭo, nanu prāptā vayaṃ Śrī|Dharma|śiv'|āśramam. tathā hi:

chaste ascetics also grew alarmed and started to leave. What do you command, master?

GRADUATE: Boy, we must quickly and respectfully appoint community leaders to keep back the virtuous. *(to the* MANSERVANT*)* You, go with them to show the way.

MANSERVANT: As the master commands. *(Exits.)*

BOY: Oh my, you have wavered in your resolution, sir.*

GRADUATE. Boy, it is improper for those living in the beginningless continuum of transmigration who follow the chaste religions to be beset by worries. For King Shánkara·varman is supremely devoted to Shiva, and he is merciful to all religious schools. So come, we shall go now straight to the ashram of the Venerable Dharma·shiva in order to soothe needless worries.

BOY: As you command, sir. 3.60

They walk about.

Offstage:

> Why are you worried and afraid, hermits? The king, master of all religious schools, is not hostile toward you. The Supreme Lord has banished those who, screening themselves with faked observances, had almost proved to be your ruin.

BOY: These must be the community leaders you appointed, sir, passing by, notifying the public.

GRADUATE: Well observed, boy. We shall quicken our pace. 3.65 *(They walk about.)* Boy, we must have arrived at the Venerable Dharma·shiva's ashram, for:*

Ete dhūlana|bhasma|dhūsara|ruco
dhūp'|âgni|saṃdhukṣaṇe
dakṣās tat|kṣaṇa|pīta|puṇya|pura|jit|
pūj''|ârtha|puṣp'|āsavāḥ
dhanyāḥ kaṃ na haranti tāpasa|jaṭā|
granthi|ślathī|kāriṇaḥ
kanthā|manthara|lāsya|dāna|rasikāḥ
śaiv'|āśrame vāyavaḥ?

BAṬUḤ: ⌜Jadhā ayyo maṃtedi. pasaṃta|ramaṇijjaṃ tavo|vaṇaṃ imaṃ ṇo dīsadi.⌟

SNĀTA°: Tad ehi praviśāvaḥ. *(praveśam abhinīya)* kathaṃ, prāṅgana ev' âbhivartate Śrī|Dharma|śivo Bhaṭṭārakaḥ! aho amuṣya sarv'|âtiśāyinī tapo|lakṣmīḥ! eṣo hi:

Bhasma|smer'|ānana|śrīḥ,
śuci|vibudha|dhunī|nīra|nirdhauta|mūrdhā,
dhāvadbhiś ceṭa|vṛttaiś
caṭula|gaṇa|nibhais tāpasair vandyamānaḥ,
gaury'' âjasraṃ sukīrtyā
śaśa|dhara|samayā nandyamān'|âmal'|ātmā
śreyaḥ Śrī|kaṇṭha|kalpo
janayati jagatāṃ darśanād eva nūnam.

3.70 Api ca:

Ātmānam āśrama|pade ca bahu|prakāra|
kāleya|kalmaṣa|viśeṣa|muṣi praviṣṭam
satyam śape Śiva|pura|stham iv' âpy avaimi
smera|Smar'|âri|nayana|traya|tarpyamāṇam.

> Their color is gray with smearing-ashes, they are able to inflame the fires of incense, they have just drunk the pure nectar of flowers used for the worship of Shiva, the Conquerer of the Forts—whom do these blessed breezes not enchant in the Shaiva ashram, loosening the knots in the ascetics' matted hair, and delighting in presenting the mendicant-garments' slow, graceful dance?

BOY: It is as you say, sir. This penance grove seems to me peaceful and charming.

GRADUATE: Come now, let's enter. *(They mime entering.)* What! The Reverend Abbot Dharma·shiva comes forward in the very courtyard! How the splendor of his asceticism outshines everyone! For:

> His beautiful face is smiling with ashes;* his forehead is cleansed by the holy water of the Ganges; he is worshiped by ascetics resembling Shiva's kind attendants, who bustle about and act as servants; his spotless soul is constantly gladdened by his bright fame, which is like camphor,* *just as Shiva is delighted by the well-praised Gauri together with the moon*—merely by being seen he, resembling Shiva Shri·kantha, truly brings about the creatures' salvation.

And what's more: 3.70

> Having entered the ashram-compound, which dispels the many stains of the Iron Age, upon my word, I also feel as if I were in Shiva's heaven, reanimated by the three eyes of Love's smiling enemy.

BAṬUḤ: ⌜Ahaṃ pi attāṇaṃ uppataṃtaṃ Bamha|bhūyaṃ pekkhāmi.⌟

*Tataḥ praviśati āsanastho yathā|nirdiṣṭaḥ Śrī|*DHARMA|ŚIVO *vibhavataś ca parivāraḥ.*

BHAṬṬĀRAKAḤ: *(savitarkam)*

3.75 Rāj" âsau bhuvaneṣu viśruta|guṇo
dharm'|âikatān'|āśayo,
mantrī śāstra|mah"|âṭavī|viharaṇ'|â-
śrāntaḥ Jayanto 'py asau.
n' âham karma yaśo|viruddham anayoḥ
śaṅke. yath"|âvasthitās
tiṣṭhantv āśramiṇaḥ. kim ākulatayā?
kiṃ vā bhayaṃ mādṛśām?

(agrato 'valokya) Katham! ayam ih' âiv' āyātaḥ snātakaḥ? sarvaṃ vyaktam idānīm.

SNĀTA°: Tad ehi baṭo, praṇamāmo Bhaṭṭārakam. *(upasṛtya)* namo bhagavate pratyakṣa|Mah"|eśvarāya Bhaṭṭārakāya.

BHAṬṬĀRAKAḤ: Svāgatam āryāya. kuśalino bhavantaḥ? āsanam.

SNĀTA°: Alam āsanena, śādvala|sthala ev' ôpaviśāmaḥ. bhagavan, apy avighnam upapadyate yathā|prastutas tapo|vidhiḥ? ko v" âtra vighnaḥ? bhagavān Mah"|ēśvara eva ātmānam ātman" ârcayati. tad amunā jana|pravādena yathā na manāg ākulatām bibhrati tapo|dhanās, tath" âinān ādeṣṭum arhati bhaṭṭārakaḥ. tapo|vighnā eva pratihatā

BOY: Me, too. I see myself flying toward absorption into Brahman.

Then enters the Venerable Dharma·shiva sitting on a stool, looking as described above, and as many followers as can be afforded.

ABBOT: *(pensively)*

> The merits of this king are celebrated all over the world, and his attention is solely devoted to social and religious order. As for this adviser, Jayánta, he never grows weary of strolling in the great forest of doctrines and sciences. I don't think they would take any measures that would be contrary to their reputation. The hermits should remain as usual. Why worry? Or, rather, what danger can there be for people like us? 3.75

(He looks ahead.) What in the world! The graduate has come right here? Everything is clear now.

GRADUATE: Come, boy, let's bow down to the Abbot. *(They approach.)* Obeisance to the Blessed Abbot, Mahéshvara manifest in front of us!

ABBOT: Welcome, sir. Are you well? Please take this seat.

GRADUATE: There's no need of seats, I'll just sit down on the lawn. Your Holiness, I hope the observance of religious austerities goes on free from impediments, as it has been established. Or, rather, what kind of impediment could occur here? The Blessed Mahéshvara worships himself by himself. So could Your Holiness please advise the ascetics that they should not be worried in the slightest rājñā. rāj" âpy anupadam āgamiṣyaty eva bhaṭṭārakaṃ draṣṭum.

3.80 BHAṬṬĀ°: *(sasmitam)* K" âsmākam ākulatā, tāpasānāṃ vā? Śrī|Śaṅkara|varmaṇi dharmeṇa medinīṃ samāgatāṃ śāsati sādhūnām eva rājyaṃ, tasya paraṃ bhṛtiḥ. n' âiv' âdy' âivaṃ, cirāt prabhṛty evam ev' ânubhavāmaḥ.

(praviśy' âpaṭī|kṣepeṇa saṃbhrāntas) TĀPASAḤ: ⌜jayadu jayadu bhaṭṭārako! eso khu ko vi vuḍḍhako paṃḍido sva|gavvaṃ uvvahaṃto assamaṃ imaṃ uvahasaṃto aṇea|sissa| parivārido †uggāhaṇakaaṇakhaṃdhaṃva† kareṃto ido āgado. tā ittha bhaṭṭārako pamāṇaṃ.⌟

BHAṬṬĀ°: *(sasmitam)* Praviśatu tapasvī. kim asmākam?

Tataḥ praviśati yathā|nirdiṣṭo VṚDDHĀMBHIḤ.

VṚDDHĀMBHIḤ: Aho vismayaḥ! aho bata kiyān anartha|kārī rājā Śaṅkara|varmā yasy' ēdṛśī sāmrājya|lakṣmīr agni|hotṛbhir vana|sthair yatibhir brahma|cāribhir ebhiś ca Śaiva| Pāśupata|Pāñcarātrik'|Ārhata|Sāṅkhya|Saugata|prabhṛtibhir anargalaṃ bhujyate! tat katham eṣa ciraṃ jīviṣyati? tad adya tāvad ayam eka|vṛkṣe mandāraka iva dṛśyate. asminn ev' âvasara īśvaraṃ parākṛtya para|lokaṃ nirasya Veda|prāmāṇyaṃ pratikṣipya rājānam amum amārgād ato nivārya yogye vartmani sthāpayāmi, yen' âyam artha|paraś ciraṃ rājyam anubhavati. atra ca Śaiv'|āśrame degree about this rumor among the people? The king has removed nothing but the impediments of asceticism. And the king himself is also coming close behind us to visit Your Holiness.

ABBOT: *(smiling)* Why should I or the ascetics be worried? As long as His Majesty Shánkara·varman righteously rules the country that has fallen to him, the kingdom belongs to the virtuous alone, but he supports it. And it is like that not just today; this has been our experience for a long time. 3.80

AN ASCETIC: *(enters with a toss of the curtain, excited)* Glory to the Abbot! Some elderly scholar has arrived, showing off his arrogance, mocking the ashram, surrounded by several disciples, making †. . . †* Your Holiness should tell me what to do.

ABBOT: *(smiling)* Let the poor fellow enter, I don't mind.

Then enters VRIDDHÁMBHI *as described above.**

VRIDDHÁMBHI: Amazing! What a great disaster-maker king Shánkara·varman is, letting Vedic priests, hermits, renouncers, celibate students, as well as these Shaivas, Pashu·patas, Pañcha·rátrikas, Jainas, Sankhyas, Buddhists and the rest consume the great riches of his kingdom without check. So how is he going to live long? He now actually looks like a heavenly tree surrounded by nothing.* I am going to take this opportunity to do away with God, set aside the world-to-come, demolish the validity of the Vedas, and thereby turn the king back from this wrong path and establish him on the

śrutaṃ mayā bahavaḥ paṇḍita|māninaḥ saṅghaṭitā iti. teṣāṃ samakṣam enam eva Śaiv'|ācāryaṃ nirbhartsayāmi. *(parikramy' ânyato 'valokya)* ayaṃ sa Śaiv'|ācāryaḥ Kaṇa|bhakṣ'|Âkṣa|pād'|ādi|darśana|pāradṛśvā, eṣa ca mahā|Mīmāṃsakaḥ Saṅkarṣaṇa, ime cānye bahavo nānā|śāstra|vidaḥ. bhavat' ûpasarpāmi. *(upasṛtya)* kuśaly asi, tapasvin? bhadraṃ te, brāhmaṇa. *(iti vadan śādvala eva śiṣyair upaviśati.)*

3.85 BHAṬṬĀ°: *(sasmitam)* Katham? upakrama eva ākṣepaḥ? *(*SAṄKARṢAṆASYA *mukhaṃ paśyati.)*

SNĀTA°: Bhagavann, evam etat. paśyāmas tāvat.

VṚDDHĀ°: Kim ittham anartha|śata|duḥstham āsyate bhavadbhiḥ?

Tapāṃsi yātanāś citrāḥ, saṃyamo bhoga|vañcanam,
Agni|hotr'|ādikaṃ karma bāla|krīḍ" êva lakṣyate.

BHAṬṬĀ°: Kiṃ kurmaḥ? īdṛśe karmaṇi bhagavat" ēśvareṇa preritāḥ smaḥ.

3.90 VṚDDHĀ°: Kaḥ puno bhagavān īśvaraḥ?

right track, so that concentrating on worldly prosperity he can enjoy his kingship for a long time. Now I have heard that a lot of self-proclaimed scholars are gathered in this Shaiva ashram. I shall make this Shaiva professor a laughingstock right in front of them. *(He takes a few steps and looks in another direction.)* Here is the Shaiva professor who is an expert in the systems of Kana·bhaksha, Aksha·pada* and others, and this here is Sankárshana, the great Mimámsaka, and here there are many other scholars belonging to various branches of learning. All right then, I'll approach them. *(He approaches.)* Are you O.K., ascetic? Hello, brahmin. *(While saying this he sits down right on the lawn with his pupils.)*

ABBOT: *(smiling)* What? Disrespect right from the start?* 3.85
(He looks at SANKÁRSHANA*'s face.)*

GRADUATE: Reverend, you're right. Well, let's see.

VRIDDHÁMBHI: Why do you live so miserably because of hundreds of useless torments?

> Asceticism is just a variety of torture; self-restraint
> is just a way to cheat yourself of pleasures; while
> sacrificial rituals such as the Agni·hotra seem to
> me just like children's games.

ABBOT: What shall we do? The Lord God impels us to perform such actions.

VRIDDHÁMBHI: But who is this "Lord God"? 3.90

Mṛga|tṛṣṇ"|âmbhasi snātaḥ, kha|puṣpa|kṛta|śekharaḥ,
eṣo vandhyā|suto yāti śaśa|śṛṅga|dhanur|dharaḥ.

BHAṬṬĀ°: Alam apabhāṣaṇena! sa hi bhagavān viśva|jagataḥ sraṣṭā saṃhart" ânanta|jantu|grāma|vṛtter vicitra|vipākasya karma|kalāpakasya yathā|viṣayaṃ viniyoktā nity'|ānandaḥ sarva|jñaḥ kṛpāluḥ Param'|ēśvaraḥ.

VṚDDHĀMBHIḤ: *(mandaṃ vihasya)* Aho bhautānāṃ bhakti|timira|hatā na kiṃ cit paśyati mugdhā dṛṣṭiḥ. kuta evaṃ bhaviṣyati? katham iva hi kartṛtvam asya sammaṃsyate lokaḥ? tathā hi:

Kṛp" êyaṃ, krīḍ" êyaṃ,
prabhu|rucir iyaṃ, preraṇam idaṃ,
sva|bhāvo 'yaṃ, dharm'|â-
rjanam idam, ath' âpy ārjavam idam:
na jāne kiṃ kṛtva
manasi kṛta|kṛtyo munir asau
purāṇo nīrāgaḥ
sṛjati jagatīṃ saṃharati ca.

3.95 Karaṇ'|ādi|kāraṇa|kalāpa|niḥspṛhaḥ
saha|kāribhiś ca rahitaḥ kathaṃ vrajet
sva|para|prayojana|<viśeṣa>|varjitāṃ
jagatāṃ sthiti|pralaya|sarga|hetutām?

There goes the son of a barren woman, fresh from bathing in the water of a mirage, a wreath of sky-flowers on his head, holding a bow made of hare-horn.

ABBOT: Enough abuse! For he is the blessed creator and destroyer of the whole world; he supervises the mass of karmas, according to their appropriate scope, which karmas are active in the infinite mass of creatures, having various effects; he is the eternally blissful, omniscient, compassionate Supreme Lord.

VRIDDHÁMBHI: *(laughing slightly)* Behold the foolish vision of idiots, obstructed by the blindness of devotion, seeing nothing. How could this be? For how on earth can people accept that God is the supreme agent? To explain:*

It is compassion, it is sport, it is a lordly whim, it is an impulse, it is his nature, this is the way he earns merit, or, rather, it is his honesty: who knows what that ancient, passionless sage, who has all he needs, has got into his head to create and destroy the universe?

How could one who has no desire for the group of causal factors like the instrumental cause, and who is also deprived of assistant factors, become the cause of the maintenance, destruction and creation of the worlds, which has no <particular> benefit for himself or others? 3.95

Kiṃ ca:

Evam eva vidhāt" âpi dhātā trīṇi jaganti vā
punar n' ânyāni bhūyāṃsi sṛjat' îty atra ko vidhiḥ?

BHAṬṬĀ°: Kṛtaṃ dūṣaṇ'|ôpanyās'|āyāsena.

Pramāṇa|śūnye viphalaṃ hi dūṣaṇaṃ,
pramāṇa|siddhe tad apāstam eva yat,
tad|ukti|maukharyam apāsya mṛgyatām
atīndriye vastuni sādhanaṃ paraiḥ.

3.100 VṚDDHĀ°: *(sasmitam)* Yady evam, Īśvara|siddhāv abhidhīyatāṃ pramāṇam.

BHAṬṬĀ°: Anumānam iti brūmaḥ.

VṚDDHĀ°: *(sasmitam)* Anumānaṃ pramāṇaṃ c' êti mano|rathaḥ.

Avasthā|deśa|kālānāṃ bhedād bhinnāsu śaktiṣu
bhāvānām anumānena prasiddhir atidurlabhā.

Moreover:

> Even if he is the creator, what rule is there to ensure that he is going to create exactly in this way as you say and only three worlds, and he does not create other and more worlds?

ABBOT: Stop exerting yourself putting forward fault-finding arguments.

> On the one hand, fault-finding argument is pointless with regard to something that lacks the support of a means of valid knowledge. On the other hand, it is totally discarded with respect to what is proved by a means of valid knowledge. Therefore disputants should stop making noise with uttering those fault-finding arguments and should seek positive arguments concerning this matter which is beyond the scope of the sense organs.

VRIDDHÁMBHI: *(smiling)* If that's what you think, then 3.100
please state a proof for establishing God.

ABBOT: I say that inference proves His existence.

VRIDDHÁMBHI: *(smiling)* To say that something is an inference and at the same time a means of valid knowledge is wishful thinking.

> It is extremely difficult to verify things with the help of inference since their capacities differ because of differences in condition, place and time.*

Kiṃ ca:

3.105 Hasta|sparśād iv' ândhena viṣame pathi dhāvatā
anumāna|pradhānena vinipāto na durlabhaḥ.

Api ca:

Yatnen' ânumito 'py arthaḥ kuśalair anumātṛbhiḥ
abhiyuktatarair anyair anyath" âiv' ôpapādyate.

BHAṬṬĀ°: Alaṃ prapañcena! prasiddham eva bārhaspatyānāṃ gṛha|kṛtyakam idam. idaṃ tu brūhi: kiṃ pratyakṣam ev' âikaṃ teṣāṃ pramāṇam?

VṚDDHĀ°: Om ity ucyate.

3.110 BHAṬṬĀ°: Na tarhi teṣāṃ kā cana kalpate loka|yātrā.

VṚDDHĀ°: Kim iti?

BHAṬṬĀ°: Kṣudh"|ākulatvād dīn' âudane pravartase, na sikatāyām. ambhāṃsy apekṣase pipāsito na vibhāvasum.

VṚDDHĀ°: Yady evaṃ tataḥ kim?

BHAṬṬĀ°:

3.115 Sakhe, pradhānatā nāma na khalv indriya|gocaraḥ.
s" ânvaya|vyatirekābhyāṃ bhāvānām avagamyate.

Moreover:

> One who relies on inference tumbles easily, just like a blind man running by touch of hand on an uneven path.* 3.105

Furthermore:

> Even if clever logicians infer something with great effort, other, extremely competent logicians account for the same thing in another way.*

ABBOT: Enough of verbosity! We know all too well this "specialty of the house" of the materialists. But tell me this: do they hold that sense perception is the one and only means of valid knowledge?

VRIDDHÁMBHI: The answer is yes.

ABBOT: Then everyday activity is impossible for them. 3.110

VRIDDHÁMBHI: How so?

ABBOT: If you suffer the torments of hunger, my poor thing, you seek rice, not sand. When you are thirsty you look for water, not for fire.

VRIDDHÁMBHI: Yes, but what's your point?

ABBOT:

> My friend, surely it does not fall into the scope of the sense faculties to be the "best thing" for a particular purpose. That is ascertained through the positive and negative concomitance of entities. 3.115

Anvaya|vyatirekau ca mukhyaṃ liṅgasya lakṣaṇam.
yatra|sthaṃ dṛśyate liṅgaṃ, tasya sā pakṣa|dharmatā.

Eta eva c' ânumānasya prāṇā anvaya|vyatirekau pakṣa|dharmat" êti.

VṚDDHĀ°: Nanv ayaṃ sukha|duḥkha|sādhanatā|niścaya|nimittako vyavahāras tiraścām iva manuṣyāṇām api pratibhay" âiva bhaviṣyati.

BHAṬṬĀ°: M" âivam. avidita|niyata|nimittaṃ hi jñānaṃ pratibh" êty ucyate. iha ca viditam eva nimittam anvaya|vyatirek'|ādi, na ca sva|saṃvedyasya nihnavo yuktaḥ.

3.120 VṚDDHĀ°: Nanu viditam api na viditam eva nimittam, avinā|bhāva|sambandhasya grahītum aśakyatvāt. tad ayam avicārita eva ramaṇīyo vyavahāraḥ, etad eva ca tattvam iti tattvavidaḥ.

BHAṬṬĀ°: Ālasyam idaṃ pāda|prasārikā vā. vicārayituṃ vastūni gṛhīta|kṣaṇā ime vicakṣaṇāḥ.

And positive and negative concomitance are the primary defining characteristics of the inferential mark. As for the condition of being the property of the subject, that holds for any inferential mark seen in a particular subject.*

These are indeed the very life-breath of inference: positive and negative concomitance, and the condition of being the property of the subject.

VRIDDHÁMBHI: Surely for humans, just as for animals, such everyday behavior, based on determining what leads to pleasure and what to suffering, takes place merely through instinct.

ABBOT: Say not so. For instinct is defined as a knowledge the specific cause of whose validity is not known. But in this case we do know the cause, namely positive and negative concomitance and the like. And one cannot deny something self-evident.

VRIDDHÁMBHI: Surely even if we know the cause, yet we do not really know it, since we cannot comprehend the connection of being invariably related. Therefore this everyday activity is pleasant only if we do not examine it, and this fact alone is real: thus say those who know reality. 3.120

ABBOT: This is laziness, or you just don't want to yield an inch. These scholars here are taking the opportunity to examine things.

VṚDDHĀ°: Nanv aśakyo 'yaṃ vicāra ānantyād dhūm'|âgni|vyaktīnām adhūm'|ânagni|vyaktīnāṃ ca. dur|adhigamau c' âsākṣāt|kṛta|sakala|tri|bhuvan'|ôdara|varti|pad'|ârtha|sārthair imāv anvaya|vyatirekau. sarva|vidāṃ tu kim anumānena?

BHAṬṬĀ°: Anvayas tāvat sāmānyam avalambya grahīṣyate. vyakty|ānantyam abādhakaṃ, dhūmatvasy' âikatvād agnitvasya ca. bhāva|sāmāny'|ânugama|puraḥ|sara eva ca tad|abhāvayor apy anugamo grahīṣyate. sa eva ca vyatirekaḥ.

Bhāvayoḥ sāha|caryaṃ yad, anvayaṃ tam pracakṣate.
vyatirekaṃ tu manyante sāhityaṃ tad|abhāvayoḥ.

3.125 Pakṣa|dharmatā tu tapasvinī su|bodh" âiva, niradhikaraṇa|liṅga|dharm'|ânavadhāraṇād iti. tad evaṃ suśakatayā nimitta|niścayasya vipaścitām iva tiraścām api pramāṇair eva vyavahāraḥ. yath" āha Bhāṣya|kāraḥ, «tad evam ebhiḥ pramāṇair deva|manuṣya|tiraścāṃ vyavahārāḥ prakalpante, n' âto 'nyathā» iti.

VRIDDHÁMBHI: Surely this examination is impossible, because there are infinite individual instances of smoke and fire, and non-smoke and non-fire, and people who have not perceived directly the multitude of all things existing in the three worlds cannot ascertain this positive and negative concomitance. As for the omniscient, what need have they for inference?

ABBOT: First of all, positive concomitance can be grasped resorting to universals. The infinitude of individual instances cannot invalidate the inference since smoke-ness is one and fire-ness is also one. And following precisely the accordance of positive universals, the accordance of their absence can also be grasped. And exactly that is negative concomitance.

> The association of two things* is taught to be positive concomitance. As for negative concomitance, it is considered to be the concurrence of their absence.

As for the inferential mark's condition of being the property of the subject, that poor thing can easily be understood, since we cannot ascertain the inferential mark as a property without it having any locus. Therefore, since the cause of validity is easily determined in this way, even animals, just like the wise, act only with the help of means of valid knowledge. As the Commentator says, "Therefore the activities of gods, human beings and animals are possible in this way, with the help of these means of valid knowledge, and not otherwise."* 3.125

VṚDDHĀ°: Nanu bhavatu loka|siddhānām utpanna|pratītīnām, <utpādya|pratītīnāṃ tv> ati|durghaṭo 'yaṃ prakāraḥ.

Na h' Īśvaraṃ pṛthivy|ādeḥ kāryād dhūmād iv' ânalam
laukikāḥ pratipadyante tārkikair apratāritāḥ.

BHAṬṬĀ°:

Nārī|jano 'pi bālo 'pi gopālo 'pi bhavān api
budhyate niyatād arthād arth'|ântaram asaṃśayam.

3.130 Avinā|bhāva|sāmarthyād dhūmen' êva vibhāvasoḥ
anumānaṃ sva|kāryeṇa kartuḥ sidhyati dhīmataḥ.

VṚDDHĀ°:

Nanv anyad eva kumbh'|ādi kāryaṃ sambhāvit'|ôdayam,
anyad eva hi śail'|ādi, tayor hi mahad antaram.

BHAṬṬĀ°:

Anya eva hi dhūmo 'sau kṛśa|janmā mah"|ânase,
anya ev' âyam adrau ca vyāpta|vyoma|dig|antaraḥ.

3.135 Kiṃ c' êdaṃ rakta|paṭ'|ôcchiṣṭaṃ bhujyate,

VRIDDHÁMBHI: Surely this may be all right for things already established in the world, regarding which cognition has already arisen,* but it is impossible <for things concerning which cognition is still to be acquired.>

For ordinary people, unless they are deceived by logicians, do not cognize God from effects like the earth, in the way they cognize fire from smoke.

ABBOT:

Even women, even a child, even a cowherd, even you, sir, comprehend one thing without doubt from some other specific thing.*

Because of the power of invariable concomitance, 3.130
one can successfully infer a sentient agent from its effect, just as one can infer fire from smoke.

VRIDDHÁMBHI:

Surely an effect like a pot, the production of which is conceivable, is one thing, and a mountain, for instance, is very different thing, for there is a great difference between them.

ABBOT:

Indeed, this smoke with its small beginnings in the kitchen is one thing, and a very different thing is the smoke on the mountain, permeating the main and intermediate directions of the sky.*

Moreover these are the leftovers of the red-robed Buddhists 3.135
that you are eating:

«Siddhaṃ yādṛg adhiṣṭhātṛ|bhāv'|âbhāv'|ânuvṛttimat
sanniveś'|ādi, tat tasmād yuktaṃ yad anumīyate.» iti.

Dharmaṃ niyatam ālambya bhavati hy anumā|kramaḥ.
kva vā sarv'|ātmanā sāmyaṃ sādhya|dṛṣṭ'|ânta|dharmiṇoḥ?

VṚDDHĀ°: Nanv anyatra vāstavaṃ sāmānyam, iha tu śabda|sāmānya|mātraṃ, na vastu|sāmānyam. śabda|sāmānye c' âtiprasaṅgaḥ.

BHAṬṬĀ°: *(sasmitam)* Kuto Bauddha|gṛhe vāstavaṃ sāmānyam?

3.140 Buddhy|ārūḍhaṃ bahiṣṭhaṃ vā,
satyaṃ sāṃvṛtam eva vā
sāmānyam avalamby' âiṣā
loka|yātrā pratīyate.

Na paras|parataḥ sāmyaṃ kāryāṇām api bhūyasām.
tad ime «yādṛk» ity asya padasy' ârthaṃ na manmahe.

VṚDDHĀ°: Nanu vilakṣaṇam ev' êdaṃ kṣity|ādi kāryam.

BHAṬṬĀ°: Nanu vilakṣaṇam eva kartāraṃ kalpayantu bhavantaḥ.

"When that particular kind of compositeness, etc., is established to be in positive and negative concomitance with the existence of the controller, it is fine that the existence of a controller is inferred from that kind of compositeness."*

In fact, the process of inference takes place depending upon a specific property.* Where is there ever a complete similarity between the thing that has the property to be established and the one in the example?*

VRIDDHÁMBHI: Surely there is a real universal in other cases, but in this case the similarity is only nominal, not real.* And to apply inference in the case of nominal similarity would be a fault of overextension.

ABBOT: *(smiling)* How could there be real universals in the house of a Buddhist?

We see that people's everyday activities depend upon some universal, whether arisen from the intellect, or external, real or conventional. 3.140

There are many things that, although they are all effects, do not resemble each other. Therefore I don't see the point of the expression "that particular kind."

VRIDDHÁMBHI: But surely these products such as the earth are quite special.

ABBOT: Surely, then, you should postulate a very special craftsman.

VṚDDHĀ°: Na kalpayitum aprasiddhaṃ śaknumaḥ.

3.145 BHAṬṬĀ°: Vayam api na kāryam akartṛkaṃ vaktuṃ śaknumaḥ.

VṚDDHĀ°: Kim atra tarhi kurmaḥ?

BHAṬṬĀ°: Kataram atra jahāmaḥ? kiṃ kartr|atiśayo duḥkh'|āvahaḥ, kiṃ vā kāryam akartṛkaṃ duḥkh'|āvaham? tatra «dṛṣṭa|siddhaye hy adṛṣṭaṃ kalpyate, na tu dṛṣṭam utsṛjyate» iti nyāyād varaṃ kartr|atiśayaḥ kāry'|âtiśayāt sahyatām, na tu kāryatāyā ev' ôpekṣaṇam.

VṚDDHĀMBHIR *bhūmim ālikhati.*

BHAṬṬĀ°: Api ca lavana|kriyayā dātram iva chidi|kriyayā paraśur iva rūp'|ôpalabdhyā yat karaṇaṃ locanam anumīyate, tatra netrasya dātra|paraśvadhābhyāṃ kiṃ sādharmyam?

3.150 VṚDDHĀ°: Tad api m" ânumāyi, kiṃ naś chinnam?

BHAṬṬĀ°: Nanu cakṣuṣā vinā kathaṃ rūpaṃ drakṣyasi?

VṚDDHĀ°: Bhavatu tarhi kim api karaṇam.

VRIDDHÁMBHI: I am unable to postulate something that is unknown.

ABBOT: And I cannot talk about an effect that has no agent. 3.145

VRIDDHÁMBHI: So what can we do in such a case?

ABBOT: Which alternative shall we reject? Is it the extraordinary nature of the agent that is troublesome or is it the effect of having no agent that is troublesome? Regarding these two alternatives, according to the general principle "We postulate something unseen in order to account for something already seen, but we cannot deny something seen," one should put up with the extraordinary nature of the agent because the effect is also extraordinary, rather than disregarding the fact that something is an effect.

VRIDDHÁMBHI *draws on the ground.*

ABBOT: Moreover, when we infer from our perception of colors the faculty of sight as the instrument, just as we infer a scythe from the action of mowing and an axe from the action of cutting, in this case what kind of property does the faculty of sight have in common with the scythe and the axe?

VRIDDHÁMBHI: Let that not be inferred, either—why should it bother me? 3.150

ABBOT: But how could you see color without your faculty of vision?

VRIDDHÁMBHI: Fine, then let there be some kind of instrument.

BHAṬṬĀ°: Bhavatv etarhi ko 'pi kartā.

VṚDDHĀ°: Na sahyate kartā. karaṇaṃ vinā kathaṃ kriyā?

3.155 BHAṬṬĀ°: Kartāraṃ vinā kathaṃ kāryam? kāryam iti hi na Ḍitth'|ādivad|abhidhānam, api tu kriyata iti kāryam. kriyate ca kartrā ca vinā ken' êti na vidmaḥ. tad evam iyam Īśvar'|ânumāna|śirortir abhaiṣajyā sahyatām. kiṃ kriyate?

VṚDDHĀMBHIR *bhūmim ālikhati.*

BHAṬṬĀ°: Api ca para|loka|vedanām api kaṣṭāṃ soḍhum arhati bhavān.

VṚDDHĀ°: Na jīvan sahiṣyate.

BHAṬṬĀ°: Nanu kṣipram eva mariṣyasi.

3.160 VṚDDHĀ°: Katham iva?

BHAṬṬĀ°: Caitanyam ayāvad|dravya|bhāvitayā sva|saṃvedyatayā ca na bhūta|dharmā bhavitum arhati. na ca jñāna|santati|pakṣe kaṃ cid ekam anusandhātāram antareṇa smaraṇ'|êcch"|ādi|vyavahāra upapadyate.

VṚDDHĀ°: Astu tarhi kim apy evaṃ pramātṛ|tattvam. tat punar ūrdhvaṃ deha|dāhād ast' îti kim atra pramāṇam?

BHAṬṬĀ°: Sādho, na pramāṇam anyat tatr' ôpayujyate.

ABBOT: Then let there be likewise some kind of maker.

VRIDDHÁMBHI: I cannot accept a maker. But how could there be action without an instrument?

ABBOT: How could there be an effect without a maker? For 3.155
the word "effect" is not just a name like Dittha, but something is an effect because it is made. If something is both made and without a maker, then by whom? We do not know. So you have to put up with this incurable headache of inferring God. What else can you do?

VRIDDHÁMBHI *draws on the ground.*

ABBOT: What's more, you also have to endure the severe pain of transmigration.*

VRIDDHÁMBHI: One will not endure it while alive.

ABBOT: Then surely you will die very quickly.

VRIDDHÁMBHI: How so? 3.160

ABBOT: Consciousness cannot be a property of material elements, because it does not exist for as long as the substance does, and because it is aware of itself. And if you hold the theory of the "stream of consciousness," the activities of remembering, desiring, etc., are not possible without a single synthesizer.

VRIDDHÁMBHI: Then I will accept the existence of some such entity to be the cognizing subject. But what proves that it exists after the cremation of the body?

ABBOT: My good fellow, that requires no further proof.

VṚDDHĀ°: Kim iti?

3.165 BHAṬṬĀ°: Svābhāvika|vināśa|bhāvo hi niṣiddha|bhāvaḥ. na ca pramātur utpattir vā vināśo vā tat|kāraṇaṃ vā kadā cid anubhūyate. na ca s'|âvayavatv'|ādinā paṭ'|āder iva tantu|vyatiṣaṅga|vimocan'|ādinā nāśaḥ kalpate. tad asya pramātṛ|tattvasya sva|rūpam ev' ôpalabhyate n' ôtpāda|vināśāv ity asti cet pramātā, nitya ev' âsau. nityaś cet, sa eva para|lokī. kim idam ucyate cārvākaiḥ, «para|lokino 'bhāvāt para|lok'|âbhāvaḥ» iti?

Anyad api: bālasya harṣa|bhaya|śok'|ādi stany'|âbhilāṣ'|ādi ca na svābhāvikaṃ n' ākasmikaṃ na pratibhā|mātra|kṛtam iti vā vaktuṃ śakyam ity ato 'pi nityat" ātmano 'numīyata eva.

VṚDDHĀ°: Nanv Īśvara|siddhi|prasaṅge para|loka|carcayā kim āyātam?

BHAṬṬĀ°: Idam āyātam: para|loke sati n' âkarma|nimitto bhūta|sarga upapadyate.

VṚDDHĀ°: Tataḥ kim?

VRIDDHÁMBHI: Why not?

ABBOT: For we deny that the destruction of something is part of its nature. In addition, we never experience either the arising or the perishing of the cognizing subject, or any cause of such arising or perishing. Nor is it the case that its destruction must be possible on the ground that it has parts, in the way that, for instance, a cloth is destroyed, when, for example, the contact of its threads with one another disintegrates. Therefore we perceive only the form itself of this real entity called "subject" but not its arising or perishing. Because of this, if the cognizing subject exists it must be eternal. If it is eternal, then it is the one that transmigrates. Why do the materialists say, "Because there is nothing which transmigrates, therefore there is no transmigration"?* 3.165

And there is a further consideration: the infant's joy, fear, sorrow, etc., and his desire for milk, and so on, cannot be said to be either innate or accidental or produced merely by instinct. So because of this, too, the Self has to be inferred to be eternal.

VRIDDHÁMBHI: But what is gained by investigating transmigration in the context of proving God?

ABBOT: This is what is gained: if there is transmigration, then the creation of the material world cannot but be caused by individual karmas.

VRIDDHÁMBHI: So what?

3.170 BHAṬṬĀ°: Karmaṇām api śarīr'|ādi|sarge hetutvam.

VṚDDHĀ°: Punas tataḥ kim?

BHAṬṬĀ°: Nanu karmāṇy acetanāni.

VṚDDHĀ°: Tato 'pi kim?

BHAṬṬĀ°: Nanv acetanaṃ cetan"|ânadhiṣṭhitaṃ san na kāraṇatām eti.

3.175 VṚDDHĀ°: Nanu cetanās teṣām eva karmaṇāṃ kartāro 'dhiṣṭhātāro bhaviṣyanti.

BHAṬṬĀ°: Na bhavitum arhanti, bhinn'|âbhiprāyāṇāṃ sammān'|ânupapatteḥ.

VṚDDHĀ°: Kathaṃ tarhi takṣṇām?

BHAṬṬĀ°: Kiṃ takṣṇām?

VṚDDHĀ°: Nanu te bahavo 'py ekaṃ mandiram ārabhante.

3.180 BHAṬṬĀ°: M" âivam. ekasya sthapater āśay'|ânuvartinas te.

VṚDDHĀ°: Kathaṃ tarhi pariṣadi dvijānāṃ sammānam?

BHAṬṬĀ°: Tatr' âpi kārya|kovidasya pariṣat|pater ekasya āśayam anurudhyate pariṣat. iha punar rāja|śarīram amātya|śarīraṃ v" âikam eva prāṇi|sahasrāṇām upakār'|âpakāra|dvāreṇa sukha|duḥkha|sādhanam iti nūnaṃ tat|karmabhiḥ sambhūya tad ārabhyate. na ca yeṣāṃ tad rāja|śarīraṃ duḥkhāya kalpate te tad|ārambhanam anumodanta it' Īśvara eva bhagavāṃs tasya tāvataḥ karma|rāśer adhiṣṭhātā nūnam eṣitavya ity evaṃ parisiddhāv Īśvara|siddhir

ABBOT: The karmas are also the causes of the creation of 3.170
bodies, etc.*

VRIDDHÁMBHI: And then what?

ABBOT: Surely the karmas are unconscious.

VRIDDHÁMBHI: And even then what?

ABBOT: Surely an insentient thing can become a cause only if it is presided over by a sentient being.

VRIDDHÁMBHI: Surely their sentient agents will preside over 3.175
those very karmas.

ABBOT: They cannot, since no accord is possible among those who have different intentions.

VRIDDHÁMBHI: Then what about carpenters?

ABBOT: Why carpenters?

VRIDDHÁMBHI: Surely they build one house although they are many.

ABBOT: That's not so. They follow the will of one architect. 3.180

VRIDDHÁMBHI: Then what about the brahmins' agreement in an assembly?

ABBOT: In that case, too, the assembly adheres to the will of a single chairman who is expert in the matter. But in this case the body of a king or the body of an adviser, a single thing, is the source of pleasure and suffering for thousands of living beings through helping or harming them, so surely it is produced by their karmas collectively. And those for whom the king's body causes suffering do not rejoice at its production.* Therefore it is the Lord God alone who must surely be accepted as the supervisor of

apratyākhyeyā. evaṃ ca tiṣṭhatu pṛthivī|sāgara|himavad|ādi mahat kāryam aparimitam, mādṛśa|kṛśa|śarīr'|ādi|kārya|mātrakeṇ' âpy anena krameṇa śakyo 'numātum Īśvaraḥ. anena ca nayen' âcetan'|âcatura|śarīr'|ādi|saṃyojita|sarit|pulina|saikata|kūṭ'|ādayo 'py akṛṣṭa|jātā giri|kandara|vana|gahana|tṛṇa|latā|vitān'|ādayo vā janasya sukha|duḥkha|karatayā tat|karm'|ākṣiptā iti karm'|âdhiṣṭhāna|dvāreṇa n' âcetana|kartṛkā bhaviṣyanti.

VṚDDHĀ° *bhūmim ālikhati.*

BHAṬṬĀ°: Āstām anyat sthūlaṃ vā kṛśaṃ vā kāryam. yo 'yam asmad|ādīnāṃ kṛṣi|sevā|vāṇijy'|ādi|vyavahāraḥ śayan'|āsana|viharaṇ'|āhār'|ādi|vyavahār'|ântaḥ, eṣo 'pi bhūyasāṃ prāṇinām upakār'|âpakāra|kāraṇam iti sukha|duḥkham upajanayati. tataś ca so 'pi pūrva|nītyā tat|karm'|ākṣiptatayā karmaṇāṃ c' âcetanatayā tat|kartṝṇāṃ ca bhūyasāṃ paras|para|virodhināṃ sammān'|âsambhavena Bhagavat" âdhiṣṭhitaiḥ karmabhir eva ārabhyata ity āha mah"|ātmā Pārāśaryaḥ:

such an immense heap of karmas. And so, once one has completely established this, the proof of God's existence is irrefutable. And thus let alone great, immeasurable products like the earth, the ocean, mountains, etc.; we can infer God following the same steps even just from such insignificant products as, for instance, slender little bodies like mine. Similarly, even heaps of sand, for instance, on a riverbank, constructed by insentient, unskillful bodies, or wild plants such as grass, vines and bushes, in mountains, caves, forests, and thickets, are dependent on the karmas of people because they cause them pleasure or pain. Therefore, since the karmas must be presided over, the maker of these things cannot be insentient.

VRIDDHÁMBHI *draws on the ground.*

ABBOT: But let us leave aside other gross or subtle effects. The daily activities of people like us, like agriculture, service or trade, and everything down to lying, sitting, strolling, eating and so on, because they cause benefit or harm for many living beings, produce pleasure or suffering. Therefore, by the above reasoning, because these activities are dependent on the karmas of those beings, and since the karmas are insentient, and since their agents are many and mutually opposed, and so cannot accord—they are also produced by those very karmas presided over by the Blessed Lord. That's why the illustrious Vyasa says:

3.185 «Ajño jantur anīśo 'yam ātmanaḥ sukha|duḥkhayoḥ
Īśvara|prerito gacchet svargaṃ vā śvabhram eva vā.»

VṚDDHĀ°: Carcayiṣyāma etat. gacchāmas tāvat.

BHAṬṬĀRAK'|*ânuvartinas tāpasā enam upahasanto bahu|prakāraṃ paribhavanti.*

BHAṬṬĀ°: *(tān nivārya* VṚDDHĀMBHIṂ *prati)* Kv' êdānīṃ gamyate? ady' âpy udvaha kṣaṇaṃ karma|viṣūcīm. Āgama|prāmāṇyād ap' Īśvaraṃ pratipadyāmahe.

VṚDDHĀ°: Āgamaḥ pramāṇam iti sāhasam.

3.190 BHAṬṬĀ°: *(*SNĀTAKAM *uddiśya)* Śrāntā vayam. tad bhavanta enaṃ bodhayantu.

SNĀTA°: Yathā Bhaṭṭāraka ādiśati. asmākaṃ tv Āgama|prāmāṇya|samarthane prayāsa eva n' ôpayujyate, nisarga|siddhatvāt.

VṚDDHĀ°:

Nisarga|siddhaṃ prāmāṇyaṃ? kim etad abhidhīyate?
na hi nityatayā Vedaḥ prāmāṇyam adhigacchati.

Kiṃ hi nityaṃ pramāṇaṃ dṛṣṭam ākāśādi? pratyakṣādi vā yad anityaṃ tasya prāmāṇye kasya vipratipattiḥ?

> "This creature is ignorant, and not master of his own pleasure and pain; impelled by the Lord, he may go to heaven, or he may go straight to hell."* 3.185

VRIDDHÁMBHI: I will give the matter some thought. Right now I am going.

The ascetic followers of the ABBOT *laugh at* VRIDDHÁMBHI *and humiliate him in many ways.*

ABBOT: *(checks them and says to* VRIDDHÁMBHI*)* Where are you going? Endure right now for a moment the suffering caused by your karma.* We know that God exists also by the authority of Scripture.

VRIDDHÁMBHI: Scripture a means of valid knowledge! That's bold.

ABBOT: *(to the* GRADUATE*)* I am tired; will you please enlighten him? 3.190

GRADUATE: Just as the Abbot wishes. Anyway, I won't have to exert myself at all to corroborate the validity of Scripture, since it is established by nature.

VRIDDHÁMBHI:

> The validity of Scripture established by nature? How can you say this? For the Veda is not authoritative simply because of its eternity.

For is any other permanent thing, such as space, seen to be a means of valid knowledge? Or who would argue about the validity of sense perception and the like, which is not eternal?

3.195 SNĀTA°: Sādho,

Na hi nityatay" âsmābhiḥ prāmāṇyam abhidhīyate
Vedasya, bodhakatvāt tu tathā|bhāvaṃ pracakṣmahe.

VṚDDHĀ°:

Nanv asti bādhyamāne 'pi śabde bodhakatā kva cit
«kareṇuḥ kara|śākhāyām» iti ken' âpy udīrite.

SNĀTA°:

3.200 N' âiv' ânvit'|âbhidhānaṃ hi śābdam atr' âpi bādhate,
bādhyate tv abhidheye 'rthe pramāṇ'|ântara|darśanam.

VṚDDHĀ°:

Pramāṇ'|ântara|dṛṣṭe 'rthe nanu śabdaḥ pravartate.
ato viṣaya|bādhena bādhitaḥ syāt sa eva te.

SNĀTA°:

Bādhyatāṃ viṣayo yasya pramāṇ'|ântara|gocaraḥ,
codanāyā niyog'|ātmā viṣayas tv anya|durlabhaḥ.

GRADUATE: My good fellow, 3.195

It's not that I assert that the Veda is authoritative because it is eternal; rather, I claim that it is authoritative since it creates awareness.

VRIDDHÁMBHI:

Surely in some cases, even though the verbal expression is contradicted, it still creates awareness, like when somebody says: "There is an elephant on my finger."

GRADUATE:

Yet even here it is not the denotation of the words 3.200
connected in a sentence which renders impossible verbal cognition. Rather, it is impossible to find any other means of valid knowledge with respect to the sense that is conveyed.*

VRIDDHÁMBHI:

Surely verbal expression operates with reference to objects known by other means of valid knowledge. Therefore by contradicting the object verbal expression itself must be invalidated for you.

GRADUATE:

Granted, a verbal expression is invalidated when its content is covered by another means of valid knowledge, but the content of an injunction, namely a command, is hardly accessible to other means of valid knowledge.*

3.205 Sa ca mān'|ântar'|ākrānter abhūmitvān nisargataḥ
anugrah'|ôpaghātābhyāṃ tat|kṛtābhyāṃ na lipyate.

Anugrahe 'nuvādatvam, upaghāte tv asatyatā,
dvayasy' ânupapattau tu kathaṃ syād apramāṇatā?

VṚDDHĀ°:

Nanu sambandha|sāpekṣaḥ śabdo bhavati vācakaḥ,
sa c' âiva puruṣ'|âdhīnaḥ. kathaṃ syāt tad|agocare?

SNĀTA°:

3.210 Sambando nanu śaktir eva vacasaḥ,
sā c' âsya naisargikī.
puṃsā kartum aśakya eva samayaḥ
śabdair vinā vacakaiḥ.
vyutpattir vyavahāratas tu ghaṭate
ceṣṭā|nimitte nṛṇām
ātmany eva tathā prathām upagate
śabd'|âika|gamye vidhau.

«Kuryād» iti padasy' ârthas tri|kāla|sparśa|varjitaḥ
na kāla|viṣayair anyaiḥ pramāṇair avagāhyate.

And since by nature it cannot be encroached upon by other means of valid knowledge, it is unaffected by any help or harm they cause. 3.205

If other means of valid knowledge help verbal testimony, then it is only repetition, and if it is contradicted, it is false; but when both are impossible, how could it be not authoritative?

VRIDDHÁMBHI:

Surely a verbal expression necessarily requires the connection of the expression and the object expressed in order to be expressive, and that connection is dependent on a person. But how could this be in the case of something inaccessible to anyone?

GRADUATE:

But connection is just the word's power, and that power is innate in it. A person cannot make a convention without words that are already expressive. As for learning this connection—it is possible with regard to an injunction the content of which can be reached only through verbal expressions, through usage, when the cause of people's action has become manifest in oneself in the same way. 3.210

The meaning of the expression "he is to perform it"—a meaning that is not temporally bound—cannot be entered into by other means of valid knowledge with temporal objects.

VṚDDHĀ°: Kathaṃ tarhi tatra vyutpattiḥ?

SNĀTA°: Nan' ûktam atra, tan na gṛhītaṃ bhavatā. sv'|ātmani hi prerak'|âvagama|pūrvikā ceṣṭā dṛṣṭā. parasy' âpi liṅ|vibhaktiṃ śrutavataś ceṣṭā|darśanāt tataḥ prerak'|âvagamo jāta iti kalpyate. kīdṛg asau preraka iti svayam eva ātmavad upalabhyate. na tv «asāv evaṃ|rūpaḥ» iti rūpavān iva parasmai darśayituṃ śakyate. paro 'py enam anubhavaty eva, na c' ânyasmai darśayituṃ śaknot' îti pramāṇ'|ântar'|âgocare 'pi siddhā vyutpattiḥ. vṛddhasy' âpi bāla|daśāyām eṣ" âiva gatir ity anādiḥ saṃsāraḥ.

VṚDDHĀ°: Kim iyat" âiva siddhaṃ codanā|prāmāṇyam?

3.215 SNĀTA°: Kiṃ vā mṛgayate bhavān?

VṚDDHĀ°: Na pramāṇ'|ântar'|ânugraha|rahitaḥ Śabdaḥ pramāṇatām aśnute. abhidhāyaka eva hy asau, n' ârtha|tathātva|samarpakaḥ.

SNĀTA°: Abhidhāyako 'pi bodhaka eva. pramāṇaṃ hi sarvaṃ bodhakam eva bhavati, na tu ghaṭam iva kaṇṭhe rajjvā baddhvā prameyam arpayati.

VRIDDHÁMBHI: Then how can one learn that injunction?

GRADUATE: I've told you already, but you didn't get it. For one perceives in oneself that action is preceded by the cognizing of an instigator. Because one observes that someone else also acts after hearing an optative ending, therefore one postulates that the other person has also cognized an instigator. And one perceives oneself, just as one perceives the Self, what kind of instigator this is. But we cannot show it to somebody else saying, "It is like this," as we can show something else that has form. Others, too, do experience it, but they cannot show it to anyone else. Therefore learning the connection of word and meaning is established even in the case of injunction, which cannot be known by other means of valid knowledge. When old people were children, they learned in the same way: so the world has no beginning.

VRIDDHÁMBHI: Is that enough to prove the validity of Vedic injunction?

GRADUATE: What else are you looking for? 3.215

VRIDDHÁMBHI: The words of Scripture cannot be valid if they are deprived of the support of other means of valid knowledge, for they are merely expressive, but they do not provide a guarantee that the object is thus.

GRADUATE: Things that are expressive can also, in fact, create awareness. For every means of valid knowledge just creates awareness; it does not deliver the object of cognition like a pot, tying a rope around its neck.

Pramāṇ'|ântara|saṃvāda|sāpekṣāṃ ca pramāṇatām
vadanto n' âdhigaccheyur antaṃ yuga|śatair api.

Bādhaḥ kāraṇa|doṣo vā dvayaṃ mithyātva|kāraṇam.
tac c' âtidurlabhaṃ Veda iti siddhā pramāṇatā.

3.220 VṚDDHĀ° *bhūmim ālikhati.* SNĀTAK'|*ânucarā enam upahasanti.* SNĀTAKAS *tān vārayati.*

BHAṬṬĀ°: Y" êyam āryeṇa Veda|prāmāṇya|veṇī darśitā, kiṃ s" âiv' âpekṣyā, kiṃ vā «tad|vacanād āmnāya|prāmāṇyam», «mantr'|Āyur|veda|prāmāṇyavac ca tat|prāmāṇyam āpta|prāmāṇyāt» ity eṣa sādhīyān panthā iti sva|gṛha|kalaho 'yam asmākam. alaṃ tena. Veda|dviṣo nāstikās tāvad evaṃ|prāyā yuṣmābhiś ca nirākaraṇīyā eva.

SNĀTA°: Yathā bhagavān ādiśati.

Nepathye kalakalaḥ.

BHAṬṬĀ°: Kim etat?

3.225 SNĀTA°: Rāj'|āgama|śaṃsī nanv ayaṃ kalakalaḥ. tad vayaṃ rājñaḥ pratyanantarī|bhavāmaḥ. bhavanto 'pi sv'|āgam'|ôcitam arghy'|ādi rājñe sajjī|kurvantu.

BHAṬṬĀ°: Yath" āha bhavān.

Those who claim that validity must depend on agreement with other means of valid knowledge couldn't reach the end of the series of these means even after hundreds of aeons.

Falsity has two reasons: invalidation or a fault on the part of the causes of cognition.* And since neither of them obtain at all in the Veda, its validity is established.

VRIDDHÁMBHI *draws on the ground. The followers of the* GRADUATE *laugh at him. The* GRADUATE *restrains them.* 3.220

ABBOT: Whether we should rely on this way of proving the validity of the Veda that you, sir, have shown, or whether it is better to follow the train of thought that "the sacred tradition is authoritative because it is His word,"* and "it is valid because the trustworthy person* is authoritative, similarly to the validity of spells or texts about medicine"*: this is a private quarrel among ourselves. Let us leave it aside. First you too must completely refute the Veda-hating unbelievers of this ilk.

GRADUATE: As Your Eminence commands.

Hubbub offstage.

ABBOT: What's that?

GRADUATE: This hubbub must announce the king's arrival. 3.225
I will go to meet him. As for you, please prepare the respectful offerings for the king, as it befits your scriptures.

ABBOT: All right, sir.

SNĀTA°: Idaṃ ca punaḥ puno vijñāpyase Bhagavan,

Na hi dviṣmo devaṃ
Śivam anupam'|âiśvarya|vibhavaṃ.
sa ev' âiko hetuḥ
sthiti|vilaya|sargeṣu jagatām.
sa Rudraḥ, sa Brahmā,
sa Harir, aparo v" âpi Puruṣaḥ
paras tebhyas. tasmin
bhuvanam akhilaṃ saṃśritam idam.

Tad ime Śaiva|Pāśupata|Kālamukhā Mahā|vratinaś ca yathā|sukham āsatām.

3.230 Guru|vidy" âpi bhavatāṃ bhāti moh'|âpasāriṇī,
sā tv astu tāvad|viṣayā yāvaty eva vyavasthitā.

BHAṬṬĀ°: Yathā bhavān āha.

Niṣkrāntāḥ sarve.

Tṛtīyo 'ṅkaḥ.

GRADUATE: And let me remind Your Eminence once again:

> We certainly do not hate the god Shiva, the power of whose majesty is incomparable. He alone is the single cause of the upholding, resorbing and emitting of the worlds. He is Rudra, he is Brahma, he is Hari, or some other Person beyond them. This entire world depends on him.

Therefore let these Shaivas, Pashu·patas, Kala·mukhas and Maha·vratins remain at ease.*

> The knowledge handed down by your teachers also seems to dispel delusion, but let its scope be limited to that with respect to which it is justly established.* 3.230

ABBOT: Precisely, sir.

Exeunt omnes.

End of Act Three.

PRELUDE TO ACT FOUR: ORTHODOX IMPOSTURES

Tataḥ praviśati ṚTVIG UPĀDHYĀYAŚ *ca.*

ṚTVIK: *(sodvegam)* Kaṣṭaṃ bhoḥ kaṣṭam! anyad eva cintitam anyad ev' ôpanatam. Veda|bāhya|sakal'|āgama|tiraskāreṇ' âsmin prasaṅge sarvam asmad|bhogyam eva bhuvanaṃ bhaviṣyat' îti cintitam. yathā|vyāsam ev' âdy' âpi bāhy'| āgamā vartanta ity upanatam. tathā hi:

Śaiva|Pāśupata|Pāñcarātrikāḥ
Sāṅkhya|Saugata|Dig|ambar'|ādayaḥ
sarva eva hi yathā|sthitā ime.
snātakasya dhig apārthakam śrutam!

UPĀ°: Bho vayasya, nanu rāja|puruṣo 'sāv adya saṃvṛttaḥ. rājā ca parama|māheśvara iti tad|ārādhan'|âikatāna|buddhinā tena bhavitavyam. yataḥ:

4.5 Samīpato bhūmi|bhṛtāṃ hi pūruṣās
tad|uktam ev' ânuvadanta āsate,
sva|vṛddhi|lubdhās tu na sādhv asādhu vā
vivecayanti pratiśabdakā iva.

ṚTVIK: Vayasya, yathā manyase. kaḥ sv'|ârtham avadhīrya madhya|stho dharm'|âikatāna|buddhir bhavati? kiṃ tu kathaṃ Ved'|âika|viṣaya|yājan'|âdhyāpan'|ādi|vṛttibhir asmābhiḥ kālo netavyaḥ?

UPĀ°: Vayasya, yath" âiv' âtikrānto nītas tath" âiv' āgāmy api grāsa|vasana|mātra|santoṣibhir neṣyate. yataḥ:

Then enters the Vedic OFFICIANT *and the Vedic* INSTRUCTOR.

OFFICIANT: *(agitated)* What an awful blow! I had one thing in mind and something completely different has happened. I had in mind that when all the extra-Vedic religions are censured, we'll be able to enjoy the whole country. But what has happened is that the heterodox religions are still just as widespread as they were before. For:

> Shaivas, Pashu·patas, Pañcha·rátrikas, Sankhyas, Buddhists, Sky-Clad Jains and the rest: all of them remain as they were. Shame on the graduate's useless learning!

INSTRUCTOR: But, my friend, he is by now the king's man. And the king is supremely devoted to Shiva, so Sankárshana has to be completely focussed on propitiating Him. For:

> In a monarch's vicinity, his men always repeat his 4.5
> words, but, eager for their own advantage, they do not distinguish between good or bad, like echoes.

OFFICIANT: Right you are, my friend. Who would disregard his own interests and impartially focus his attention on Dharma alone? But how should we spend our time? Our profession—officiating at sacrifices, teaching and the like—is concerned exclusively with the Veda.

INSTRUCTOR: My friend, we shall spend the future just as we have spent the past: content merely with something to eat and wear. For:

Adurjana|giro goṣṭhyo, vīta|māna|grahāḥ priyāḥ
puṇyair vinā na labhyante, niḥsapatnāś ca sampadaḥ.

ṚTVIK: Evam eva. kiṃ kriyate? kiṃ tv idam adhikaṃ me karṇa|śalyam.

4.10 UPĀ°: Kim iva?

ṚTVIK: Yad amī Pāñca|rātrikā Bhāgavatā brāhmaṇavad vyavaharanti. brāhmaṇa|samāja|madhyam anupraviśya nirviśaṅkam abhivādaya iti jalpante. viśiṣṭa|svara|varṇ'|ānupūrvīkatayā Veda|pāṭham anusaranta iva Pañca|rātra|granthamadhīyate. «brāhmaṇāḥ smaḥ» ity ātmānaṃ vyapadiśanti vyapadeśayanti ca. Śaiv'|ādayas tu na cāturvarṇya|madhya|patitāḥ śruti|smṛti|vihitam āśramam avajahataḥ śāsan'|ântara|parigraheṇ' ânyathā vartante. ete punar «ā janmana ā santater brāhmaṇā eva vayam» iti bruvāṇās tath" âiva cāturāśramyam anukurvant' îti mahad duḥkham.

UPĀ°: Vayasya, kiyad idaṃ duḥkham?

Yājane 'dhyāpane yaune sambandhe 'nyatra vā kva cit
dūrāt parihṛtā eva śrotriyaiḥ Pāñcarātrikāḥ.

Without merit one cannot find assemblies exempt
from villains' talk, lovers immune from sulkiness,
and treasure not claimed by another.

OFFICIANT: Quite right. What to do? But this other thing annoys me more.

INSTRUCTOR: What is it? 4.10

OFFICIANT: That these Pañcha·rátrika Bhágavatas should adopt brahminical manners. They mix with brahmins and have no scruples about using the form of greeting that only we may use to our equals. They recite the Pañcha·ratra scriptures with a special pattern of accented syllables, as if they were taking the text of Veda as their example.* "We are brahmins," they say of themselves, and demand that others speak of them in the same way. Take the Shaivas and their ilk: they are not part of the system of the four social estates, they reject the life-periods determined by the Veda and the Smritis and they set themselves apart by adopting a different doctrine.* But these fellows say that "We have been truly brahmins ever since our birth, for a long succession of ancestors," and in the same way they imitate the system of the four life-periods: this is a great torment.

INSTRUCTOR: How great is this torment, my friend?

In officiating, teaching, matrimonial relations or
any other context, brahmins learned in the Veda
give the Pañcha·rátrikas a wide berth.

Brāhmaṇā iti tu vyapadeśas teṣām sva|samaya|saṃvyavahāra|mātram.

4.15 ṚTVIK: Kim etad alpaṃ duḥkham?

UPĀ°: Kiyad v" âitad? Śruti|Smṛtī adhyetuṃ Mīmāṃsāṃ ca, śrautaṃ smārtaṃ ca karm' ânuṣṭhātum ete kva cid api na labhante. brāhmaṇīṃ ca kāṃ cana śīlāc cyutām upayacchantaḥ prātilaumy'|ôdantena yojyante. Ved'|âṅgāni tu kāni cit kiyad v" âpy adhigacchanto 'pi na kva cin niṣidhyanta ity alam udvegena. tad āstām etat. idaṃ tu śrutaṃ mayā.

ṚTVIK: Kim iva?

UPĀ°: Adya khalu bhāgavat'|āgama|vicāram eva kartuṃ Śrī|saṅkarṣaṇo Vaiṣṇav'|āyatanaṃ Bhāgavata|śata|sahasra|sambādhaṃ gataḥ. brāhmaṇāś ca Brahma|dvīpe vidvāṃsaḥ sahasra|saṅkhyāḥ saṅghaṭitāḥ. tatra mahatyā goṣṭhyā bhavitavyam. tad ehi tatr' âiva gacchāmaḥ.

ṚTVIK: Dṛṣṭaḥ Saṅkarṣaṇa|pratāpaḥ, sa hi sarv'|āgama|prāmāṇya|vādī. rājñī ca Śrī|Sugandhā|devī teṣv eva sānukrośā śrūyate. rāja|puruṣo 'pi kaś cid anugrāhakaḥ Sātvatānām ast' îti vārttā.

As for the fact that they label themselves "brahmins": this is merely the usage of their own sect.

OFFICIANT: Is this a small nuisance? 4.15

INSTRUCTOR: Why, how big is it? They will never get to study the Veda, the Smritis, or Mimámsa, or to perform solemn or domestic rituals. And if they marry some brahmin woman who has strayed from the path of decorum, they will gain a reputation for having married "against the grain."* No need to get upset that they will not be banned from some places, even if they learn just a few of the Vedic ancillary sciences to some small extent. Let's drop the subject. But this is what I've heard.

OFFICIANT: What is it?

INSTRUCTOR: Today, apparently, the Honorable Sankárshana went to the Váishnavas' sanctuary, which is crowded with hundreds and thousands of Bhágavatas, precisely to scrutinize their religion. And thousands of brahmin scholars have assembled in Brahma·dvipa.* There must be a great conference there. So come, that is where we shall go.

OFFICIANT: We've seen Sankárshana's ardor, for he is an advocate of the theory that all religions are authoritative. On the other hand, the queen, Her Majesty Sugándha·devi, is reported to sympathize with these people especially. Rumor has it that there is a royal functionary who also supports the Sátvatas.*

4.20 UPĀ°: Alam asad|āśaṅkābhiḥ. na yathā|prastutād vyavahārād adhikaṃ tṛṇam api te kubjī|kartum īśate. tad ehi bāhy'|āgamānāṃ Mīmāṃsaka|sarasvatī|sāgare nimajjatām unmajjatāṃ ca vihvala|vepitam anekavidhaṃ draṣṭuṃ tatr' âiva gacchāvaḥ.

Iti niṣkrāntau.

INSTRUCTOR: Don't always fear the worst. They couldn't even bend a blade of grass if this was beyond the established customs. So come, let's go there and see the manifold, desperate floundering of the heterodox religions as they are ducked again and again in the ocean of the Mimámsaka's streaming eloquence. 4.20

Exeunt ambo.

ACT FOUR: QUALIFIED TOLERANCE

Tataḥ praviśati Śrī|SAṄKARṢAṆO, BAṬUR, *vibhavataś ca parivāraḥ.*

SNĀTA°: *(sodvegam)* Baṭo, saṅkaṭe nipatitāḥ smaḥ. yataḥ:

Ye viśva|sthiti|sarga|saṃhṛti|daśā|
paryāya|sampādana|
krīḍ"|āsakta|mater mataṃ bhagavato
Nārāyaṇasy' āśritāḥ,
tad|dṛṣṭeḥ katham anyathātvam anayā
brūmo vayaṃ jihvayā?
śakṣyāmaḥ kṛtināṃ trayī|maya|dhiyāṃ
sthātuṃ kathaṃ v" âgrataḥ?

4.25 BAṬUḤ: ⌜Ayya, atthi yyeva edaṃ. taha vi cirādo pahudi paütto jaha|ṭṭhido saṃvavahāro rakkhīadi. kiṃ ettha ayyo visaṃṭhulo? tā saṃpadaṃ pekkhadu Paṃca|rattia|ppamuha|mahā|paṃḍita|saya|sahassa|saṃbādhaṃ imaṃ padesaṃ ayyo.⌟

SNĀTA°: *(parikramy' âgrato 'valokya savismayam)* Aho mahatī paras|para|spardh"|ânubandha|pratanyamān'|ânalpa|jalpa|vikalpa|kolāhal'|ākulita|dig|antar" âiṣā paṇḍita|pariṣat! asyāṃ hi

Ito vākyeṣv ālo-
cita|vividha|tātparya|gataya,
ito nām'|ākhyāta|
prakṛti|kṛta|yatnāḥ pada|vidaḥ,
ito hetu|vyāpti|
graha|paṭu|dhiyas tarka|kuśalā,
itaś c' âite vṛddhāḥ
Smṛti|Naya|Purāṇ'|ādi|nipuṇāḥ.

Then enters the Honorable SANKÁRSHANA, *the* BOY, *and as many attendants as can be afforded.*

GRADUATE: Boy, I am in a tight corner, for:

> Those who adhere to the teaching of the Blessed Vishnu Naráyana, whose mind is absorbed in the play of accomplishing the revolution of the states of the universe, that is, its continuation, emission and resorption—how shall I say with this tongue of mine that their worldview is false? But, if I don't, how could I stand before the learned whose intellect is completely occupied by the three Vedas?

BOY: Oh dear, you have a dilemma, sir. Nevertheless the 4.25
customs that were set up long ago continue as they were. Why be uneasy about this matter, sir? So now please take a look at this place thronged with hundreds and thousands of Pañcha·rátrikas and other great scholars.

GRADUATE: *(walks about, looks ahead, amazed)* Good Lord! What a big conference of scholars! It fills the quarters with a great hullabaloo of dispute and disagreement spreading with mutual emulation. For in this assembly:

> There are Mimámsakas who have reflected on the ways of the various meanings in sentences; grammarians who have scrutinized the roots of nouns and verbs; logicians whose minds are sharp in ascertaining the concomitance of the logical reason; and over here are the senior masters of the Smritis, Polity, Puránas and the like.

Aho bata Pura|hara|hṛdayasya spṛhaṇīya|guṇ'|ôdadher vibudha|guṇ'|ākarṇana|karṇ'|âlaṅkārasya pūrita|sakala|sādhu|jana|manorathasya puṇya|yaśasaḥ Śrī|Yaśo|varma|devasya Brahma|loka|nirviśeṣam ev' êdaṃ dṛśyate rāṣṭram! *(kṣaṇaṃ vicintya svagatam)* iha khalv itar'|êtara|viruddh'|âbhidhāyi|bahu|vidha|vibudha|prabandha|sambodhana|praśāsanam anurudhyamāne jane katham iva mayā vartitavyam?

Pathi Veda|virodha|dāruṇe
  nipuṇen' âpi na śakya|nirṇaye
kim ahaṃ karavāṇi? hanta! me
  śaraṇaṃ śārṅga|rath'|âṅga|śaṅkha|bhṛt.

4.30 Bhavatu, Bhagavantam eva tāvat samprati śaraṇaṃ prapadye. *(prakāśam)* baṭo, pratyāsannam ito Bhagavad|āyatanam. tad atra praviśya Bhagavantam aśeṣa|jana|śaraṇaṃ Raṇa|svāminaṃ praṇipatya tataḥ sabhā|madhyam adhyāsiṣye.

BAṬUḤ: ⌜Jaṃ āṇavedi.⌟

Parikrāmataḥ.

SNĀTA°: *(praveśam abhinīya bhūmau jānunī nidhāya)*

Namaḥ krama|samākrānta|citra|trailokya|sadmane,
kukṣi|koṇ'|âika|deś'|âṃśa|līna|viśvāya Viṣṇave.

How wonderful! Now the kingdom looks exactly like Brahma's heaven—the kingdom of His Majesty Yasho·varma·deva* of holy fame, whose heart is with Shiva, Destroyer of the Triple City, an ocean of enviable virtues, who adorns his ear by listening to the valuable advice of the learned, and fulfills the wishes of every virtuous man. *(He muses for a moment, and says aside:)* I wonder how I should behave among these people, for they adhere to the guidance and instructions of diverse, mutually contradictory, scholarly works.

> What shall I do on a path that is rough because
> it opposes the Veda, and on which even an expert
> could not arrive at a decision? I know! My refuge
> is Vishnu, the god who holds a bow, a discus and
> a conch shell.

So be it! First I take refuge at once with the Blessed Lord himself. *(aloud)* Boy, the Blessed Lord's temple is close by. I'll enter there, do obeisance to the Blessed Vishnu Rana·svamin, everyone's refuge, and then I shall take my seat in the assembly. 4.30

BOY: As you command.

They walk about.

GRADUATE: *(mimes entering and kneels down on the ground)*

> Homage to Vishnu, who is the abode of the diverse
> triple world that he spanned with his steps, in the
> fragment of one part of the corner of whose belly
> the universe rests absorbed.

4.35 Namaḥ kara|tal'|ālambi|kambu|cakrāya Cakriṇe,
vyañjate mokṣa|san|mārgaṃ, nirmal'|ānanda|dīpine.

Namaḥ parama|nirvāṇa|kāraṇāya Rath'|âṅgine . . .

(<ākarṇya> saharṣam) Amunā śaṅkha|dhvani|maṅgalena tarkayāmi . . .

<MAÑJĪRAḤ>: . . . mahān eṣa varṇ'|āśrama|virodho vartate. tad atra|bhavato brāhmaṇān ānetuṃ Brahma. . . kṣa|mantri|pravara|prārthitā Devī prahit" âbhūt. tayā sa āgatya kathitaḥ —« ‹tīrth'|ântarāṇāṃ trayī|vidāṃ c' âtra vivāde stheyatayā sarveṣāṃ sammataḥ pratīta|guṇo mahā|naiyāyiko Dhairya|rāśir iti prathit'|âpara|nāmā Bhaṭṭa|Sāhaṭas, tam atra vivāda|pada|nirṇetāraṃ kuru› iti tair vayam abhyarthitās †tadvatātha† . . . » . . . pagatam. tato na bhavān gantum arhati. atr' âiva vivāde sabhā|vartinam anudgrāhayantam atra|bhavantam icchāmo vayam iti . . .

SNĀTA°: Sakhe Mañjīra, tad ehi, sah' âiva sabhāṃ praviśāmaḥ.

4.40 *Parikrāmanti.*

Nepathye:

Vaṃśe kv' âpi
prakaṭa|mahima<ny>. . .

. . . ko 'pi dhanyaḥ
yasy' ânyonya|
pratihata|dṛśāṃ sarva|sandeha|mokṣāt
tuly'|ākārā
bhavati viduṣāṃ dṛṣṭir utkṛṣṭatāyām.

Homage to Chakrin,* in whose palms a conch shell and a discus rest, who shows the true path of liberation and illuminates spotless beatitude. 4.35

Homage to Rathángin,* who is the cause of final extinction . . .

(<He listens> and says joyfully:) From this auspicious conch shell sound I assume . . .

<MAÑJÍRA>: . . . this is a great risk for the social estates and life-periods. So the queen, solicited by the chief minister Brahma. . . ksha, has been induced to summon these respected brahmins. Returning from there she told the chief minister that she had been requested: "All accept Bhatta Sáhata, the great Naiyáyika, also known by the name of Dhairya·rashi, as an umpire in this debate between those who are learned in the Three Vedas and the preceptors of other religions: please make him the arbitrator in the affair of this debate." . . . Therefore, sir, please do not leave. I would like Your Honor to be present in the assembly of the same debate, without adducing your view. . . .

GRADUATE: My friend Mañjíra, come then, we shall enter the assembly together.

They walk about. 4.40

From offstage:

In a distinguished family of well-known dignity . . . remarkably fortunate, eliminates every doubt in those with opposing views, and thereby scholars have a shared vision of what is supreme.

Śrī|Sāhaṭo nāma lalāma|bhūto
jāto jagatyāḥ Parameṣṭhi|kalpaḥ,
guṇair analpair adhikī|kṛtasya
virodhitāṃ yasya gato na lokaḥ.

SNĀTA°: Āgacchato Dhairya|rāśer eṣa stavaḥ. aho Dhairya|rāśi|pakṣa|pātī lokaḥ. na c' âyam asthāne lokasya pakṣa|pātaḥ. īdṛśa ev' âsau. sakhe Mañjīra, bhavad|anugrahān mahataḥ saṅkaṭād uttīrṇā vayaṃ yad evaṃ|vidheṣu karmas' ûdāsmahe.

4.45 MAÑJĪ°: Ārya, kutas tava yāvaj|jīvaṃ jan'|ânugraha|mahā|vyāpārasya saṅkaṭ'|âvataraṇam ajar'|âmare Param'|ēśvare?

BAṬUḤ: ⌜Ajja idaṃ sabhā|majjhe ayyassa uvavesaṇa|ṭṭhāṇaṃ ciṭṭhadi. tā pavisadu bhavaṃ.⌟

SNĀTA°: Sakhe Mañjīra, prathamaṃ praviśya devasy' ājñāṃ śrāvaya sadasyān.

MAÑJĪ°: Evaṃ karomi. *(parikramya)* yathā|sannihitā vidvāṃsaḥ, śrūyatām!

Vaktā tīkṣṇa|matiḥ, satāṃ bahu|mataḥ,
vidy"|āpagā|sāgaro,
vidvat|saṃsadi paṇḍit'|ôttamatayā
prāptaḥ pratītiṃ parām
tīrtha|prārthanayā gato 'dya sa nṛp'|ā-
deśād iha stheyatām.
svasthāḥ santu, samutsṛjantu vimatiṃ,
nandantu sarvāḥ prajāḥ!

The Honorable Sáhata was born a true ornament of the world, nearly equal to the Highest Lord. No small virtues have elevated him so that no one confronts him.

GRADUATE: The approaching Dhairya·rashi is being praised. Clearly, people are on Dhairya·rashi's side! And their sympathy is appropriate, for he is exactly as they describe him. Mañjíra, my friend, thanks to Your Honor's favor I've got out of a bad fix, and can stay away from such matters.

MAÑJÍRA: When the ageless and deathless Supreme Lord is 4.45
there by your side, how could you have any difficulty, sir, in your lifelong mission to help people?

BOY: There is this seat for you, sir, in the present assembly, so please enter.

GRADUATE: My colleague, Mañjíra, please enter first and announce the king's order to the assembly members.

MAÑJÍRA: All right. *(He walks about.)* Scholars, now that you are all in your places, may I have your attention!

There is a sharp-witted speaker, highly esteemed by the virtuous, an ocean of the rivers of sciences, who has achieved great reputation in the society of scholars as the greatest pandit. Today, on the king's order and at the request of religious leaders, he is made the arbitrator in this affair. May all the people be at ease, give up their differences and rejoice!

4.50 *Tataḥ praviśati yathā|nirdiṣṭo* DHAIRYA|RĀŚIR *vibhavataś ca vādi|samājaḥ.*

DHAIRYA°: *(savismayam)* Aho vidyā|samāgamaḥ! citram! ih' âiva Jambu|dvīpe Bharata|varṣe ca Parameṣṭhi|puraṃ paśyāmaḥ! tathā hi:

Iha vinihitaṃ
vidyā|sthānaiś catur|daśabhiḥ padaṃ,
sthitam iha samā-
cāraiś citrair, ito vividhair vrataiḥ,
prakṛti|viśadā-
ny atra svairaṃ tapāṃsi ca śerate,
nara|patir api
Brahmā sākṣād dhruvaṃ. kim ataḥ param?

(agrato 'valokya) Katham! ih' âiva maha|rṣi|nirviśeṣaḥ Śrī|saṅkarṣaṇaḥ. bhavatv, enam abhivādaye. *(tathā <karoti>.)*

SNĀTA°: *(gāḍham enaṃ pariṣvajya)* Ayam aprayāsa|sulabho 'nubhūyate sakala|tīrtha|salil'|âbhiṣekaḥ.

4.55 *Sarva upaviśanti.*

SNĀTA°: Bho iha|bhavantas tīrthikā, nanv idānīm atra|bhavatāṃ chinnāḥ samagrāḥ saṃśaya|granthayaḥ. eṣo hi sākṣād Akṣa|pāda iva ānvīkṣikī|Prajā|patir upasthito nar'|âdhip'|ânurodhena Dhairya|rāśiḥ.

VĀDINAḤ: Tīrtha|kar'|ânurodhena yathā na tathā rāj'|ânurodhena.

SNĀTA°: *(*DHAIRYA|RĀŚIM *uddiśya)* Bho naiyāyika|tilakā vidita|vṛtt'|ântā eva yathā|prastuta|vastuni bhavantaḥ. tad upakramyatāṃ sva|pratibhān"|ânusāreṇa yath"|ôcitam abhidhātum.

Then enter DHAIRYA·RASHI *as described above, and as large a gathering of disputants as can be afforded.* 4.50

DHAIRYA·RASHI: *(amazed)* What a confluence of sciences! Amazing! I see the City of the Supreme Being right here, on the continent of Jambu and in Bhárata's country! For:

> Here the fourteen branches of knowledge* stand firm; various practices are present; there are manifold observances here, and naturally pure austerities are unhindered and at peace. As for the king, he is clearly Brahma in the flesh: what can be better?

(He looks ahead.) I see that the Honorable Sankárshana, the equal of legendary sages, is present. Very well, let me salute him. *(<He does> so.)*

GRADUATE: *(embraces him closely)* Your embrace is a well-met ablution in all the holy waters!

All sit down. 4.55

GRADUATE: Respectable theologians, all your knotty doubts are now as good as cut. For, on the king's order, one we may call the living Aksha·pada, the Praja·pati of Philosophy, is present among us: Dhairya·rashi!

DISPUTANTS: On the religious leaders' request rather than at the king's command.

GRADUATE: *(to* DHAIRYA·RASHI*)* Ornament among logicians, you must already be acquainted with the facts of the matter presently under discussion. So please pronounce as you find proper, according to your inspiration.

DHAIRYA°: Ārya, viditam etāvat: Pañca|rātr'|ādy|āgamāḥ pramāṇam apramāṇaṃ v" êti vādinām iha vipratiprattiḥ. atra|bhavatsu punaḥ sannihiteṣu kīdṛśo mādṛśām abhidhān'|âdhikāro? yadi paraṃ bhavad|anujñā|sṛṣṭyā bhavat|prasūtā iva kim api vaktuṃ śakṣyāmaḥ.

4.60 SNĀTA°: Kim evam abhidhīyate? sraṣṭāro 'tra|bhavantaḥ. sarva|vādināṃ ca tvayy eva viśvasiti hṛdayam. tad abhidhīyatām.

DHAIRYA°: *(pravādakān uddiśya)* Bho bhavantaḥ āryāḥ, pakṣa|dvaye 'pi yuktayo bhavad|uktāḥ śrutā gṛhītāś ca nirākāṅkṣā asmābhiḥ. tato 'virata|vacasi mayi n' ântarā kim api vaktum arhanti bhavantaḥ.

VĀDI°: Ārya, yathā bhavān āha. na kiṃ cid apṛṣṭāḥ santo 'ntarāle bhavatāṃ vacanam ākṣipya brūmaḥ.

DHAIRYA°: Tad idānīm avahitaiḥ śrūyatām.

VĀDI°: Avahitāḥ smaḥ.

4.65 DHAIRYA°:

Mīmāṃsakais tāvad avādi: Vedaḥ
svataḥ pramāṇaṃ kila bodhakatvāt,
anāditā|darbha|nirasta|kartṛ|
pram"|âpavāda|dvaya|pāṃsu|pātaḥ.

Tathā c' āhuḥ:

DHAIRYA·RASHI: Sir, I know this much: the disputants here disagree whether such scriptures as the Pañcha·ratra are valid or not. But when Your Honor is present, what sort of authority do people like me have to speak? Only if you grant us your permission are we allowed to speak, like Your Honor's child, as it were.

GRADUATE: Why do you say so? It is Your Honor who ordains. And every disputant has placed his confidence in you alone. So please speak. 4.60

DHAIRYA·RASHI: *(addressing the disputants)* Respected gentlemen, I have heard and understood the arguments put forth by you concerning both positions, and they are complete. Therefore please do not interject anything while I deliver my speech uninterrupted.

DISPUTANTS: All right, sir. We shall not interject anything to interrupt your speech without being asked.

DHAIRYA·RASHI: Then listen carefully now.

DISPUTANTS: We hang upon your lips.

DHAIRYA·RASHI: 4.65

> First of all, the Mimámsakas say that the Veda is a means of valid cognition by itself, since it creates awareness. The *darbha* grass* of beginninglessness has swept away its author and the dust of both challenges to its validity.*

Accordingly they say:

Sarve bodhāḥ svato 'mī
samucita|viṣay'|āvedakatvāt pramāṇam.
n' âiṣāṃ bādh'|ôpapātaḥ
karaṇa|kaluṣatā|pratyayo vā yadi syāt.
nitye Vede 'pavāda|
dvayam anavasaraṃ, bodhakatvaṃ ca siddham.
kārye v" âtīndriy'|ârthe
na bhavati sutarāṃ bādhakasy' âvakāśaḥ.

Pratyakṣa|gocare hy arthe grahītuṃ śaknuyur narāḥ
tathātvam atathātvaṃ ca. teṣāṃ k" âtīndriye gatiḥ?

4.70 Tasmād bodhakatvād apavāda|dvay'|âbhāvāc ca svata eva Vedaḥ pramāṇam.

Atra brūmaḥ:
sarala|sugamaḥ satyam eṣo 'sti panthās
tat|prāmāṇye,
na punar amunā cittam āvarjyate naḥ.
śabde 'rthe vā
kva khalu racanā dṛśyate 'pauruṣeyī?
svādhyāyo 'pi
prathama|samaye saṃpravṛttaḥ kutaś cit.

Śruteḥ ko 'sāv ādyaḥ
samaya iti cet: kalpaya varaṃ,
na hi vyūho nityo
'yam avayava|nityasya ghaṭate.
dhruvān varṇān kāmaṃ
kathaya, racanānāṃ punar idaṃ
na rūpaṃ dṛśyaṃ te:
nanu jagati tāḥ kartṛ|vaśa|gāḥ.

All cognitions we have are valid by themselves because they give information about their appropriate object. But they are not valid if a contradiction* occurs, or if we realize that the instrument* is defective. In the case of the eternal Veda, both challenges are out of place, and the fact that it creates awareness is established. Or, rather, there is even less room for objection if an imperceptible object* is to be accomplished.

For people can ascertain about an object that is within the scope of sense perception that it is or is not thus.* What means do they have in the case of an imperceptible object?

Therefore the Veda is a source of valid cognition by itself alone because it creates awareness and because neither of the challenges of validity obtain. 4.70

To this I say: This path concerning the Veda's validity is indeed straight and easy. Nevertheless it does not win my heart. Where can we see a non-human arrangement in the case of words and their meaning? The recitation of the Veda also started from somewhere on the first occasion.

If you ask when this "first occasion" of the Veda was, it is up to you to imagine it. For this arrangement of the Veda, which is eternal in its components, cannot itself be eternal. You may say that sounds are permanent, yet you cannot observe this nature in the case of structures: surely in our world they depend on a maker.

«Dvaipāyan'|ādi|vad iha smaraṇam na kartur
ast' îti»: hanta! na bhay'|āvaha eṣo doṣaḥ.
kartā vilakṣaṇatayā hi na dṛśya eṣa.
mādṛkṣa|dṛṣṭi|viṣaye smṛtayo bhavanti.

Api ca, Hiraṇya|garbham aniśaṃ kathayanti janā
janakam udāra|vaidika|vaco|racanāsu ciram.
«smṛtir iyam artha|vāda|janit" êti» viśeṣa|dhiyāṃ
na khalu bhavān pramāṇa|kaṇikām api vaktum alam.

4.75 Kiṃ ca:

Yath" Âṣṭak"|ādi|Smṛti|mūla|bhūtā
nity'|ânumeyāḥ Śrutayas tvay" ôktāḥ,
nity'|ânumeyo 'stu tath" âiva Vede
kartā, viśeṣo yadi v" âbhidheyaḥ.

«Nanu ten' ânumeyena vinā kim avasīdati?»
Śruti|vāky'|ânumānena vinā kim avasīdati?

Smṛtiś cen n' ôpapadyeta, racanā n' ôpapatsyate.
smṛtiḥ kārya|svabhāvā ced, racan" âpi tathā|vidhā.

You may object: "We do not remember an author of the Veda, in the way that we remember Vyasa and others."* Come now! This charge is not a dangerous one. For his extraordinary nature makes this maker imperceptible. We can have memories only about something or somebody perceptible to ordinary people like me.

Furthermore, since ancient times people have always said that Hiránya·garbha was the author of the rich Vedic verbal compositions. If you say, "This tradition is the product of explanatory exegesis," you cannot adduce even a morsel of proof to ascertain this distinction.*

Furthermore: 4.75

Just as you say that Vedic texts are always to be inferred as the bases of such Smritis as the one dealing with the *Aṣṭakā* ritual,* in the same way one must always infer an author for the Veda, or else the difference* must be stated.

You may well ask in that case: "What fails without that* which is to be inferred?" What fails without the inference of Vedic sentences?*

If you say that the memory of the prescribed ritual* would be impossible, my answer is that a composition will be an impossibility.* If you say that memory* has the nature of an effect, then a composition is also of that kind.

«Mithyā nanu Manor vākyaṃ
bhaven mūla|śrutiṃ vinā.»
prayojan'|ânurodhena
kiṃ pramāṇa|vyavasthitiḥ?

4.80 Athavā:

Mithyā santu Manor vacāṃsi, na punaḥ
śākhā|śat'|âdhyāyinām
ekasy' âpi mukhe kva v" âpy apatitā
śaky" ânumātuṃ śrutiḥ.
kalpyā Veda|vidām ath' ādara|vaśāt
tan|mūla|bhūtā Śrutiḥ,
kartā Veda|<pada|>kram'|ādi|racanā|
yogāt tathā kalpyatām.

«Vedasy' âdhyayanaṃ sarvaṃ
gurv|adhyayana|pūrvakam,
Ved'|âdhyayana|vācyatvād»
iti hetur asādhakaḥ.

Aprayojakatā c' âivaṃ|prāyāṇām ucyate svayam,
svayaṃ c' âite prayujyanta iti k" êyaṃ viḍambanā?

Kva cana cirantana|racane
'bhrama|janita|paramparā|prathite
asmaryamāṇa|kartriṇi
mūle kartā bhavaty eva.

You may object: "Surely Manu's sentences would be false without a Vedic text as their basis." Why are you positing a source of valid knowledge according to your purpose?

Or, rather: 4.80

Let Manu's propositions be false, but we cannot infer a Vedic text that is nowhere, not in the mouth of even one of those who have studied hundreds of Vedic recensions. If you say that out of respect for those who are learned in the Veda* a Vedic text should be postulated as its basis, likewise we should postulate an author as a consequence of such structures as the sequence of Vedic <words>.

"The regular study of the Veda presupposes its regular study from one's teacher, since that is referred to by the expression 'the study of the Veda:'"* this logical reason is indecisive.

You yourself say that such logical reasons are not effective, and yet at the same time you yourself use them—this is ridiculous.

In the case of an ancient composition that has become well known through a transmission whose source is not error, even though the memory of its author has not been retained, there is obviously an author at its origin.

4.85 Vede hi pauruṣeye
tat|karmasu vitata|vitta|sādhyeṣu
puruṣam ananusmarantaḥ
katham iva santaḥ pravartante?

Anumānen' âpi mite
kartari viduṣāṃ pravṛttir ucit" âiva,
smārte 'ṣṭak"|ādi|kārye
śruty|anumānād yathā bhavatām.

Ataś ca nity'|ânumeyo Vede 'sti kartā:

Viśva|jity ucitam aśrutaṃ phalaṃ
kalpyate kim api vidhy|apekṣayā.
tatra kasya tad|apekṣitā bhavet?
cetanau na khalu vācya|vācakau.

Avagati|dharmo 'yaṃ ced,
avagatir api kasya? na svatantr" âsau.
asmākaṃ cet, puruṣa|
prabhavaḥ prāpnoti Ved'|ârthaḥ.

4.90 Avagantāro hi vayaṃ
boddhṛtayā kartur āśayaṃ vidmaḥ.
iha kasy' âbhiprāyaḥ?
śabdasy' ârthasya vā n' âsau.

For, given that the Veda is authored, how is it indeed that virtuous people who have no recollection of that person perform its rituals, which can only be accomplished with a lot of money? 4.85

The effort of the wise* is very much appropriate in that case, too, if the author is inferred, just as your effort to perform such rituals as the *áshtaka* ceremony enjoined in the Smritis is suitable on the basis of inferring a Vedic text.*

And for the following reasons, too, the Veda does have an author, who is always to be inferred:

In the case of the All-conquering sacrifice,* a particular fruit* is rightly postulated, even though it is not mentioned explicitly in the Veda, because of the expectation generated by the ritual injunction. In that case who could be the one who expects that fruit? The signified sense and the signifying word are surely not conscious.

If you claim that this is characteristic of comprehension,* then whose comprehension are you talking about? For it is not autonomous. If you say that it is ours, then it will follow that the Veda's authors are human beings.

Since whenever we understand,* we become aware of the intention of the author,* inasmuch as he is the one who knows.* Whose is the intention here? Not the word's or the meaning's. 4.90

Yad|ākāṅkṣā|balād aṅgaṃ phalaṃ vā kalpyate kva cit,
so 'sya kart" âsti puruṣaḥ. kasy' ākāṅkṣ" ânyathā bhavet?

Ato nity'|ânumeyo 'pi kartā Vedasya vidyate,
na hi tena vinā ko 'pi vyavahāro 'vakalpate.

Yac ca kartā na smaryata iti bhaṇyate, tatr' âyaṃ vivekaḥ:

Kartāro ye hi yānti
smaraṇa|patham iha Vyāsa|Vālmīki|mukhyāḥ,
sarve mādṛg|dṛśāṃ te
viniyata|tanavo gocare saṃcaranti.
kāmaṃ vyom'|âika|kāyaḥ
śrita|vividha|tanur niḥśarīro 'thav" âsau
devo Vedasya kartā
katham iva viṣayatvaṃ prayāti smṛtīnām?

4.95 Ata eva ca tatra kartari
pratibh" âneka|vidhā vipaścitām.
param'|ârthata eka eva sa
tri|jagat|kṣema|niyojana|kṣamaḥ.

Samāna|saṅkalpatay" ēśvarāṇām
anekatā kalpayituṃ na śakyā.
viruddha|saṅkalpita|siddhy|abhāvān
nūnaṃ tataḥ ke cid anīśvarāḥ syuḥ.

Tasmāt sarva|vid eka eva. jagato
'dhiṣṭhātṛ|bhede punar
niṣpadyeta na tat, kṛtaṃ na ca ciraṃ
tiṣṭhet ku|rāṣṭram yathā.

> He whose expectation is postulated as the reason for an ancillary of or a result of a given ritual is the author of that ritual. Whose expectation other than his could it be?
>
> Therefore the Veda does have an author, even if he must always be inferred, for without him no Vedic activity would be possible.

As for the statement that no author is remembered, we analyze the problem as follows:

> Those authors who reach the path of recollection in this world, such as Vyasa and Valmíki, all have a limited body and so walk about in the range of sight of people like me. Maybe space alone is his body, or he might occupy various forms, or he may have no body at all: in any case, how on earth could God, the author of the Veda, become an object of memories?
>
> That is exactly why the wise have various fanciful ideas about this author. In reality He is only one, able of securing the welfare of the three worlds. 4.95
>
> One cannot postulate a plurality of gods, all with the same intention. On the other hand, since opposed intentions cannot be simultaneously accomplished, some of them would clearly be non-gods.
>
> Therefore there is only one omniscient person. But if there were many managers of the world, either it could not be created at all or, if somehow produced, it would not last long, like a misgoverned

ekasya sthapater mat'|ânusaraṇāt
prāsāda|sampādanaṃ
bhūyobhiḥ kriyate narair iti bhaved
eka|praṇītaṃ jagat.

Vyāpāribhiś ca bahubhiḥ puruṣair idaṃ hi
śakyaṃ jagad yuga|śatair api na praṇetum,
ekas tu nirmala|matiḥ sahas" âiva satya|
saṅkalpa evam upapādayat' îti yuktam.

Uktaṃ ca:

4.100 «Ekasya kasya cid aśeṣa|jagat|prasūti|
hetor anādi|puruṣasya mahā|vibhūteḥ
sarga|sthiti|pralaya|kārya|vibhāga|yogād
Brahm" êti Viṣṇur iti Rudra iti prasiddhiḥ.»

Vidhātā viśv'|ātmā
sakala|jagatām eṣa ca yathā,
praṇetā Vedānām
api sa hi tath" âiv' âmala|matiḥ.
yath" ânyony'|âdhīna|
sthitaya iha lokās traya ime,
tath" ânyony'|âpekṣān
abhidadhati Vedā api vidhīn.

Sanniveśo hi yo 'nyonya|vyatiṣakte 'vadhāryate
arthe vā vāci vā n' âsau saṃbhaved iti kalpyate:

kingdom. The construction of a building is accomplished by many only because they follow the instructions of one architect: thus the world must have been created by a single agent.

For many people bustling about could not create this world even in hundreds of aeons. But one pure-minded person whose intentions are always realized brings it about in no time: this is the right view.

And it is taught:

"Because of his association with the elements of his task, namely creation, maintenance and dissolution, the unique, wonderful, unborn, supremely powerful Person, who is the cause of the emission of the whole world, is known as Brahma, Vishnu, and Rudra."* 4.100

And just as this Self of the universe is the creator of all worlds, in the same way He, the pure-minded one, is indeed the author of the Vedas, too. Just as the condition of these three worlds is interdependent, in the same way the Vedas also proclaim interrelated injunctions.

Since the arrangement that is perceived in interconnected topics or words would not be possible otherwise, thus we postulate the following:

Vedānām eka ev' â-
tula|kuśala|path'|ādeśak'|âneka|śākhā|
vikṣiptānāṃ vidhātā
kavir amalamatiḥ ko 'pi devaḥ purāṇaḥ.
tad|vat sarv'|āgamānāṃ
bhavatu sa bhagavān eka eva praṇetā,
nānātvaṃ kartur itthaṃ
na suvacam iti hi prāg upanyastam etat.

«Aho!

4.105 Paraspara|virodhino nanu ca sarva eva āgamāḥ,
samānam abhidheyam eṣu na hi kiṃ cid īkṣāmahe.
ta eka|nara|nirmitā iti kathaṃ nu manyāmahe?
pramāṇam itar'|êtara|pratihatāś ca te vā katham?»

Yat tāvad bravīṣi «paraspara|virodhe kathaṃ prāmāṇyam?» iti tatr' ânuyujyase:

Paraspara|virodhitāṃ pratikaroṣi Vede katham?
sa nitya iti ced, aho gṛha|kathāsu sakto bhavān!
vibhāgam avalambya kaṃ cana virodhit" âpāsyate
yadi Śrutiṣu, s" āgam'|ântara|vacaḥsu tulyā gatiḥ.

Śrutāv āyuṣ|kāmaṃ
prati hi vihitaḥ kṛṣṇala|carus,
tathā sarva|svāraḥ
kila maraṇa|kāmasya paṭhitaḥ.
virodhaś c' âitasyāṃ
yadi viṣaya|bhedāt parihṛto
bhavadbhiḥ, s" âiva syāt
saraṇir iha tīrth'|ântara|girām.

The only creator of the Vedas, which show us the path to unequalled happiness and which are scattered in several recensions, is a pure-minded sage, a wonderful, ancient god. Likewise let the Blessed Lord be the one and only author of all scriptures, for, as it has already been stated, a plurality of authors is not easy to account for.

"Oho!" you may exclaim,

"Surely all scriptures without exception are mutually contradictory, for we do not see any common subject matter therein. How could we accept that they were created by one man? Or how could they be authoritative when they annul each other?" 4.105

First, your assertion will be examined, namely: "How can there be validity if there is mutual contradiction?"

How do you prevent mutual contradiction in the case of the Veda? If you say that it is eternal: aha! You are caught fast in your family tales. If the contradiction is averted by somehow differentiating Vedic texts, the procedure is the same with regard to the texts of other scriptures.

In the Veda, blackberry-oblation is prescribed for a man who wishes for a long life,* and, as we learn, the *Sarvasvāra* ritual is recited for someone who wants to die.* If you obviate the contradiction in these Vedic passages through differentiating the object of injunction, the course of action must be the same here, regarding the propositions of other religions.

Evaṃ tāvad itar'|êtara|virodhinīṣv api Veda|codanāsv iva na tīrth'|ântara|deśanāsu doṣaḥ. athavā:

4.110 Paramaṃ puruṣ'|ârthaṃ prati
na c' āgamānāṃ virodhitā kā cit,
ādiśyate hi sarvaiḥ
kaivalyaṃ tulyam eva phalam.

Mārga|bhedās tv anugrāhya|sattva|buddhy|anusāriṇaḥ
tatra tatr' ôpadiśyante vicitrās trāṇa|kāriṇaḥ.

«Amī hi c' ânena pathā yatheṣṭaṃ
śakyāḥ śubhaṃ prāpayituṃ manuṣyāḥ.»
it' Īśvaraḥ sarva|vid eṣa paśyan
nānā|vidhān ādiśati sma mārgān.

Praveṣṭu|kāmā bahavaḥ pumāṃsaḥ
pure yath" âikatra mahā|gṛhe vā
dvār'|ântareṇ' âpi viśanti ke cit,
tath" ôttame dhāmni mumukṣavo 'pi.

Ata eva hi bāla|kaver
avalokita|sakala|śāstra|sarasya
sūktam idaṃ tattva|vido
bhraṣṭa|bhrānter Jayantasya:

4.115 «Nānā|vidhair āgama|mārga|bhedair
ādiśyamānā bahavo 'bhyupāyāḥ
ekatra te śreyasi saṃpatanti
sindhau pravāhā iva jāhnavīyāḥ.»

Iti. yat punar abhidhīyate, «virodhinām āgamānāṃ katham eka|kartṛkatvam» iti, tatr' âpy uktam eva:

Thus, first, there is no more fault in the instructions of other sacred texts than in Vedic injunctions, even if they are mutually contradictory. Or, rather:

With regard to the highest human goal, there is no contradiction among scriptures, since all teach the very same reward: deliverance. 4.110

Nevertheless, differing salvific paths are taught, according to the intellect of the beings to be favored.

This omniscient Lord taught various kinds of approaches when he saw that "these people can be helped to reach beatitude in the way they prefer on this path."

Just as people from a crowd that wants to enter a single fort or a big house also enter through different doors, liberation-seekers too enter the highest abode in the same way.

The following wise saying of Jayánta, the prodigy, who has mastered the essence of all sciences, who knows reality, and who has shaken off error, refers to the same thing:

"The many means taught by various scriptural approaches converge in the single *summum bonum*, as the currents of the Ganges meet in the ocean."* 4.115

As for the objection "How can contradictory scriptures have one and the same author," this has also been dealt with:

Vedānām Īśvar'|ôktatvāt prāmāṇyaṃ, na punaḥ svataḥ.
na c' ēśvara|bahutve 'pi yuktiḥ kā cana vidyate.

Kartṛ|bheda|vyapadeśaḥ punar anyathā|siddhaḥ.

Eko 'py asau sakala|sattva|hitāya kāyam
icchā|vinirmitam anekam upādadhānaḥ
nān"|āgamān upadiśan vividhā bibharti
tās tāḥ samasta|bhuvana|prathitāḥ samākhyāḥ.

4.120 Ekaḥ Śivaḥ Paśu|patiḥ Kapilo 'tha Viṣṇuḥ
Saṃkarṣaṇo Jina|muniḥ Su|gato Manur vā,
saṃjñāḥ paraṃ pṛthag imās tanavo 'pi kāmam,
avyākṛte tu Param'|ātmani n' âsti bhedaḥ.

Anyatve 'pi naro yaḥ
s'|âtiśayo bhavati ko 'pi, nūnam asau
tejo bibharti Bhagavata.
iti hi Dvaipāyanaḥ prāha:

«Yad yad vibhūtimat sattvaṃ śrīmad ūrjitam eva vā,
tat tad ev' âvagacches tvaṃ mama tejoṃśa|saṃbhavam.»
iti.

Yad vā Jina|prabhṛtayo bahavo bhavantu
bhinn'|āgama|praṇayana|pravaṇā mun'|îndrāḥ,
paśyantu te 'pi Bhagavat|praṇidhāna|labdha|
śuddh'|âvinaśvara|dṛśaḥ kuśal'|âbhyupāyān.

The Vedas are authoritative not by themselves, but because they were pronounced by God. And, on the other hand, there is no argument for the plurality of gods.

As for the reference to different authors, it is established in another way.

Though He is one, inasmuch as he assumes various bodies fashioned by His will and teaches all kinds of scriptures for the benefit of all beings, he bears all those diverse names which are celebrated in all the worlds.

Shiva, Pashu·pati, Kapila and Vishnu, the divine Sankárshana, the Sage Jina, the Buddha and Manu are one, only these designations differ, and maybe their bodies as well, but there is no plurality in the undifferentiated Supreme Self. 4.120

Even if he is different from God, an extraordinary, eminent man clearly bears the Lord's luster. For thus taught Krishna:

"Whenever a being is powerful, thriving or mighty, know that he has arisen from a particle of my luster."*

Or let there be many illustrious sages, like Jina, who are devoted to propagating different religions: they, too, will recognize the means leading to beatitude inasmuch as they have a pure, imperishable vision acquired through devoted meditation on the All-holy.*

Eṣa eva viśeṣo hi yogināṃ Param'|ēśvarāt:
tasya naisargikaṃ jñānaṃ, dhyāna|yogena yoginām.

4.125 Evaṃ tāvad Vedam āpta|praṇītaṃ
ye manvānās tat|pramāṇatvam āhuḥ.
sa pratyekaṃ Pañca|rātr'|ādi|śāstra|
prāmāṇye 'pi nyāya|mārgaḥ samānaḥ.

Ekas teṣām Īśvaro vā praṇetā,
bhinnā v" āptāḥ santu mārg'|ântara|jñāḥ,
na prāmāṇyāt sarvathā tat|praṇītā
granthā ete Vedavat pratyavetāḥ.

Yadi v" ânādayo Vedāḥ svata eva pramāṇatām
yāntu kāmaṃ, tath" âiv' âitāḥ Pañca|rātr'|ādi|codanāḥ.

Kartṛ|smaraṇam atr' âpi na spaṣṭam upalabhyate,
Saṃkarṣaṇ'|ādayas tv āsāṃ pravaktāraḥ Kaṭh'|ādivat.

«Nanu catvāra ev' âite Vedāḥ su|prathitā jane.
Itihāsa|Purāṇe 'pi tad|uktir upacārataḥ.

For only this much differentiates a yogin from the Supreme Lord: His knowledge is inherent, while the yogin's is acquired through the practice of meditation.

At all events, those who believe that the Veda was composed by a trustworthy person assert its authority in this way. The course of reasoning is the same with regard to the validity of every single scripture, such as the Pañcha·ratra. 4.125

Their author may either be one, namely the Lord, or various trustworthy persons who know different approaches. In either case, these texts composed by Him or them do not lose their validity, any more than the Veda does.*

Or let us suppose instead that the Vedas are beginningless and that they become authoritative by themselves alone: very well, these injunctions of the Pañcha·ratra and the like may become valid in the same way.

We have no clear memory of an author in this case either. As for the divine Sankárshana and others, they are the propagators of these propositions, just like Katha and others.*

"But surely," one might object, "people know well that these Vedas are only four. As for the Narratives of the Way Things Were and the Ancient Lore, in their case the name 'Veda' is used in a figurative sense.

4.130 ‹Vedo 'yaṃ brāhmaṇo 'yaṃ
salilam idam ayaṃ vahnir eṣā mah" îti›
spaṣṭe śabd'|ârtha|bodhe
praṇihita|matayo hanta vṛddhāḥ pramāṇam.
tat ko 'smin Pañca|rātre
śiśur api sahasā Veda|śabdaṃ prayuṅkte?
ke vā tac|chāsana|sthaṃ
muni|sadṛśam api brāhmaṇaṃ vyāharanti?»

Vayam api na vadāmaḥ pañca ṣaḍ v" âtra Vedān,
vidita|niyata|saṃkhyās te hi catvāra eva.
bhavati tu bahu|śākhā|vistaras tatra citras,
tad ayam api hi teṣām astu śākhā|viśeṣaḥ.

Āha:

«Nanu ca sakala|śākhā|pratyayaṃ kāryam ekam
abhidadhati vidhi|jñāḥ Soma|paśv|ādi|yāgam.
vadata yadi kadā cit Pañca|rātr'|ânuṣaktaṃ
kva cid api paridṛṣṭaṃ vaidikaṃ karma kiṃ cit?»

Ucyate:

4.135 Aneka|guṇa|yuktam ekam upadiśyate karma yair,
bahūny api vacāṃsi tāni dadhate samāveśitām.
tatasya kila karmaṇaḥ kim api coditaṃ śākhayā
kayā cid abhidhīyate, bhavatu s" âiva saṃsargitā.

'This is the Veda, this is a brahmin, this is water, this is fire, this is earth': in this clear understanding of a word's meaning, the elders, their minds well focussed, are the source of authoritative knowledge. So what child even would recklessly apply the word 'Veda' to this Pañcha·ratra? Or who would call the follower of that doctrine a brahmin, even if he resembled a sage?" 4.130

Nor do I say that there are five or six Vedas here, for their number is well known to be limited: they are only four. But they diversely branch into many recensions, so let this Pañcha·ratra be one of their particular recensions.

Someone may object:

"But surely those who know the Vedic ordinances speak about a single duty that is learned from all recensions, namely sacrifice, such as the Soma-offering or the immolation of animals. Tell me, have you ever seen anywhere any Vedic ritual that was connected with the Pañcha·ratra?"

We reply:

Those sentences which teach a single ritual action furnished with several components, though many, have a common applicability. Certain rules of this extended ritual action are, as we learn, prescribed in certain recensions: let precisely this be their connected nature. 4.135

Niyata|viṣayaṃ śāstraṃ śāstr'|ântareṇa na pṛcchyate.
visadṛśa|vidhau Vede 'py eṣā sthitir na na dṛśyate.
iha hi niyatā Sautrāmaṇyāṃ surā|graha|codanā
kratubhir itaraiḥ saṃsargaṃ sā na hi pratipadyate.

Śruti|Smṛty|uditā dharmāḥ pṛthag|āśrama|gocarāḥ
anye 'pi pratipadyante kiṃ paraspara|saṃkaram?

Sādhāraṇaṃ punar ahiṃsana|satyavāda|
santoṣa|śauca|dama|dāna|day"|ādi|dharmam
tīrtheṣu nityam akhileṣv api varṇayanti.
s" êyam Śruti|Smṛti|samanvayat" âpi teṣām.

Yas tu Veda iti ca vyapadeśaḥ
Pañca|rātra|vacaneṣu janānām,
so 'nya|gocaratayā. na ca śakyaṃ
vastu loka|vacanena niyantum.

4.140 Kiṃ vā sat" âsatā v" âpi vyapadeśena? nanv asau
Āyur|veda|Dhanur|veda|prabhṛtiṣv api dṛśyate?

Tac|chāsana|sthe Bhagavat|pradhāna|
karm'|ântar'|âvāpta|viśeṣa|saṃjñe
sāmānyato brāhmaṇa|śabda|mātraṃ
brūte parivrājakavac ca lokaḥ.

A doctrinal work with a determined object cannot be interrogated by another doctrinal work.* This state of affairs obtains within the Veda, too, with its diverging ordinances. For here the prescription of using beer cups is specified to the *Sautrāmaṇī* sacrifice;* it is certainly not connected with other rites.

As for other pious acts taught in the Vedas and the Smritis which pertain to separate life-periods: do they confound one another?

At the same time, people have always praised piety common to all sacred traditions, which consists of nonviolence, sincerity, contentment, purity, self-control, munificence, compassion and the like. This is also the point where these traditions are concordant with the Vedas and the Smritis.

As for the designation "Veda" that people apply to the texts of the Pañcha·ratra, it refers to something else. And in any case the matter cannot be settled on the basis of common usage.

Or, rather, why bother whether the designation is 4.140
true or false? Do we not find it in such names as Ayur·veda or Dhanur·veda, too?

People refer to the follower of this teaching* in general terms as a brahmin, even though he has a more specific designation* derived from a different* ritual devoted to Bhágavat, the Blessed Lord Vishnu, just as people refer to wandering mendicants in general terms as brahmins.

Na ca jagati na prasiddhā
brāhmaṇa|śabd'|âbhidheyatā teṣām.
vyavaharati janaḥ kāmaṃ
sāmānya|viśeṣa|saṃjñābhiḥ.

Brāhmaṇatv'|ādi|jātau ca vivadante vipaścitaḥ
vadantaḥ śabda|mātreṇa cāturvarṇya|vyavasthitim.

«Gotv'|ādi|jāti|vad iyaṃ prakaṭ" ânyathā vā
vipr'|ādi|jātir?» iti tattva|vicāraṇ" âiṣā
aprastutā. kim anay" âkhila|śāstra|loka|
siddhā sthitis tu na kathaṃ cana tarkaṇīyā.

4.145 Tad āstām iyaṃ jāti|sad|asad|bhāva|cintā. prakṛtam anusarāmaḥ.

Ten' ânādaya eva Vedavad ime
sarve bhavantv āgamāḥ,
kāryā eva hi vā, na teṣu kaluṣaṃ
vācyaṃ vaco dhārmikaiḥ.
yac c' âiṣām apabhāṣaṇaṃ kṛśam api
syād, Veda|nind"|âiva sā.
prāyaścittina eva te hata|dhiyo
ye teṣv asūyā|parāḥ.

Atha vā Pañca|rātr'|ādi|vākyānāṃ Veda|mūlatā
prāmāṇya|hetur Manv|ādi|vacasām iva varṇyatām.

Everyone knows that they are designated by the word "brahmin." People use general and specific names as they please.

The learned disagree about such caste universals as "brahminness." Some say that the system of the four estates is arranged on the basis of mere words.

"Are such caste universals as 'brahminhood' perceptible in the same way as the genus universal 'cowness,' or differently?": such deliberation about the true state of affairs is beside the point, it makes no difference. The status quo, established in all doctrines and for everyone, should not be speculated about in any way.

So let us not worry about the existence or nonexistence of castes. I shall continue with the present subject. 4.145

Thus, whether all these sacred scriptures are beginningless, like the Veda, or are after all just products, the pious should not bad-mouth them. If they were reviled, however slightly, it would be the same as abusing the Veda. Those fools who are given to finding fault with them are guilty of a sin.

Or, rather, one should say that the sentences of such sacred texts as the Pañcha·ratra are valid because they are based on the Veda just like the words of Manu and other Smritis.*

Kāryeṇa pratiniyataḥ sva|siddhi|hetur
dhūmena jvalana iva prakalpanīyaḥ,
na hy artha|grahaṇam idaṃ vinā smṛtīnām
utpādaḥ kva cid avalokitaḥ śruto vā.

Na lobha|mohau, na jana|pratāraṇā,
na bīja|śūnyā nṛ|vacaḥ|paramparā
abādhite vastuni yāti mūlatām.
na c' êha bādhā, kṛtibhiḥ parigrahāt.

4.150 Anādi|Veda|vādibhir na yogi|bodha|mūlatā
viṣahyate sma. tad|girām ath' âvaśiṣyate Śrutiḥ.

«Nanv atra kartṛ|sāmānyaṃ na kiṃ cid upalabhyate,
na ca tena vinā yuktam anumānam iha Śruteḥ.»

Ucyate:

Pravibhakta|kartṛkatayā
kāmaṃ tulya|prayogatā mā bhūt,
kāryaṃ tv anuguṇa|kāraṇa|
kalpana|yogyaṃ bhavaty eva.

Āha:

4.155 «Traivarṇikānām upapadyamāno
Ved'|ânvayaḥ kalpayituṃ hi śakyaḥ.
kāryaṃ punaḥ kāraṇa|mātra|mūlaṃ,
taj jāyatām atra yataḥ kutaś cit.»

An effect determines in each case the cause of its accomplishment, as smoke determines fire: one has to postulate this cause, for without the perception of an object no memory* could ever be seen or heard of about anything.

Neither greed nor delusion, nor deceiving people, nor a series of human utterances lacking any substance become the basis of an incontrovertible fact. And in this case there is no controverting factor, since competent people accept it.*

Those who profess that the Veda has no beginning cannot accept that the validity of scripture is based on yogic perception. In which case the Veda is left as the basis for the Pañcha·ratra's words. 4.150

"But surely," one might object, "we do not perceive here any identity among the performers,* and without that the inference of a Vedic text* is in this case not correct."

We reply:

Fine, their practice* may not be similar, inasmuch as they* have different performers, but an effect is undoubtedly fit for assuming an adequate cause.

One could object:

"Association* with the Veda can be assumed inasmuch as it is theoretically possible for the members of the first three social estates. On the other hand, the source of an effect is only its cause, and 4.155

Ucyate:

Dharme pramāṇam Śrutir eva n' ânyad
ity evam atra Śruti|mūlat" ôktā,
na kartṛ|sāmānya|balena, yogi|
pratyakṣa|vādo 'py ata eva neṣṭaḥ.

Tad idaṃ kartṛ|sāmānyam astu mā v" âtra, sarvathā
kārye 'sti dharma|rūpe 'smiñ Chruter eva hi mūlatā.

Ih' âiṣāṃ sarveṣāṃ Jina|Kapila|Buddh'|ādi|vacasāṃ
na yogi|pratyakṣam Śrutir api na mūlaṃ yadi bhavet,
kathaṃ syād vyāmohād anavadhir anek'|ārya|viditaḥ
praroho? nanv eṣāṃ kva cid api ca saṃvāda|bahulaḥ.

4.160 Vyāmohāc ca hi vartante kāmaṃ katipayair dinaiḥ,
so 'yaṃ yuga|pada|sthāyī vyāmoha iti vismayaḥ.

«Pur" âpi Saugatā āsann iti ken' âvagamyate?»
pur" âpi śrotriyā āsann iti ken' âvagamyate?

Lobh'|ādi dṛśyamānaṃ vā yadi mūlam ih' ôcyate,
Vedo 'pi jīvik"|ôpāya iti jalpanti nāstikāḥ.

in this case* it could have arisen for any reason whatsoever."*

To which we would reply:

With respect to piety, the Veda alone is the means of valid knowledge, nothing else: that's why it has been said that the Veda is the source in this case, not on the strength of the identity of the performers. Nor is the theory of yogic perception needed, for the same reason.

So the performers may or may not be identical in this case. At any rate, it is the Veda alone that is the source of this duty, namely, piety.

Here,* if neither yogic perception nor even the Veda were the basis of all these teachings, such as that of the Jina, Kápila or the Buddha, how could delusion be the cause of their unlimited reproduction, acknowledged by many Aryas? What's more, at some places it even meets their full accord.

For delusion might make them last for a few days, 4.160
but it would be fantastic to say that such delusion persists for aeons.

You might ask: "Who knows if there were Buddhists in former times, too?" Who knows if there were brahmins learned in the Veda in former times, too?

Or, if you say that greed and the like are the visible source in this case, the heterodox will retort that the Veda is also a means of livelihood.

Mahā|jana|parigrahād yadi punaḥ śrutau vāryate
Bṛhas|pati|mat'|āśrita|pralapito 'pavāda|kramaḥ,
sa vārayitum āgam'|ântara|vacaḥsu śakyas tathā.
kṛtaḥ kila parigrahaḥ kuśala|dhībhir eṣām api.

Yāvāñ ca kaś cana nyāyo Veda|prāmāṇya|siddhaye
bhavadbhir varṇyate, so 'yaṃ tulyas tīrth'|ântareṣv api.

4.165 Na kadā cid anīdṛśaṃ jagat
kathitaṃ tatra|bhavadbhir eva yad,
itarair api tat tath" ôcyate.
satataṃ te 'pi babhūvuḥ āgamāḥ.

Kṛtam ativācālatayā.
dveṣyā bahu|bhāṣiṇo bhavanti janāḥ.
tad idam upasaṃharāmo
rasanāyāś cāpalaṃ vipulam.

Satyaṃ|vad'|āpta|puruṣ'|ôktatayā pramāṇaṃ
tīrthāni, Vedavad anāditayā svato vā,
āmnāya|saṃmitatayā Manu|vākyavad vā.
sarvaṃ pramāṇam iti nīti|vido vadanti.

On the other hand, if the series of abuses jabbered by a follower of the teaching of Brihas·pati* is averted in the case of the Veda because it is accepted by exemplary persons, it can be beaten off with regard to the teachings of other scriptures in the same way: we are told that these, too, are accepted by intelligent people.*

However many arguments of whatever kind you put forth in order to establish the authority of the Veda, they are equal in value with respect to other religious doctrines as well.

Your contention, namely, that the world has always been as it is now, is also said by others in the same way. Those religions, too, have always existed. 4.165

But let's cut the discussion short. People who talk too much incur odium, so now I curb the excessive jabbering of my tongue.

Religious scriptures are authoritative because they have been enunciated by a truthful, trustworthy person, or by themselves, like the Veda, inasmuch as they have no beginning, or because they are in harmony with Vedic tradition, like Manu's teachings. All scriptures are authoritative: thus say the political scientists.

Āha:

«Nanu c' âivam atiprasaṅga|doṣād
ati|mātraṃ bhuvi viplaveta dharmaḥ.
kva nu nāma na śakyam etad itthaṃ
gadituṃ yādṛśa|tādṛśe 'pi vākye?»

4.170 Uktam atra,

Avicchinnā yeṣāṃ
vahati saraṇiḥ sarva|viditā,
na yatr' āryo lokaḥ
paricaya|kath"|ālāpa|vimukhaḥ,
yad|iṣṭ'|ânuṣṭhānaṃ
na khalu jana|bāhyaṃ na sabhayaṃ,
na rūpaṃ yeṣāṃ ca
sphurati navam abhyutthitam iva,
Pramatta|gītatvam alaukikatvam
ābhāti lobhādi na yatra mūlam,
tathā|vidhānām ayam āgamānāṃ
prāmāṇya|mārgo, na tu yatra tatra.

Āpt'|ôktatvam anāditvam athav" āmnāya|mūlatām
tatr' âiva śaknumo vaktuṃ, na punar yatra kutra cit.

Ādiśyate kim api kutsitam eva kāryaṃ
yeṣu tv agamya|gaman'|âśuci|bhakṣaṇ'|ādi,
prāmāṇya|varṇanam idaṃ tu tathā|vidhānām
ete tu vādi|vṛṣabhā na sahanta eva.

You may object:

> "But surely in this way, because of the logical fault of unwarrantable extension* socio-religious order on earth would be utterly ruined. Tell me a case when one could not say this about any proposition in the same manner, however worthless it may be."

This objection is answered as follows: 4.170

> Provided it has a widely acknowledged, unbroken tradition, provided the Aryas are not repulsed by associating with it or discussing it, provided its accepted practice is neither antisocial nor dangerous, provided it has not just recently sprung into being, provided it is not based on the ramblings of a madman, nor on something outlandish, nor simply on something like greed: for such scriptures this method of validation is applicable, but it cannot be used for just any text.*
>
> We can say about such scriptures alone, and not in any instance whatsoever, that they have been enunciated by trustworthy persons, or that they have no beginning, or that they are based on Vedic tradition.
>
> But these masters among disputants will definitely not allow this claim of validity for any scripture in which any contemptible duty is taught, such as making love to women one must not have sex with, or eating impure things.

(ity uktvā kṣaṇaṃ ca tūṣṇīṃ sthitvā SAṄKARṢAṆAṂ *prati)*

4.175 Ārya, yathā|pratibhānam etāvad abhihitam asmābhiḥ. tad idānīṃ yathā|sannihitaṃ pṛcchyantām atra|bhavanto vādinaḥ, api hṛtaṃ hṛdayam eṣām asmad|vacasā na v" êti.

SAṄKA°: *(saharṣam)* Ārya Dhairya|rāśe, vayaṃ tāvad ucchvāsitā iva śālitā iva pavitrī|kṛtā iv' āpyāyitā iva jīva|loka|phalam anubhāvitā iva bhavat|prabhavay" âbhinavayā sarasvatyā. aho āścaryam!

Sūkṣmā dṛṣṭir aho! aho gatir iyaṃ
vācām! aho kauśalam
śāstreṣv etad! aho manaḥ parihṛtaṃ
doṣair asūy"|ādibhiḥ!
ko 'sau v" âsti guṇo na yo 'tra paramāṃ
kāṣṭhāṃ gato vartate?
loko 'nāratam āha: Sāhaṭa|samaḥ
satyaṃ na jāto naraḥ.

Ete 'pi mahā|vidvāṃsaḥ sahṛdayā eva, kathaṃ n' āvarjitā āryeṇa? apy enān pṛcchāmi? *(vādy|abhimukhaṃ sthitvā)* bho bhavanto mahā|vidvāṃsaḥ, api bhavatām āvarjitaṃ Dhairya|rāśi|vacasā hṛdayam?

VĀDINAḤ: Ārya, iyaṃ tāvad amānuṣī.

4.180 <SAṄKA°: > Ābhiḥ punar aparimita|nīti|dhārā|varṣiṇībhir asadṛśa|gatibhir apagata|mātsaryābhir ārya|Dhairya|rāśi|vāgbhir brahma|ṛṣi|kalpa|nirmala|manasaḥ sarvatra bhavanto vartante. tath" âpi punaḥ punar idam avabodhyante bhavantaḥ: dvayam idam avaśya|rakṣaṇīyam āryaiḥ.

(At the end of his speech DHAIRYARASHI *remains silent for a second, and then turns to* SANKÁRSHANA:*)*

Sir, I have spoken to the best of my intellectual capabilities. Let us now ask these estimable disputants according to seating if our speech captured their heart or not. 4.175

SANKARSHANA: *(delighted)* Honorable Dhairya·rashi, be sure that, in a manner of speaking, we have been revived, beatified, purified, nourished, made to experience the goal of this worldly existence by this novel river of erudition that Your Honor has generated. How wonderful!

> What a subtle intellect! What a fluent speech! What a skill in the doctrinal and scientific works! What a mind, exempt from such faults as envy! Or is there any virtue that has not reached its highest limit in this person? People have always said that truly no match for Sáhata has been born.

These professors are also very much capable of appreciation, so how could Your Honor not win them over? Shall I ask them? *(He turns toward the* DISPUTANTS.*)* Respected Professors, has your heart been won over by Dhairya·rashi's speech?

DISPUTANTS: Sir, his erudition is superhuman at the very least.

<SANKÁRSHANA: > Besides, your intellect will always be pure, like that of brahmin sages, thanks to these words of the honorable Dhairya·rashi, which shower inexhaustible streams of political wisdom and are uniquely fluent and immune from malice. Nevertheless you are reminded 4.180

VĀDĪ°: Kim iva?

SAṄKA°: Etāni kila parasparam asaṃkīrṇāni pṛthak|prasthānāni yath"|âvasthāni tīrthāni. tad eṣām itar'|êtara|saṃkara|parihāre satatam avahitair bhavitavyam āryaiḥ.

VĀDĪ°: Ārya, yāvān iha sve sve śāsane samāmnātaḥ kaś cid ahiṃs"|ādiḥ sādhāraṇo mānavo dharmas, tatra kim ucyate? tad|atiriktaṃ tu niyat'|ôpadiṣṭa|viśiṣṭa|kriyā|kāṇḍa|saṃkaraṃ sva|śāstra|kathita|pratyavāya|bhayāt pariharāma ity ekaṃ tāvat sthitam. atha dvitīyaṃ kim?

SAṄKA°: Bhavadīyaṃ nāma mukhe dattvā durācāratayā ye viplāvayanti śāstraṃ Dharmaṃ ca, teṣāṃ sv'|āśrameṣv avakāśo na deyaḥ.

4.185 VĀDĪ°: Etad api satyam anuṣṭhīyate. kiṃ tv ayam artho n' âsmad|adhīnaḥ. āryeṇa rāja|niyuktaiś ca nirvāhyo 'yam.

SAṄKA°: Evam etat. gṛhīta|kṣaṇa ev' âtra devo varṇ'|āśrama|maryād"|ācāryaḥ. bhavadbhir api tathā|vidheṣ' ûdāsitavyam. na teṣāṃ dayitavyam.

again and again of the following: there are two things that you, gentlemen, must by all means observe.

DISPUTANTS: What are they?

SANKÁRSHANA: These religious traditions, as we have been told, are not intermixed, inasmuch as each of them has its respective scope, existing in the way they have been set up. So you, gentlemen, must always pay attention to prevent their confusion.

DISPUTANTS: Sir, what can we say concerning all the universal piety taught by Manu, such as nonviolence, which is handed down here in everyone's own doctrine? Apart from that, however, we avoid the mixing of the specifically taught, particular ritual sections, since we are afraid of acting against what is said in our own scriptures. Thus the first point has been settled. But what is the second one?

SANKÁRSHANA: You must not admit into your religions those who take your name in their mouth and then overthrow both scripture and Dharma with their wicked behavior.

DISPUTANTS: This too will be done, absolutely. But it does 4.185
not depend on us. You, sir, and the officers of the king can see it is accomplished.

SANKÁRSHANA: You are right. Assuredly His Majesty, the instructor in the established rules of social estates and life-periods, grasps the opportunity to do so. As for you, you must keep yourselves apart from such people. Don't sympathize with them.

VĀDI°: Yath" ārya āha.

SAṄKA°: Tad idānīm utthāya yathā|yathaṃ gamyatām. āśrameṣu ca sveṣu sveṣu yathā|vyavastham āsyatām. ārya Dhairya|rāśe, tad ehi vayam ap' îdānīṃ yathā|vṛttaṃ svāmine nivedayāmaḥ.

Iti niṣkrāntāḥ sarve.

4.190 *Caturtho 'ṅkaḥ.*

DISPUTANTS: As you say, sir.

SANKÁRSHANA: So now let us get up and go about our business. Each should adhere to his own religion according to the established customs. Honorable Dhairya·rashi, come now, we shall report to our master the events as they have happened.

Exeunt omnes.

End of Act Four. 4.190

CHĀYĀ

The following is a Sanskrit paraphrase (chāyā) of the Prakrit passages (marked with ⌜corner brackets⌟*) in the play. References are to chapter and paragraph.*

1.29 Bho bhadanta, kiṃ khalv etaj janana|maraṇa|vyavahāra|bāhyaṃ sthānaṃ? kena v" ôpāyen' âitat prāpyate?

1.31 Bho bhadanta, kāni punas tāni catvāri ārya|satyāni?

1.33 Bho bhadanta, iyan|mātreṇa na me prabodha utpannaḥ. savistareṇ' ôpadiśatu bhavān.

1.36 Bho bhadanta, ken' êdānīm upāyena ātm" âitad dīrgha|prabandha|pravṛttaṃ muktvā dustaraṃ duḥkha|gahanaṃ nirvāṇe nivasati?

1.42 Bho bhadanta, yadā tāvan nāsty eva ko 'py ātmā, ka idānīṃ saṃsāra|duḥkham anubhavati? ko vā etad uttīrya nirvāṇ'|âgārakaṃ pratipadyate?

1.44 Bho bhadanta, yadi n' âsti sthira ātmā, paraloke kasya karmabhogaḥ? idānīm api kasya smaraṇa|nibandhanā bhavanti vyavahārāḥ?

1.50 Yadi sakalaḥ kṣaṇa|bhaṅguro bhāva|sārthaḥ, n' âsty ev' âitasya dvitīye kṣaṇe 'vasthitiḥ, tat katham eṣa vijñānena viṣayī|kartuṃ pāryate? arthaḥ khalu vijñānena sah' ânu vā tena prakāśyate, vijñānaṃ vā janayann api no niyantraṇam ākāraṃ vā aprāptena tena viṣayī|kriyate. anyath" êdaṃ pratyakṣaṃ kṣaṇa|bhāvino durlabham.

1.55 Bho bhadanta, eṣa khalu sakala|bhikṣu|saṅgha|saṅghaṭana|velā|piśuno gaṇḍi|śabdaḥ samucchalitaḥ. tad atra bhavān pramāṇam!

1.57 Bho bhadanta, ko 'pi ca kāla etasya brāhmaṇa|yūna iha sthitasya vartate. yasminn eva kṣaṇe 'smin vṛkṣa|mūle bhadanta upaviṣṭas tasminn eva kṣaṇa iha praviṣṭo bhadantena na lakṣitaḥ.

latā|jāl'|ântariten' âitena sakala ev' ākarṇito bhadanta|varṇita upadeśaḥ.

1.64 Ārya, upanītaṃ may" âitat snān'|ôpakaraṇam. snātuṃ prasthita āryaḥ.

1.66 Na khalv anukūlam upatiṣṭhate. vihāra|gāmī khalv eṣo mārga| janaḥ sakalaḥ sañcarati.

1.68 Yad ārya ājñāpayati.

1.74 Ārya, paśy' âitāsāṃ mṛduka|pavan'|āndolita|vicitra|dhvaja|paṭa|maṇḍita|meru|gaṇḍikā|nirviśeṣa|prāsād'|âbhyantara|viniveśitānāṃ kanaka|mayīnāṃ prakṣaran|nirantara|prabhā|vistāraka|sundara|varṇ'|ābharaṇa|bhūṣitānāṃ Buddha|pratimānāṃ candana|ghanasāra|ghusṛṇa|mṛganābhi|vilepana|kusuma|dhūp'|ôpahāra|samṛddhīḥ. aho āścaryam!

1.78 Ārya, paśya paśya, etasmin dhavala|gṛha|śikhare surabhi|kusuma|dhūpa|gandha|prāgbhāra|nirbhara|bharita|daśa|diśā|mukha ete vandakā bhojan'|ônmukhā iva dṛśyante.

1.82 Tiṣṭhatu snānam, ambara|parivartana|mātram api na kṛtam!

1.84 Ārya, n' êyad ev' âitat. paśya, etāsāṃ pariveṣayantīnāṃ bhakṣya|dān'|ônmukhīnāṃ sthūla|stana|maṇḍalāṇāṃ dāsīnām vividha|vibhramāḥ kaṭākṣā bhikṣu|vadaneṣu nipatanti. etac ca kim api nirmala|kalaśa|nikṣiptaṃ pānakam upanītam.

1.87 Ārya, paśya paśya, eṣa bhikṣuḥ

1.88 Tṛṣito 'pi pibati na tathā jihvayā bhramat|kuvalayaṃ pānam,
dṛṣṭibhir yathā dāsīnāṃ vikāsita|locanaṃ vadanam.

1.91 Udyāneṣu nivāsaḥ, sulabhaṃ pānaṃ ca, sulabham annam api,
na ca kim api niyama|duḥkhaṃ: dhanyo vandatvaṃ labhate.

1.95 Punar api bhadanto 'nugrahaṃ kariṣyati.

1.106 Nanu catvāri me ārya|satyāni guruṇ" ôpadiṣṭāni, duḥkhaṃ samudayo nirodho mārga iti.

1.168 Are re duṣṭa|brāhmaṇa, kathaṃ bhadantam adhikṣipasi?

1.169 Are re varṇa|saṅkara, upādhyāyasy' âivaṃ vyāharasi?

1.170 Kasy' âiṣa upādhyāyaḥ? kevalam asy' ôṣṭra|mukhasya.

2.3 Na pīyate śītalā surā, na ca dāsyā samaṃ ramyate, sulabhaṃ ca na māṃsa|bhojanaṃ viṣame brāhmaṇa|vāsaka itaḥ.

2.4 Tat kiṃ kriyate? n' âsty eva nija|bhaṭṭakān parihṛtya ātmano garbha|dāsānāṃ gatiḥ. ājñām api tādṛśīṃ bhaṭṭako 'pekṣate ('vekṣate?) yatra na khādyate na pīyate. yato 'dya ājñapto bhaṭṭaken' âham: «are kajjalaka, gaccha paśya kṣapaṇaka|vasatau kiṃ Jinarakṣita|bhikṣur asti na v" êti». na ca jānāmi kutra sā kṣapaṇaka|vasatiḥ. atra vistīrṇa|luñcita|loma|kiṃśāru|visara|śabalitā ete pāṃśu|kaṇā lakṣyante. tad atr' âiva vṛkṣa|gahane kṣapaṇaka|vasatyā bhavitavyam. iyam eva sā kṣapaṇaka|vasatir, yato 'tra nirantara|latā|pañjar'|ândhakāre vṛkṣa|mūle kupitāṃ kṣapaṇikāṃ prasādayan eṣa kṣapaṇako dṛśyate. atikopanā khalv eṣā duṣṭā kṣapaṇikā yā caraṇa|patitam apy etaṃ kṣapaṇaka|yuvānaṃ parihṛtya dūraṃ gatā. eṣo 'pi tapasvī paruṣa|vadanaḥ kṣapaṇako dṛśyate.

2.6 Hā dhik, para|loke durāśayā prathamaṃ kṣapaṇatvaṃ mayā gṛhītam. skhalitasya tatr' êdānīṃ dṛṣṭ'|âdṛṣṭāḥ khalu me naṣṭāḥ, yata eṣ" âpi duṣṭā tāpasī caraṇa|patitasy' âpi me na prasīdati. ayi duṣṭe bandhaki, gaccha tvam! kiṃ tvayā visadṛśīṃ kām api kṣapaṇikāṃ na prāpsyāmi?

2.7 Yāvad eṣa kṣapaṇako māṃ na prekṣate, tāvad ahaṃ kṣapaṇikā|veṣaṃ kṛtv" âitaṃ kṣapaṇakam upahasiṣyāmi. lamba|karṇaḥ khalv aham. n' ānane śmaśru|lomāni ma udbhinnāni. na ca kṣapaṇikāṇāṃ veṇī|bandhaḥ śīrṣe sambhāvyate. tat sukaro me kṣapaṇikā|veṣaḥ. picchikā|mātra|śūnyaṃ sāmprataṃ me kṣapaṇikā|rūpaṃ vartate. sādhu, kṣapaṇikāyāḥ sandhārita|parityaktāṃ (?) picchikāṃ gṛhītv" ôpasarpiṣyāmi. ārya, praṇamāmi.

pariśrānt" âsmi sāmpratam. tad ācakṣva mām adya kutra bhaṭṭako Jiṇa|rakṣita|bhikṣur vartate.

2.8 N' âitad ātma|parāṅ|mukham iva me daivaṃ lakṣyate. anyā khalv eṣā taruṇa|kṣapaṇik" ôpanatā. ayi bāla|tapasvini, kiṃ tava Jinarakṣita|bhikṣuṇā? pariśrāntā khalu dṛśyase. tad ih' âiva nirjane śiśira|latā|gahana upaviśya viśrāmya muhurtakam.

2.9 Kuto me nitya|duḥkhitāyā manda|bhāgyāyā viśrāmaḥ?

2.10 Kim asmin bāla|bhāve 'pi te duḥkha|kāraṇam?

2.11 Ārya, tiṣṭhatv eṣa mama dagdha|vṛttāntaḥ. Jinarakṣita|bhikṣu|pravṛttiṃ me ācaṣṭāṃ bhavān.

2.12 Bālike, eṣa khalu Jinarakṣita|bhikṣur abhyantara ātma|śiṣyāṇāṃ madhye vyākhyānakaṃ kurvan nyagrodha|vṛkṣa|mūle tiṣṭhati. tvaṃ punaḥ kṣaṇam upaviśya varṇaya tāvad ātmano nirveda|kāraṇam.

2.13 Ārya, kim atra saṃsāra|hatāyā lajjā|nidhānaṃ varṇyate?

2.14 Bālike, varṇaya. hṛdaya|nirviśeṣaḥ khalv eṣo jano bālikāyāḥ.

2.15 Bāla|kumārik" âiva pravrajit" âsmi manda|bhāginī.

2.16 Tataḥ punaḥ?

2.17 Tata īṣad|īṣad|udbhidyamāna|virala|yauvana|lakṣaṇāyā anicchantyā eva me 'śikṣita|madana|rasāyāḥ ken' âpi taruṇa|kṣapaṇakena śīla|khaṇḍanā kṛtā.

2.18 Amṛta|nady eva me upanatā. bālike, īdṛśy eva saṃsāra|sthitiḥ. tataḥ punaḥ?

2.19 Ārya, tataḥ kāl'|ântare śanaiḥ śanair jñāta|madana|rasāṃ māṃ parihṛtya sa kṣapaṇako 'nyasyāṃ drdha|muṣṭyāṃ vṛddha|kṣapaṇikāyāṃ prasaktaḥ.

2.20 Tena hi sammukhataḥ (?) †. . . †. paṅgul'|ândha|nyāyaṃ karavāva.

2.22 Bālike, kiṃ māṃ na prekṣase?

2.23 Kathaṃ nu prekṣiṣye? tvay" âpi māṃ parihṛtya anyato gantavyam.

2.24 Bālike, m" âivaṃ bhaṇa. dāsa|vartanikaṃ te kariṣyāmi. kim ady' âpi te stanakau n' ôdbhinnau?

2.25 Kiṃ hat'|āśā kariṣyāmi?

2.26 Hā dhik, hat'|āśa, dṛḍhaṃ tvayā khalī|kṛto 'smi.

2.27 Are re tāpasa|kāmuka, yadi kim api ācakṣe tadā Jinarakṣita|bhikṣoḥ phut|kariṣyāmi.

2.28 Na tvay" âiṣaḥ parihāsaḥ kasy' âpi prakāśitavyaḥ.

2.29 Ko ma utkocakaḥ?

2.31 Kṛtaḥ parihāsaḥ. prāptaḥ kārṣāpaṇakaḥ. adhigatā bhikṣoḥ pravṛttiḥ. tat sāmpratam gatvā bhaṭṭakaṃ vijñāpayāmi. adya diṣṭyā vardhase! āgatā te hṛdaya|vallabhā.

2.33 Ayi duṣṭa|tāpasi, etāṃ pārakyāṃ picchikāṃ gṛhītvā kutra gamyate?

2.34 Ārye, gṛhāṇ' âitāṃ picchikām. ahaṃ punar anicchanty ev' âitasmin latā|gahana etena kṣapaṇakena khalī|kṛtā. na me doṣaḥ.

2.35 Are re duṣṭa|kāmuka tāpasī|lampaṭa! picchikā me vismṛt" êti yāvat pratinivṛty' āgat" âsmi, tāvad etasminn antare kṣaṇa|mātrakeṇ' âiv' âitasmin latā|gahane 'nyā kṣapaṇik" āliṅgitā. tat sāmpratam anubhav' ātmano vinayasya phalam.

2.36 M" âivaṃ sambhāvayatu bhavatī. ceṭakaḥ khalv eṣa strī|veṣaṃ kṛtvā mām upahasitum āgataḥ. tena hat'|āśena kopitā bhavatī. yat satyam, kośaṃ te pibāmi.

2.37 Kutas te mukhe satyaṃ yasy' âiṣa upaśamaḥ?

2.38 Anyām api krīḍāṃ duṣṭa|ceṭaka eṣa karoti. tad etu bhavatī, anyato gacchāva. eṣa khalu brāhmaṇaḥ ko 'p' îta āgacchan dṛśyate. tat tvaratāṃ bhavatī.

2.43 Āryasya sā krīḍā. teṣāṃ punas tapasvināṃ sarvasva|nāśaḥ.

2.45 Nanu bhaṇāmi. para|lokasya kṛte dāruṇaṃ duḥkha|prāgbhāraṃ te tapasvino 'nubhavanti. tad āryasya sarasvatī|pravāhe nipatanti. tad asminn āgama|vṛkṣake niṣphala ev' âiteṣāṃ sa prayāsaḥ.

2.53 Bho bhikṣavaḥ, praharati kṛtānta|vyādho, viṣamāḥ saṃsāra|vāgurā|pāśāḥ. kathaṃ taratu jīva|hariṇaḥ prajvalitaṃ duḥkh'|âraṇyam idam?

2.55 Athavā, Jina|caraṇa|smaraṇ'|ôdgata|nisarga|śuci|puṇya|pudgala|balānāṃ kupito 'pi kiṃ kariṣyaty aśaraṇa|śūro hata|kṛtāntaḥ?

2.57 Tat sāmpratam, dhyāyate Jina|vacanaṃ, tapo|niyamaiḥ kṣapyate śarīram: etāvan|mātraṃ gṛhṇīt' ôpadeśa|rahasya|sarvasvam.

2.58 Yad bhaṭṭaka ājñāpayati.

2.75 Bhaṭṭaka, bhikṣavo vijñāpayanti, cirāyate bhaṭṭakaḥ. tat sāmpratam asmākaṃ prastuta|kārya|vel" âtikrāmat' îti.

2.78 Are re tvarita|tvaritaṃ gatvā bhikṣūṇāṃ bhaṇa yath" âpramattāḥ kṣaṇaṃ tatr' âiva vilambadhvam, eṣa āgato 'sm' îti!

2.81 Ārya, kas tava vāda|samare sammukhaḥ sthātuṃ śaknoti? tad anena vyapadeśa|palāyanena rakṣito 'nen' ātmā.

2.84 Mṛduko 'pi ghaṭṭate hṛdayaṃ vāda|niyuktānām(?) ārya|vyāhāraḥ. mīnānāṃ sthala|gatānāṃ †. . . †

2.86 Nanu snātuṃ kasmān na gamyate?

2.88 Evaṃ kriyatām.

2.95 Ved'|ântā dustar'|ântāḥ, trayī|kathita|kathā|vistarāḥ saṃkul'|ârthāḥ. āryais tatra cintyate gahana|gatir asti n' âst' îty ātmā; dūre tiṣṭhantu te me. parihartum idaṃ ghora|saṃsāra|duḥkhaṃ saṃkṣiptaṃ nirmal'|ârthaṃ Jina|muni|bhaṇitam āgamam ādharāma.

2.96 Ārya, eṣa khalu kāṣāya|vasanas tāpasa īdṛk kim api mantrayan tvarita|tvaritaṃ parikrāmati...

2.98 Ady' âpi Jina|śāsana ev' âiteṣām abhiniveṣaḥ?

2.100 Brāhmaṇaḥ khalu tvam. tat kim ātmano bubhukṣā|vedanaṃ na jānāsi?

2.102 Atha kim?

2.104 Nanv ih' âiva Jinarakṣita|bhikṣu|tapo|vane 'dya mahā|bhojanaṃ vartate.

2.106 Ken' âpi bhagavato Jina|guroḥ śāsana|gatena ṭhakkureṇ' âdya tatra mahā|bhojanam upapāditaṃ, yatra pravrajita|sahasrāṇi saṃghaṭitāni. teṣāṃ ca saktūnāṃ rāśayas, taila|ghaṭikāḥ, kāñjika|kumbhayo, guḍa|kūṭakās, taila|pakvānāṃ bhakṣyāṇāṃ parvatā upanītāḥ.

2.108 Ahaha, yuṣmākaṃ brāhmaṇānām ete samācārāḥ. vayaṃ punas tapo|dhanāḥ prāṇi|sambhavaṃ kim api n' âśane, na pāne, na vasane, na śayane, n' āsane, n' ânyatra kutr' âpi śarīr'|ôpakaraṇe viniveśayāmaḥ. nanu mam' âiv' êmau vṛkṣa|vidala|nirmitāv upānahikau kiṃ na prekṣase? tad bhavatv anena kathā|vistareṇa. bhojana|samayo me 'tikrāmati.

2.110 Evaṃ kriyatāṃ, evaṃ kriyatām. tad etu bhavān.

2.113 Asmākaṃ ca Sugato bhagavān Jina|guruḥ. kiṃ ca Jina|guruḥ Sugato bhavati. aho bhadrā vayam Ārhatāḥ, ke 'pi dig|ambarāḥ, ke 'pi vṛkṣa|vidala|mātra|vasanāḥ, ke 'pi rakta|vāsasaḥ, ke 'pi śveta|paṭāḥ. prekṣasva tāvat. ita ime nirdaya|luñcana|prasaṅga|lakṣyamāṇa|loma|mūla|vigalat|pravirala|tanuka|śoṇita|kaṇā dig|ambarāḥ. itaḥ khalv ime †. . . †carcyamāna|komala|valkal'|âñcalāś cīra|vasanāḥ. ita ime tat|kṣaṇa|pakva|kand'|ûddhṛta|śarāva|sadṛśa|varṇa|vasanāś ca brahma|cāriṇas tapodhanāḥ. ita ime haṃsa|pakṣa|pāṇḍura|pavana|lulita|paṭa|pallavāḥ śveta|paṭāḥ. tad aho puṇya|bhājanaṃ sa ṭhakkuro yasy' ême 'dy' ânugrahaṃ kariṣyanti!

2.118 Dṛṣṭā dig|ambarāś cīra|vasanāḥ kāṣāya|vāsasaḥ śveta|paṭāḥ. tat sāmpratam ita ime nīl'|âmbarā dṛśyantām.

2.120 Aham etan na jānāmi ka eṣa catura|niyama|mārgaḥ. etat khalu tarkayāmi, iha mahā|bhojana|kiṃvadantīṃ śrutvā bhojana|mātra|lālasāḥ ke 'py ete paribhramanti. tad bhavatv eteṣāṃ vṛtt'|ântena, samāna|caryāṇām eva madhyaṃ vrajāmi.

2.122 Jayati munir Nīl'|âmbara|nātho, yena śamito bhava|saṃvara|grāhaḥ.

2.123 Yasya bhagavan tava śāsanam apūrvaṃ, pīyate kim api rasāyana|saukhyam.

2.124 Bhave bhujyate strī|saukhyaṃ, paraloke prāpyate mokṣaḥ.

2.125 Tat sidhyati śarīraṃ, laṅghyate saṃsāraḥ.

2.126 Ato 'nye ye punar āśramāḥ, teṣāṃ nibandhat' āśāṃ mā: pariśoṣyate deho, mokṣe punaḥ sandehaḥ.

2.127 Śikṣā|yoge kiṃ vidhāpyate (= arjyate)? puruṣaḥ para|vaśaḥ parisamāpyate.

2.128 Guṇānāṃ paryarjito yadi visaraḥ, so 'pi ca puruṣāṇāṃ bhoga|haraḥ.

2.129 Pariveṣṭitaḥ saṃgamo yena hy eṣa, †. . . †.

2.130 Iti yadi yugaṃ yugaṃ vijānāti (?) . . . punar bhogam (?)

2.131 Śarīre kaṃ pradeśaṃ bhramantaḥ kim padam arjanty aniṣṭhita|janmānaḥ?(?)

2.132 Yadi param'|ātma|vivarta idam, yadi vā śabda|vivarta idam.

2.133 Tad" âpy avidyā|paśamena vinā katham idaṃ sakalaṃ . . . ?

2.134 †. . . † evaṃ ye 'nye 'pi āgamāḥ, viphalān sakalān jñātvā.

2.135 Atra paratr' âpi sukhaṃ labhadhvaṃ muni|Nīl'|âmbaraṃ lātvā . . .

2.142 Evaṃ nv etad yathā āryo mantrayate.

2.145 Āryasya kiṃ jātam? na khalv āryeṇ' âdy' âpi dāra|saṃgrahaḥ kṛtaḥ. asmākaṃ punar dūre tāvad eṣā kathā.

2.147 Sā khalu sāmpratam ato 'narthād uttīrṇā yā jīvan|mṛtikā vṛddhikā vartate.

2.149 Ārya, na me pratibhāti. tvam eva jānāsi. idāniṃ punaḥ pravardhamāna eṣa kali|yugaḥ. tat kuto 'tr' ēdṛśānām anarthānāṃ pratīkāraḥ?

2.151 Kaḥ punar eṣo bhaviṣyati?

2.153 Bhos tapasvino, nanv atra tapovane bhojana|kālo yuṣmākaṃ vartate. tat kasmād atikramyate?

3.2 Astaṃ|gataḥ khalv asmin samaye Mah"|ēśa|lāñchanaṃ nava|śaśāṅkaḥ. śūnyam andha|kāraṃ gaganaṃ hṛdayam iv' âsmākam. sāmprataṃ bhavaty eṣa palāyan'|âvasaraḥ. tat kutra me priya|vayasyaḥ Śmaśāna|bhūtir gato yena samaṃ palāyiṣye? eṣa Śmaśāna|bhūtir ita ev' āgacchan lakṣyate.

3.4 Eṣā sā vayasya|Kaṅkāla|ketor maṭhikā. mayā s" âitasminn andha|kāre 'p' īṣad|īṣad dṛśyate. tad utprekṣy' ôtprekṣya padāni gamiṣyāmi. pada|śabda iva. bhagavan, manye nagara|rakṣakā ito hiṇḍanti, ye samprāpya cauryam iti śaṅkayā bandhan'|āgāraṃ nayanti, śūle vā nikṣipanti, vṛkṣe vā pāśen' ôllambayanti.

bhavatu, bhagavān Bhairava|nāthaḥ śaraṇam. vayasya|Kaṅkāla|ketor iva vyāhāraḥ śrūyate. vayasya Kaṅkāla|keto, tav' âiva sakāśam upasamprāptaḥ. nagara|rakṣakāṇāṃ śaṅkito 'smi.

3.5 Are Śmaśāna|bhūtis tvam? śobhanaṃ tvayā kṛtaṃ yad atra tvam āgataḥ. tat tvaritaṃ hiṇḍāvaḥ. ayam andha|kāro na viramati yāvat, samam eva palāyāvahai.

3.6 Kiṃ cora|śaṅkayā nagara|rakṣakā māṃ mārayant' îti saṃbhāvayasi?

3.7 N' âiṣā me śaṅkā. bhavaty apy upaśāmyati. anyaḥ punar anartha upasthitaḥ.

3.8 Kasmāt?

3.9 Ayi, asti tāvat, kiṃ tvayā na śrut" âiṣā kiṃvadantī? anyad eva sāmpratam etad duṣṭa|rāṣṭraṃ vartate.

3.10 Uttāmyati me hṛdayam. tat tvaritam āviṣkarotu vayasyaḥ!

3.11 Dāruṇaḥ khalu rājā Śaṅkara|varmā, tato 'pi viṣama eṣo brāhmaṇas tasy' âmātyo dur|ācāra|Jayanto, yābhyāṃ te tapasvino nīl'|âmbarā gṛhītvā piṭṭhvā Veda|bāhyā iti rāṣṭrān nirvāsitāḥ. anyaś ca yo Veda|bāhyas tapasvī labhyate, sa piṭhyate, māryate, badhyate, kṣipyate. tad vayam api teṣām eva madhye gaṇanīyāḥ smaḥ. surāṃ pibāmo, māṃsam bhakṣayāmaḥ, striyaṃ gacchāmaḥ. nanu vayam api sabrahma|cāriṇo nīl'|âmbarāṇām. tat sāmpratam etaṃ sādhaka|veśam ācchādya tvarita|hiṇḍanen' âsminn andhakāre 'lakṣitau gacchāva.

3.12 Evaṃ karavāva.

3.14 Vayasya Kaṅkāla|keto, kathaṃ punar eṣo 'nartha upanataḥ?

3.15 Śṛṇu, asti tāvat sa snātaka|brāhmaṇaḥ saṅkarṣaṇa|nāmā, yena Jinarakṣita|bhikṣu|vasati|kānane viraḥanti gāyanty asaṃkhyāni nīl'|âmbara|mithunāni dṛṣṭāni.

3.16 Tataḥ?

3.17 Tatas tena sa Jayanto jñāpitaḥ. tena ca rājā prabodhitaḥ.

3.18 Tataḥ?

3.19 Tato rājñā sa snātaka|brāhmaṇaḥ Saṅkarṣaṇa ānāyya vivāhya mānaiḥ paṭṭa|bandhena śrī|śabdena ca saṃskārya sakalāyā eva vasundharāyā dharma|rakṣ"|âdhikāre niyuktaḥ. ten' âiṣaḥ prajvālito 'gniḥ.

3.20 Nanu dur|ācāra|Jayantena prajvālita iti ācakṣva.

3.21 Asty ev' âitat. tat sāmpratam kutra gacchāva?

3.22 Nanu yog'|ēśvaryāḥ Kāl'|âgni|śikhāyā agrato vrajāva. tatr' âiṣa upasargaḥ kad" âpi na bādhate.

3.23 S" âpy asmin kāle pālyate?

3.24 Evaṃ śaṅke rājñaḥ parama|vallabhayā sakala|śuddh'|ânta|svāminyā sā str" îti kad" âpi rājñyā Sugandhā|devyā rakṣyate.

3.25 S" âpi rakṣyamāṇā kim āvāṃ rakṣitum pārayati? bhavatu, kasminn api gahvara|paryante dūre dig|antare gacchāva.

3.26 Yad ācaṣṭe vayasyaḥ. tad yāvat prabhātaṃ na pravartate tāvat tvaritaṃ hiṇḍāva.

3.28 Are Śmaśāna|bhūte, yathā mantrayasi. prabhāte punar hiṇḍitum ev' âtra ku|rāṣṭre na pāryate.

3.29 Kasmāt?

3.30 Viṣaye viṣaye nagare nagare grāme grāme sthale sthale Ved'|âdhyayana|śabdena truṭyataḥ karṇau, ājya|gandhena truṭyati ghrāṇaṃ, yajña|dhūmena galato 'kṣiṇī. tad etat ku|rāṣṭraṃ rajanībhir eva laṅghyatām. divasāḥ punaḥ keṣu cid vana|gahaneṣv ativāhyantām.

3.31 Evaṃ nv etat. saṅkarṣaṇa|bhayen' âpi rajanīṣv eva āvābhyāṃ hiṇḍitavyam. divasāḥ punar araṇyeṣv alakṣitābhyāṃ netavyāḥ.

3.33 Are Śmaśāna|bhūte, pravibhaktā iva diśaḥ sakalāḥ. śanair galanti nakṣatrāṇi. tāvad upanataṃ prabhātam. āvayoḥ kiṃ nu kartavyam?

3.36 Āgata eva saṅkarṣaṇa|vyapadeśena jaṅgama āvayor mṛtyuḥ. tad anyatas tvarita|tvaritaṃ gacchāva.

3.40 Ārya, m" âivam śaṅkatāṃ bhavān. durācārair alīka|tāpasair abhibhūyamānaḥ praṇaṣṭa eva punar āryeṇa pratiṣṭhitas trayī|dharmaḥ.

3.42 Ārya, Śaiva|vyapadeśena yat kim apy ācaranta etāvat|kālaṃ dṛṣṭā duṣṭās tāpasāḥ. sāmprataṃ punar agaṇitā ārya|pratāpena (°prabhāvena?) te 'pi praviralā bhavanti.

3.45 Yath" āryo mantrayate.

3.47 Teṣām api sa kalaṅka eva māheśvarāṇāṃ yeṣām vyapadeśena te vyavaharanti.

3.50 Yuktaṃ nv idam.

3.52 Yad ārya ājñāpayati. ārya, praṇaṣṭā rāṣṭrāt. anyaḥ punaḥ ko 'pi praṇidhiḥ saṃbhrānta āryam anviṣyann āgataḥ. tad atra āryaḥ pramāṇam.

3.55 Jayatu bhaṭṭakaḥ! ye nāma māheśvarā māṃsa|śīdhu|dāsī|vyavahāra|śīlā nīl'|âmbara|kiṃ|vadantīm eva śrutvā te sakalā rāṣṭrāt praṇaṣṭāḥ. anye punaḥ śuddha|tapasvino 'pi śaṅkitāś calituṃ pravṛttāḥ. atra bhaṭṭakaḥ pramāṇam.

3.57 Yad bhaṭṭaka ājñāpayati.

3.58 Aho, āryasya prabhāva ucchalitaḥ.

3.60 Yad ārya ājñāpayati.

3.64 Ete khalu āryeṇa niyuktāḥ pradhāna|puruṣā udghoṣayanto gatāḥ.

3.67 Yath" āryo mantrayati. praśānta|ramaṇīyaṃ tapo|vanam idaṃ no dṛśyate.

3.72 Aham apy ātmānam utpatantaṃ Brahma|bhūyaṃ paśyāmi.

3.81 Jayatu jayatu bhaṭṭārakaḥ! eṣa khalu ko 'pi vṛddhaḥ paṇḍitaḥ sva|garvam udvahann āśramam imam upahasann aneka|śiṣya|parivāritaḥ †. . . † kurvann ita āgataḥ. tad atra bhaṭṭārakaḥ pramāṇam.

4.25 Ārya, asty ev' âitat. tath" âpi cirāt prabhṛti pravṛtto yathā|sthitaḥ saṃvyavahāro rakṣyate. kim atr' āryo visaṃṣṭhulaḥ? tat sāmpratam prekṣatāṃ Pāñcarātrika|pramukha|mahā|paṇḍita|śata|sahasra|sambādham imaṃ pradeśam āryaḥ.

4.31 Yad ājñāpayati.

4.46 Ady' êdaṃ sabhā|madhya āryasy' ôpaveśana|sthānaṃ tiṣṭhati. tat praviśatu bhavān.

NOTES

Bold *references are to the English text;* ***bold italic*** *references are to the Sanskrit text. An asterisk (*) in the body of the text marks the word or passage being annotated.*

1.26 The First Act of Jayánta's play begins with an introductory scene *(viṣkambhaka)*, set in the garden of a Buddhist monastery, most probably in or near Srinagar. The characters are: a Buddhist monk, who is a distinguished scholar (his name, Dharmóttara, echoes the name of the great logician of the eighth century, cf. *Āgama/ḍambara (ed. pr.)*, p. xxiv; *Rāja/taraṅgiṇī* 4.498.), well versed in the teaching of the Buddha, confident in his knowledge, and his disciple, who is ready to learn, although perhaps not blessed with great acumen. The disciple speaks *Śaurasenī*, one of the literary Prakrit languages used in classical Indian dramas.

1.38 The Buddhist opponent in the *Nyāya/mañjarī* (vol.II, p. 298) calls the attachment to a Self "the royally anointed, principal delusion" *(mūrdh'/âbhiṣiktaḥ prathamo mohaḥ)*, the termination of which entails that the attachment to anything belonging to a Self *(ātmīya/graha)* also ceases. The realization of having no Self *(nairātmya/darśana)* is said to be the door to Nirvana, and the way leading to it is to establish that all things are momentary, which helps one to realize that cognition, too, has no permanent substratum *(āśraya)* such as a Self.

1.44 The disciple's question alludes to a common objection against the Buddhist position: if there is no permanent substratum, i.e., no Self, functioning as the basis of the stream of cognitions, the one who performs an action and the one who experiences its result cannot be the same person. This would entail the impossibility of karmic retribution and all other activities (e.g., memory) that require the permanence of the agent's self-identity. According to the Buddhist position, the connection between actions and their results is established on the basis of causality alone, without any need for a stable Self. In fact, causality is possible only in the case of momentary entities, and this is precisely what the monk is going to demonstrate.

1.46 The monk's exposition of the doctrine of momentariness is based on two well-known arguments: "the inference of momentariness from the perishing nature of produced entities" (*vināśitv'|ânumāna*) and "the inference of momentariness from the existence of things" (*sattv'|ânumāna*). Cf. *Hetubindu* p. 4*, 6f.: "Whatever is existent must be momentary. If it were not momentary, because non-momentariness contradicts causal efficacy, it would be deprived of the condition of being a real thing, since this condition has causal efficacy as its defining mark." *(yat sat tat kṣaṇikam eva, akṣaṇikatve 'rtha|kriyā|virodhāt tal|lakṣaṇaṃ vastutvaṃ hīyate.)*

1.47 Cf. *Pramāṇavārtika with svavṛtti* (GNOLI) p. 84, v. 166ab.

1.48 In the following verses the Monk puts forward "the inference of momentariness from the perishing nature of things" *(vināśitv'|ânumāna)*.

1.48 **Useless**, if the pot is perishable by itself, and **incapable**, if the pot has an imperishable nature.

1.49 No pot exists, only the series of momentary "pot-phases."

1.50 The translation of the disciples's speech is based on a reading containing several conjectures.

1.56 **Delicious meals served in the monastery** were one of the main attractions of Buddhism according to satirical literature.

1.62 Pronunciation *(śikṣā)*, ritual *(kalpa)*, grammar *(vyākaraṇa)*, explanation of obscure words *(nirukta)*, prosody *(chandas)* and astronomy *(jyotis)*.

1.62 Vedic hermeneutics.

1.62 The graduate's career starts as a glorious campaign against heretics, but by the fourth act it will prove to be a complete failure for the representatives of Vedic orthodoxy.

1.63 The *Mīmāṃsaka* looks upon the Buddha as simply the mortal son of a human king.

1.66 I.e., not favorable to hold a debate with the Buddhists.

1.70 The following description of a gorgeous Buddhist monastery might seem exaggerated, but we know from the *Rāja/taraṅgiṇī* that several Kashmirian *vihāra*s were very rich indeed, owing to generous donations. The treasures of Buddhist monasteries often aroused the interest of Kashmirian kings, who plundered and sometimes, just for good measure, even burned down some of the *vihāras*. These atrocities became more frequent from the end of the tenth century. King Shánkara·varman, whom Jayánta served as an adviser (*amātya*), often resorted to confiscations in order to fill his treasury, and *vihāras* like the one described by the graduate and his pupil could easily become a choice morsel for the king. On the other hand, the high taxes introduced during his reign were probably very effective in holding the rich back from making further donations.

1.79 Brahmanical invective against Buddhism insinuates that as soon as Buddhist monks think they are out of the range of the pious brahmins' severe sight they fling themselves wholeheartedly into pleasures. Public censure is the only retarding force.

1.86 Satire insinuates not just that Buddhist monks run after women and drink wine, but also (what is even worse) that they pretend the opposite is the case. Hypocrisy is one of the most important targets of satire, and not just in classical Indian literature.

1.86 **Meat allegedly fit for vegetarians**, lit. "free from the three conditions of impurity," this means that the monks have neither seen nor heard that the meat has been prepared for them, nor do they have any doubts in this respect.

1.87 The following two verses are in *Māhārāṣṭrī*, one of the literary Prakrit languages.

1.103 The grammatical rule in question is *Aṣṭādhyāyī* 1.4.29. Patañjali's examples for the use of the verb *śru-* with the genitive-case ending are *(Mahā/bhāṣya ad loc.)*: *naṭasya śṛṇoti, granthikasya śṛṇoti*, "He hears from the actor, he hears from the narrator."

1.104 Angle brackets mark text supplied by the editor.

1.140 The graduate's objection asserts that the Buddhist "inference of momentariness from the existence of things" *(sattv'/ânumāna)* is not valid because of the fault of "the impossibility of drawing a conclusion due to exclusiveness of the logical reason" *(asādhāraṇ'/ânaikāntikatā)*. The classical example of this fallacy is the fifth syllogism in Dig·naga's *hetu/cakra*: "Sound is eternal because of its audibility," *(śabdo nityaḥ śrāvaṇatvāt)*. The problem with this syllogism is that the logical reason or middle term *(hetu)*, namely "audibility," belongs exclusively to the subject or minor term *(pakṣa)*, namely "sound," and therefore it is impossible to produce an example *(dṛṣṭ'/ânta)* which is different from the subject *(pakṣa)*. In the case of the syllogism "everything is momentary because of its existence" *(sattv'/ânumāna)*, we face a similar problem, since all existing things are part of the minor term *(pakṣa)*, and nothing else is left to serve as a similar instance *(sa/pakṣa)*. On the other hand, the Buddhist cannot show a counterexample *(vi/pakṣa)*, either, since the thing that does not possess the inferential mark *(hetu)*, namely "existence," is nonexistent in this case. Compare with the standard Indian example of syllogism: "this mountain is fire-possessing, because it is smoke-possessing, like a kitchen *(sa/pakṣa)*, unlike a pond *(vi/pakṣa)*." Cf. MIMAKI 1976, pp. 46ff.

1.141 This means that it is possible to show the concomitance of "existence" *(sattva)* and "momentariness" *(kṣaṇikatva)* in the following way: "something that is not momentary does not exist."

1.142 **Existence** is nothing else but causal efficacy for the Buddhist.

1.142 The monk replies to the graduate's objection by putting forward "a means of valid cognition which refutes the possibility of the opposite of the property to be proven co-occurring with the proving property, i.e., the logical reason *(hetu)*" *(sādhya/viparyaya/bādhaka/pramāṇa)*. In the case of the syllogism "everything is momentary because of its existence" *(sattvānumāna)*, this means to establish that the assertion "something that is not momentary exists" is not valid.

1.144 The invariable concomitant property in question is gradual and instantaneous efficacy.

1.147 Ratna·kirti's *Sthira/siddhi/dūṣaṇa* illustrates how causality operates in the stream of consciousness (118,14 in MIMAKI 1976, p. 164): "To explain, the determination of the ascertainment of causality is also well-established resorting to the stream of consciousness which consists in the relation between the material cause and its effect, so why should one resuscitate the Self? First of all, the ascertainment of causality in that stream presents no problem. Still, to go into further details, the determination of positive concomitance in the form of 'when there is A, there is B' comes about through a cognition of an object that exists subsequently (C^B), which cognition is the effect (*upādeya*) of another determining cognition (C^A, being the material cause, *upādāna* of C^B) of an object that existed previously (A), and which cognition, (i.e., C^B) contains the impression imprinted by that (i.e., C^A)." *(tathā hi, upādān'/ôpādeya/bhāva/sthita/citta/santatim apy āśrity' êyaṃ vyavasthā susth" êti katham ātmānaṃ pratyujjīvayatu? tatra kārya/kāraṇa/bhāva/pratītis tāvad anākulā. tath" âpi prāg/bhāvi/vastu/niścaya/jñānasy' ôpādeya/bhūtena tad/arpita/saṃskāra/garbheṇa paścād/bhāvi/vastu/jñānen' âsmin sat' îdaṃ bhavat' îti niścayo janyate.)*

1.149 I.e., in the state of affairs the Buddhists assert.

1.149 I.e., among the cognition-phases belonging to the same continuum.

1.153 Note the similarity between the Buddhist's "means of valid cognition which refutes the possibility of the opposite of the property to be proven co-occurring with the proving property, i.e., the logical reason *(hetu)*" *(sādhya/viparyaya/bādhaka/pramāṇa)*, and the graduate's claim that "the proving property inheres in a locus that possesses the opposite of the property to be proved" *(sādhya/viparyaya/sādhana)*. In other words, the Buddhist put forth an argument that refuted that non-momentary entities exist, while the *Mīmāṃsaka* proves that only those things exist which are non-momentary, since only permanent things have causal efficacy, which is a defining characteristic of existence.

1.158 I.e., both for perishing and for arising.

1.159 I.e., the assumed cause of destruction, such as a hammer.

1.159 Such as the continuum of shard-phases, and not of the perishing of the pot. The Buddhist certainly denies that perishing is an effect.

1.159 I.e., it cannot be otherwise accounted for.

1.160 This is possibly a reference to the view of the *Mīmāṃsakas*, who hold that when one pronounces the eternal *śabda* it is only manifested, and not actually produced, so it is different from other effects.

1.166 I.e., just as the pot is not destroyed, as you claim, according to our position.

1.173 I.e., in the case of the perception of someone who is not winking.

1.177 I.e., "That thing is blue."

1.181 Namely cognition, word and fire.

1.181 Cf. *Svopajña/vṛtti ad Vākya/padīya* 1.12 (VP(V) 1966, p. 43): "In this world there are three lustres, three lights which illuminate their own form and the form of other things: namely, that which is called *jātavedas*, i.e. fire, that which is the inner light inside men, i.e. consciousness, and that which illuminates both shining entities (that is all the three lights) and non-shining ones (e.g. pots), and which light is called 'word.' " *(iha trīṇi jyotīṃṣi trayaḥ prakāśāḥ sva/rūpa/para/rūpayor avadyotakāḥ. tad yathā, yo 'yaṃ jātavedā yaś ca puruṣesv āntaraḥ prakāśo yaś ca prakāś'/âprakāśayoḥ prakāśayitā śabdākhyaḥ prakāśaḥ.)*

1.181 I.e., when the object is grasped.

1.181 I.e., in the way speckled cows are established through **positive and negative concomitance** to be cows.

1.185 As we shall see, the graduate is going to postpone bathing yet again, because he cannot help entering into a discussion with potential opponents, which also means that he is postponing lunch, to the great regret of his pupil.

2.1 The theme of the following introductory scene is not without parallels in Sanskrit dramatic literature. Among the dramatists preceding Jayánta are two examples one might think of: Harsha's *Nāg'/ānanda* (Third Act) and Bhava·bhuti's *Mālatī/ Mādhava* (Seventh Act).

2.2 The dogsbody speaks *Māgadhī*, the mendicant and the nun speak *Śaurasenī*, two literary Prakrit languages.

2.4 Pulling out the hair in five handfuls is part of the ceremony *(dīkṣā)* that initiates the aspirant into Jain mendicancy (see JAINI p. 245). Both Buddhist and Brahmanical authors frequently refer to this practice as the most striking example of the various "unnecessary" austerities of the Jains.

2.6 I.e., both this life and the next one, together with their pleasures.

2.7 Both the reading and the interpretation of this sentence are uncertain.

2.19 The meaning of this expression is not certain.

2.20 The interpretation of this sentence is uncertain. Judging from the context, it may mean something like "So our lucky star has risen."

2.50 From the Jain standpoint, it seems that the monk has fallen victim to one of the "attitudes that spoil the correct (i.e., Jain) view" (*samyaktva/dūṣaṇas*), namely "uncertainty" *(vicikitsā)*.

2.62 In Sanskrit the pun is based on the double meaning of *prastuta*: "praised" and "declared as the subject of discussion."

2.67 "Many-sidedness" *(anek'/ânta/vāda)* was perhaps the best-known concept of Jain philosophy for Brahmanical and Buddhist thinkers. It claims that every single entity possesses innumerable characteristics or natures, even mutually incompatible ones. The soul, for example, is eternal with respect to its qualities (which inhere forever in their substance), but it is non-eternal with respect to the modes of these qualities (which last for only a moment) (cf. JAINI p. 90; UNO pp. 423f.). Even existence and nonexistence are present simultaneously in the object. For example, a pot is existent inasmuch as it is black, which also means that it is not red, blue, etc. On the other hand, a pot is nonexistent inasmuch as it is red, blue, etc., that is, not black. This means that the pot is characterized by all colors in a positive or a negative way, and the same can be said about its other attributes as well. This also explains why the knowledge of a single thing in all its aspects entails the knowledge of all things.

2.84 The second half of this line cannot be deciphered. The whole verse seems to be in *Māhārāṣṭrī*, a literary Prakrit language.

2.95 According to Bha·sarva·jña, a thinker of the *Nyāya* school, Jainism and other heretical religions first spread among the lowborn, but later certain slow-witted and impoverished brahmins also showed interest in their teachings about the cessation of suffering *(duḥkh'/ôpakṣaya)* (*Nyāya/bhūṣaṇa*, p. 393).

2.107 Jains distinguished ten *vikṛtis*, i.e., certain types of food that have changed their nature, or, according to the traditional interpretation, "that by which the tongue is perverted": milk *(kṣīra)*, curd *(dadhi)*, butter *(navanīta)*, ghee *(ghṛta)*, oil *(taila)*, molasses *(guḍa)*, alcohol *(madya)*, honey *(madhu)*, meat *(māṃsa)*, and the first three cookings of rice in a pan filled with ghee or oil *(avagāhima)* (see WILLIAMS pp. 39f.). Four of these *vikṛtis* are considered unfit to be eaten *(abhakṣyas)*: the three "m"s (alcohol, honey, meat: *madya, madhu, māṃsa*) and butter (see WILLIAMS p. 54, 110). Curd, milk and ghee do not seem to have been forbidden.

2.112 I.e., the Buddha.

2.113 I.e., "one who has fared well."

2.113 These statements sound suspiciously like a parody of the Jain "doctrine of maybe" *(syād/vāda)*, which asserts that everything can be looked at from many different points of view.

2.113 *Ārhata* can mean both Buddhist and Jain ("follower of the Venerable One").

2.113 In the *Harṣa/carita* (p. 89), red *(kāṣāya)* is associated with the followers of *Sāṅkhya (kāpilaṃ matam)*. *Yājñavalkya/smṛti* (3.157), however, prescribes wearing red *(kāṣāya/dhāraṇa)* for ascetics in general who strive for liberation.

2.113 In the majority of texts written by the followers of Brahmanical religions we find a lack of comprehension and the expression of actual disgust with regard to Jain doctrine and practice. The Jains were certainly aware of this repugnance and its dangerous influence on the mind of the mendicants. One of the "attitudes that spoil the correct view" (*samyaktva/dūṣaṇas*) is called *vicikitsā*, which can be interpreted as becoming doubtful about the effectiveness of the various self-mortifications with regard to the final goal: deliverance, but it can also refer to the disgust that learned people feel toward Jain monks *(vidvaj/jugupsā)*.

2.113 It has not been possible to interpret the reading of the manuscripts.

2.113 On the color of the ascetic brahmin student's garment see *Āpastamba/dharma/sūtra* 1.1.2.41–1.1.3.1.

2.113 The mendicant describes an immense crowd of ascetics, some naked, some wearing white, some red, others black robes (*nīl'/âmbaras*), but amalgamated into a single flock by the goal of their journey: the feast. There might be differences among these heretic sects concerning their tenets, but on the mundane level they are just part of the same ever hungry plebs—at least, this is what the brahmin Jayánta insinuates. While "Jains took great pains to establish and maintain an identity for themselves that was distinct both from Hindu society and from the Buddhists as well," observes GRANOFF (1994 p. 258), "throughout classical and medieval times Jains and Buddhists had been closely linked together by all of their opponents."

2.120 **Lovely**: or "ingenious."

2.121 We know from the *Nyāya/mañjarī* that King Shánkara·varman banned the sect of the black-blankets (*nīl'/âmbaras*, *Nyāya/mañjarī*, vol. I, p. 649.4–7). The same sect was extirpated by King Bhoja of *Dhārā* (1018–1060), as it is related in the *Purātana/prabandha/saṅgraha* (p. 19, *Nīla/paṭa/vadha/prabandha*). Other sources mentioning the black-blankets are referred to in WEZLER pp. 346f. According to GRÖNBOLD they were Christian missionaries. The language of their song in the play is *Apabhraṃśa*. Unfortunately, both manuscripts are very lacunose at this point, which makes the interpretation of the song extremely difficult.

2.125 Both the reading and the interpretation of this verse is highly tentative.

2.127 I am following Raghavan and Thakur's reading and interpretation.

2.129 It has not been possible to interpret the second half of this verse. It is also uncertain if the fragment *ṇira* belongs to the same verse.

2.131 Both the reading and the interpretation of this verse are conjectural.

2.133 I have conjectured a lacuna at this point, since nothing seems to rhyme with *viṇu*. *satattu* may be the corrupted form of the rhyming word, or it may rather belong to the next verse.

2.135 Again, the rhyming word (possibly an imperative) seems to be missing.

2.143 **Great Vow** is probably a reference to the *kāpālika Śaiva* ascetic observance of the skull *(kapāla/vrata)*. On the other hand, the learned graduate might also allude to the ancient solemn Vedic ritual, which involved joyful singing, music and dance, as well as an obscene altercation and sexual intercourse between a celibate Veda-student *(brahma/cārin)* and a prostitute.

3.1 "Worshippers in all these Śaiva cults [i.e., the *Siddhānta*, the *Netra/nātha* cult, the *Svacchanda/bhairava* cult, the *Trika*, and the *Krama*] were of one of two kinds. This was a matter of individual choice and it determined both the form of initiation received and the form of the subsequent ritual discipline. On the one hand were those whose chosen goal was nothing but liberation *(mokṣaḥ)* from the bondage of transmigration *(saṃsāraḥ)*. On the other hand were those who elected to pursue supernatural powers and effects *(siddhiḥ)* while they lived and—or at least—to experience fulfilment in the enjoyment of rewards *(bhogaḥ)* in a paradisal world of their choice, either in this life through Yoga, or after death. So worshippers were either seekers of liberation *(mumukṣuḥ)* or seekers of rewards *(bubhukṣuḥ)*." (SANDERSON 1995, p. 24.) It is the second kind of worshippers we meet in the prelude of the third act (the language they speak is *Māgadhī*, one of the Prakrits used in classical Indian dramas). The *sādhaka*s, "masterers [of powers]" (SANDERSON 1995, ibid.) or "mantra-masterers" (SANDERSON 1995, p. 79, n. 208), were characterized by antinomian behavior in all Shaiva cults, from the *Siddhānta*, which adapted itself to the orthodox norms of purity in the highest degree (see SANDERSON 1985, p. 565), to the more esoteric traditions. In belletristic works *sādhaka*s are usually depicted as evil magicians who practice the black art in the cremation-grounds.

3.58 This may not be the correct interpretation of this sentence. Another translation, suggested by Dr. KATAOKA, could be: "Your power is too strong."

3.65 The inscriptions of the *Śaiva* monasteries in the *Kalacuri-Cedi* country, whose *ācārya*s belonged to the *Mattamayūra* clan, provide important historical parallels to the following description of the ashram (for more details see MIRASHI 1955).

3.69 The color of laughter is white, like the ashes smeared on the ascetic's body.

3.69 The color associated with fame is white.

3.81 The reading of the manuscripts is unclear.

3.83 Vriddhámbhi puts forth the anti-religious, materialistic and hedonist ideas of the *Cārvākas*. The *Mīmāṃsaka* graduate and the *Śaiva* professor defeat their *Cārvāka* opponent with an exemplary division of labor. Dharma·shiva proves the existence of the soul, transmigration and God, while Sankárshana keeps his own counsel: it would indeed be strange if a *Mīmāṃsaka* brought up arguments in support of the existence of an omniscient, omnipotent Creator. But he immediately hurls himself into the fray when the authority of the Veda is to be established, while the *Śaiva ācārya* keeps in the background, perhaps because *Śiva*'s scriptures are nearer to his heart, or because, as he himself points out to the *Mīmāṃsaka*, he would use the *parataḥ/prāmāṇya* argument ("validity is established through another cognition") instead of *svataḥ/prāmāṇya* ("the validity of a cognition is given by itself") to prove the validity of scripture. The moral is that, notwithstanding a few doctrinal differences, *Mīmāṃsakas* and *Saiddhāntika Śaivas* should join their forces to defeat the *nāstikas* and thereby prevent the king from ruling in an inordinately materialistic way.

3.84 The expression *eka/vṛkṣe* (actually a conjecture in the text) often occurs in Tantric context, indicating a suitable place for performing a ritual. Another possible conjecture, suggested by Prof. SANDERSON, is *maru/deśe*, "in the desert."

3.84 I.e., in *Vaiśeṣika* and *Nyāya*.

3.85 Presumably the *Cārvāka*'s behavior is disrespectful because he does not wait to be offered a seat, or, as Prof. SANDERSON pointed out, because he uses impertinently familiar forms of address to both the ascetic and Sankárshana.

3.93 The following verses could also have been spoken from a *Mīmāṃsaka* position.

3.103 *Vākya/padīya* 1.32, also quoted in *Nyāya/mañjarī* vol. I, p. 314. *Bhartṛhari* illustrates this assertion in his commentary to the *Vākya/padīya* (p. 89), e.g., "things such as water in a well feel and look, etc. very different in summer, in winter, or in other seasons" (*grīṣma/hemant'/ādiṣu kūpa/jal'/ādīnām atyanta/bhinnāḥ sparś'/ādayo dṛśyante*, an illustration of difference in time *(kāla/bheda)*, which makes it impossible to infer the exact temperature of the water). Thus, as *Vṛṣabhadeva* notes in his subcommentary, "among all things in the world there might exist such a smoke which does not arise from fire, just as some frogs are born from frogs, others from cow-dung" *(tatra syād api kaś cid dhūmo yo n' âgneḥ, yathā śālūkād api śālūkaḥ, gomayād api)*.

3.105 *Vākya/padīya* 1.42, also quoted in *Nyāya/mañjarī* vol. I, p. 316. Bhartri·hari himself intended to emphasize the importance of scripture with this verse.

3.107 *Vākya/padīya* 1.34, also quoted in *Nyāya/mañjarī* vol. I, p. 316.

3.116 In the standard Indian example of syllogism ("the mountain is fiery because it is smoky"), "mountain" is the subject *(pakṣa)* and "smokiness" is the inferential mark *(liṅga)*. "Smokiness" is invariably comcomitant with "fieriness" ("whatever is smoky is fiery"), just as "non-fieriness" is invariably concomitant with "non-smokiness."

3.124 I.e., the association of the proving property (*hetu*, "smokiness" in the example) and the property to be established (*sādhya*, "fieriness").

3.125 *Nyāya/bhāṣya ad Nyāya/sūtra* 1.1.7 (p. 14).

3.126 I.e., for things we already know through sense perception.

3.129 I.e., from an invariably concomitant thing.

3.134 In the case of the standard Indian example of syllogism ("there is fire on the mountain, because there is smoke on it"), kitchen is adduced as an example of a place (*sapakṣa*, "similar subject") where the invariable concomitance between smoke and fire is directly observable for everyone.

3.136 According to the Buddhist position, not every kind of composite thing presupposes a maker. Cf. *Pramāṇa/vārttika* (Pandey), *pramāṇa/siddhi* 13.

3.137 I.e., the inferential mark.

3.137 In the classic example of inference, the mountain's similarity to the kitchen in the example is only the fact that both possess smoke, and since in the kitchen smoke is always visibly accompanied by fire, we infer that the mountain possesses fire, too.

3.138 According to *Vṛddhāmbhi*, smoke in general allows us to infer fire in general, but pots and mountains are not products in the same way, and thus we cannot say that both require a maker.

3.157 The universe created by God must have a function: it helps souls to gather the fruits of their actions through a long series of rebirths. But this theory comes to nothing if no eternal Self exists attached to our perishable body.

3.165 Cf. BHATTACHARYA, p. 605, IV.2.

3.170 Since our pleasurable and painful experiences are the results of our former deeds, the creation of our body, which is the sine qua non of these experiences, is also determined by karma.

3.182 Therefore if it depended on them they would probably hinder its creation.

3.185 *Mahā/bhārata* 3.31.27.

3.188 More precisely, "cholera of your karma." One might consider emending the text to "*karṇe 'pi sūcīm*," meaning "Endure still a needle in your ear, too, for a moment."

3.200 I.e., the sentence makes sense, but the information it gives is contradicted by perception and other means of valid knowledge.

3.204 For the *Mīmāṃsakas*, ritual injunctions form the essential part of the Veda; everything else is just exegesis.

3.219 E.g., the faulty working of the sense faculties.

3.221 *Vaiśeṣika/sūtra* 1.1.3; 10.21.

3.221 I.e., the person who revealed it.

3.221 *Nyāya/sūtra* 2.1.68.

3.229 As SANDERSON pointed out ("Hinduism," Handout 3, 22. ii. 1999), the same fourfold division of Shaivas in general (1. *Pāśupatas* or *Pāñcārthikas*, 2. *Lākulas* or *Kālamukhas*, 3. *Soma-siddhāntins* or *Kāpālikas* or *Mahāvratins*, and 4. *Śaivas*) also appears in several other texts.

3.230 A similar idea occurs at the end of the play, when the graduate warns against the confusion of various religious traditions.

4.11 This might be a reference to the (now "lost") *Ekāyana/śākhā* (belonging allegedly to the White *Yajur/Veda*), which was regarded by the *Pāñcarātrika*s as the Vedic foundation of their religion, and which they found mentioned in the *Chāndogya-upaniṣad* (7.1.2).

4.11 The *Vaiṣṇava Yāmuna* emphasizes that one should not judge *Śaiva* and *Vaiṣṇava tantra*s by the same standard just because they happen to share the name *"tantra"* (likewise we do not put an equals sign between killing a brahmin and performing a Horse Sacrifice just because both are "actions," see *Āgama/prāmāṇya* p. 101). The *Śaiva* scriptures—and on this point *Yāmuna* shares the view of the *Mīmāṃsakas*—are indeed heretical (*Āgama/prāmāṇya* p. 91).

4.16 I.e., having married a woman from a higher caste.

4.18 As Kálhana relates (*Rāja/taraṅgiṇī* 3.439ff.) the *Raṇa/svāmin-temple* was built by King *Raṇ'/āditya*. According to a legend, the queen made a certain holy man *(siddha)* called *Brahman* consecrate the images of the *Raṇa/svāmin* and the *Raṇ'/ēśvara* temples. Having consecrated the *liṅga*, *Brahman* placed himself on the seat *(pīṭha)* of the idol in the *Raṇa/svāmin* temple (*Rāja/taraṅgiṇī* 3.458: *sa svayaṃ pīṭham avātarat*). In honor of this holy man the queen built the splendid *Brahma/maṇḍapa* (ibid. 3.459), which might be connected with the *Brahma/dvīpa* mentioned in our text.

4.19 *Sātvata* is another name of the *Vaiṣṇava Pāñcarātrika*s / *Bhāgavata*s.

4.28 *Śaṅkaravarman* used the same name on his *Kārkota*-style coins (see Ray).

4.35 Chakrin is Vishnu manifest as the wielder of the Sudárshana discus.

4.36 Rathángin is Vishnu manifest as the wielder of the Sudárshana discus.

4.52 The four Vedas, the six ancillary sciences (*ved'/âṅgas*), *Dharma/śāstra*, *Mīmāṃsā*, *Nyāya*, and the *Purāṇas*.

4.66 Cf. *Baudhāyana/dharma/sūtra* 1.13.30 (prescribing purification with *darbha* grass and water, *darbhair adbhiḥ prakṣālanam*, at the *Agni/hotra* and other rituals); also *Śata/patha/brāhmaṇa* 5.5.4.22.

4.66 Another possible interpretation has been suggested by Dr. Kataoka: "The *darbha* grass of beginninglessness has swept away the dust of both its author and its invalidation by another *pramāṇa*."

4.68 In the form of a subsequent cognition.

4.68 The instrument of cognition, e.g., the sense organ in the case of sense perception.

4.68 I.e., heaven.

4.69 I.e., as the first perception has found it.

4.73 We remember that Vyasa composed the Maha·bharata, Valmíki the Ramáyana, etc.

4.74 The tradition that Vyasa was the author of the Maha·bhárata might also have been created by explanatory exegesis *(artha/vāda)*.

4.76 For a description of the *Aṣṭakā* (a domestic ritual honoring the ancestors), see, e.g., *Āśvalāyana/gṛhya/sūtra* 2.4, cf. *Manu/smṛti* 4.119, 4.150. Shábara and Kumárila in their commentary to *Mīmāṃsā/sūtra* 1.3 refer to the *Aṣṭakā* as an example of a ritual that is prescribed in *Smṛti* texts but is not enjoined in the Vedas themselves. According to the view of *Prābhākara Mīmāṃsā*, the Vedic texts from which such prescriptions derive had never actually been perceptible to the compilers of these *Smṛti* texts, but only always inferable *(nity'/ânumeya)* on the basis of the acceptance of these *Smṛti*s by the moral majority, *mahā/jana* (see POLLOCK 1997, pp. 409f).

4.76 I.e., the difference between inferring a Vedic text as the basis of a ritual prescribed only in the *Smṛti*s, and inferring God as the maker of Vedic compositions.

4.77 I.e., that author of the Veda.

4.77 I.e., as the basis of *Smṛti* texts.

4.78 I.e., the memory as articulated in the *Smṛti* text. According to this theory, the authors of *Smṛti* texts always recalled the Vedic injunctions pertaining to the ritual they were prescribing, and even if we do not possess that Vedic injunction anymore we must infer that it was the basis of the *Smṛti* text.

4.78 No composite entity can exist without a maker.

4.78 I.e., *Smṛti*.

4.81 Those who are learned in the Veda also follow such *Smṛti* texts as Manu's Lawbook.

4.82 *Śloka/vārttika, vāky'/âdhikaraṇa* 366. This implies that the study of the Veda has no beginning, and thus the Veda has no author.

4.86 I.e., their effort exhibited in performing Vedic rituals.

4.86 I.e., a Vedic text as the ground of that *Smṛti*.

4.88 The *Viśva/jit* is a one-day Soma-sacrifice *(ek'/âha)*, which requires the sacrificer to pay extensive fees to the officiants (see MYLIUS, Glossar s.v., ibid. pp. 301, 357). As the name of this sacrifice suggests, it is performed "in order to conquer everything" (*Taittirīya-saṃhitā* 7.1.10.4: *sarvasy' âbhijityai*).

4.88 I.e., heaven.

4.89 I.e., to expect an appropriate result.

4.90 I.e., whenever we understand the meaning of an injunction.

4.90 I.e., the injunction's author.

4.90 It is the author who knows and communicates the meaning.

4.100 Quoting *Nyāya/mañjarī* vol. I, p. 636.8–11 (v.l. *pratītiḥ* for *prasiddhiḥ*).

4.108 Cf. *Kāṭhaka-saṃhitā* 11.4; *Maitrāyaṇī-saṃhitā* 2.2.2.

4.108 Cf. *Tāṇḍya/mahā/brāhmaṇa* 17.12.1; *Śāṅkhāyana/śrauta/sūtra* 15.10.1.

4.115 Quoting *Nyāya/mañjarī* vol. I, p. 640.17–18, cf. *Mahā/bhārata* 12.336.77.

4.122 *Bhagavad/gītā* 10.41.

4.123 See *Yoga/sūtra* 1.23, 1.28–29, 2.1, 2.32, 2.45.

4.126 Contrast with the *Mīmāṃsaka* position, according to which when the heterodox proclaim that their scriptures have authors they necessarily admit that these scriptures cannot be authoritative.

4.128 *Kaṭha* is connected with a particular Vedic recension.

4.136 Similarly, as Yámuna argues, just because the *Pāñcarātrika*s follow the prescriptions of a different, but equally valid, Vedic school, i.e., the *Ekāyana/śākhā*, it does not follow that they are not brahmins at all (see *Āgama/prāmāṇya* p. 169).

4.136 The *Sautrāmaṇī* is an expiatory sacrifice that involves the offering of alcohol. (See Mylius, Glossar s.v., ibid. p. 144; *Śata/patha/brāhmaṇa* 5.5.4.)

4.141 I.e., the *Pañcarātra.*

4.141 I.e., *Bhāgavata.*

4.141 I.e., non-Vedic.

4.147 Jayánta observes in the *Nyāya/mañjarī* (vol. I, p. 645) that all of Kumárila's arguments proving that *Smṛti* texts are based on the Veda can be applied to other scriptures as well.

4.148 I.e., *Smṛti.*

4.149 I.e., respectable people accept the authority of the *Pañcarātra*.

4.151 I.e., among the performers of the pious acts enjoined in the Veda on the one hand, and in the *Pañcarātra* on the other. The *Pāñcarātrika* does hold that the postulation of a Vedic basis is appropriate since the performers of these Tantric rituals are also brahmins. On the other hand, a *Mīmāṃsaka* would certainly never acknowledge even the twice-born status of the *Bhāgavatas*.

4.151 I.e., the inference of a Vedic text as the basis of *Pañcarātra*.

4.153 I.e., the practice of Vedic and *Pāñcarātra* religion.

4.153 I.e., Vedic and *Pāñcarātra* rites.

4.155 I.e., the association of a sacred text, e.g. the *Manu/smṛti*.

4.155 I.e., the case of the *Pañcarātra*.

4.155 As Kumárila points out, although such *Smṛti* passages as the one prescribing the *Aṣṭakā* ritual can be inferred to be based on lost Vedic texts, this fact does not mean that any scripture can be nominated for having a Vedic basis. See *Tantra/vārttika ad Mīmāṃsā/sūtra* 1.3.2 (TV^{P}, p. 265; TV^{A}, p. 164).

4.159 I.e., among scriptures.

4.163 I.e., by a *Cārvāka* materialist.

4.163 The *Mīmāṃsaka* Kumárila holds that every anti-Vedic scripture must be explicitely rejected. It is not enough to show that the adherents of Vedic religion have always been learned and respectable, since the heretics can assert the same about their own followers (*Tantra/vārttika ad Mīmāṃsā/sūtra* 1.3.4 TV^P, p. 329, $TV^Ā$, p. 194).

4.169 I.e., because of the extension of the category "valid scripture" to virtually everything.

4.171 This would certainly be an unacceptably generous view for the *Mīmāṃsaka Kumārila*, in whose interpretation *Mīmāṃsā/sūtra* 1.3.5–6 excludes such a liberal position (*Tantra/vārttika* ad *Mīmāṃsā/sūtra* 1.3.5–6, TV^P, p. 360–362, $TV^Ā$, p. 201–203).

BIBLIOGRAPHY

Aṣṭādhyāyī = Böhtlingk

[*Āgamaḍambara (ed. pr.)*] *Āgamaḍambara, otherwise called Ṣaṇmatanāṭaka of Jayanta Bhaṭṭa*, edited by Dr. V. Raghavan and Prof. Anantalal Thakur, Mithila Research Institute, Darbhanga, 1964.

Āgamaprāmāṇya of Yāmunācārya, ed. by M. Narasimhachary, Gaekwad's Oriental Series No. 160, Oriental Institute, Baroda, 1976.

Āśvalāyana Gṛhyasūtra, ed. with Sanskrit Commentary of Nārāyaṇa, English Translation, Introduction, and Index, by Narendra Nath Sharma, Delhi, 1997^2.

Āśvalāyana-Śrautasūtra. Erstmalig vollständig übersetzt, erläutert und mit Indices versehen von Klaus Mylius, Wichtrach, 1994.

Kâṭhakam. Die Saṃhitâ der Kaṭha-Çâkhâ, herausgegeben von Leopold von Schroeder, Erstes Buch, Leipzig, 1900.

Kādambarīkathāsara, Kāvyamālā 11, ed. Pt. Durgāprasād and Kāśīnāth Pāṇḍuraṅg Parab, Bombay, 1886.

[$TV^{Ā}$] *Śrīmaj-Jaimini-praṇīte Mīmāṃsādarśane ādita ārabhya dvitīyādhyāyaprathamapādāntaḥ prathamo bhāgaḥ / tatra ca prathamas Tarkapādaḥ mīmāṃsākaṇṭhīravamīmāṃsāratnetyādipadavībhūṣitaśrī- Vaidyanātha- Śāstri- praṇīta- Prabhābhidha- vyākhyāsameta- Śābarabhāṣyopetaḥ, dvitīyapādaprabhṛti śrī- Kumārila- Bhaṭṭa- viracita- Tantravārtikākhya- vyākhyāsahita- Śābarabhāṣyasametaś ca /*, ed. Subbā Śāstrī, vol. I, Ānandāśrama-Saṃskṛta-Granthāvaliḥ 97, Trivandrum, 1929.

[TV^{P}] *The Mīmāṃsā Darśana of Maharṣijaimini, with Śābarabhāṣya of Śabaramuni with the commentaries of Tantravārtika of Kumārila Bhaṭṭa and its commentary Nyāyasudhā of Someśvara Bhatta, Bhāṣyavivaraṇa of Govindāmṛtamuni and Bhāvaprakāśikā, the Hindi translation by Mahāprabhulāla Gosvāmī*, edited with an introduction by Mahāprabhulāla Gosvāmī, Prācyabhāratī Series 22, vol. I, Tara Book Agency, Varanasi, 1984.

Tattvopaplavasiṃha of Jayarāśi Bhaṭṭa, ed. Pt. S.L. Sanghavi and Prof. Rasiklal C. Parikh, Gaekwad Oriental Series 87, Baroda, 1940.

Táṇdya Mahábráhmaṇa; with the commentary of Sáyaṇa Ácharya, ed. Ánandachandra Vedántavágíśa, vol. II, Calcutta, 1874.

[*Nyāyabhūṣaṇa*] *Śrīmadācāryabhāsarvajñapraṇītasya Nyāyasārasya svopajñaṃ vyākhyānaṃ Nyāyabhūṣaṇam*, ed. SWAMI YOGINDRANANDA, Varanasi, 1968.

[*Nyāyamañjarī*, vol. I, II] *Nyāyamañjarī of Jayantabhaṭṭa, with Ṭippaṇi – Nyāyasaurabha by the editor*, critically edited by K. S. VARADACHARYA, vol. I, Oriental Research Institute Series No. 116, Mysore, 1969; vol. II, Oriental Research Institute Series No. 139, Mysore, 1983.

[*Nyāyasūtra, Nyāyabhāṣya*] *Gautamīyanyāyadarśana with Bhāṣya of Vātsyāyana*, edited by ANANTALAL THAKUR, Nyāyacaturgranthikā Vol. I, Indian Council of Philosophical Research, New Delhi, 1997.

Purātanaprabandhasaṅgraha, ed. by JINAVIJAYA MUNI, Singhi Jaina Series 2, Calcutta, 1936.

[*Pramāṇavārtika*] *The Pramāṇavārttikam of Ācārya Dharmakīrti, with the commentaries Svopajñavṛtti of the Author and Pramāṇavārttikavṛtti of Manorathanandin*, edited by R. C. PANDEYA, Motilal Banarsidass, Delhi, 1989.

Pramāṇavārtika with svavṛtti (GNOLI) = GNOLI 1960.

Baudhāyanadharmasūtram, Govindasvāmipraṇītavivaraṇasametam, ed. Cinnasvāmiśāstrī, Kashi Sanskrit Series, Karmakāṇḍa Section no. 11, Benares, 1991.

[*Manusmṛti* with Medhātithi's comm.] *Manusmṛti with the 'Manubhaṣya' of Medhātithi*, vols. I–II, Sanskrit text, ed. GANGANATH JHA, Second Edition, Motilal Banarsidass, Delhi, 1999.

[*Mahābhārata*] *The Mahābhārata, for the first time critically edited*, ed. V. S. SUKHANTAR (1927–43) and S. K. BELVALKAR (from 1943) with the co-operation of Shrimant Balasaheb Pant PRATINIDHI, R. N. DANDEKAR, S. K. DE, F. EDGERTON, A. B. GAJENDRAGADKAR, P. V. KANE, R. D. KARMAKAR, V. G. PARANJPE, Raghu VIRA, V. K. RAJAVADE, N. B. UTGIKAR, P. L. VAIDYA, V. P. VAIDYA, H. D. VELANKAR, M. WINTERNITZ, R. ZIMMERMAN and other scholars,

19 vols., Poona: Bhandarkar Oriental Research Institute, 1927–1959.

Mâitrâyaṇî Saṃhitâ, herausgegeben von LEOPOLD VON SCHROEDER, Zweites Buch, Leipzig, 1883.

Yājñavalkyasmṛti of Yogīśvara Yājñavalkya, with the Commentary Mitākṣarā of Vijñāneśvara, Notes, Variant Readings, etc., ed. with notes etc. by Narayan Ram Acharya, Fifth Edition, Bombay, 1949.

Yogasūtra of Patañjali with the commentaries of Vyāsa, Vācaspatimiśra, and Vijñānabhikṣu, ed. Nārāyaṇa Miśra, Benares, 1971.

Rājataraṅgiṇī of Kalhaṇa, ed. by VISHVA BANDHU, in collaboration with BHĪMA DEV, K. S. RĀMASWĀMI SĀSTRĪ and S. BHĀSKARAN NAIR. Part I, Taraṅgas I–VII, Hoshiarpur, 1963.

[RT(S)] *Kalhaṇa's Rājataraṅgiṇī*, vol. I–II: translated with an introduction, commentary, and appendices by M. A. STEIN, Motilal Banarsidass, Delhi, 1989 (reprinted from the edition of 1900); vol. III: Sanskrit text with critical notes, edited by M. A. STEIN, Motilal Banarsidass, Delhi, 1988 (reprinted from the Bombay edition of 1892).

[*Vākyapadīya*, VP(V)] *The Vākyapadīya of Bhartṛhari, with the Commentaries Vṛtti and Paddhati of Vṛṣabhadeva*, ed. K. A. SUBRAMANIA IYER, Deccan College, Poona. Kāṇḍa I: 1966.

[*Vaiśeṣikasūtra*] *Vaiśeṣikasūtra of Kaṇāda, with the Commentary of Candrānanda*, ed. Muni ŚRĪ JAMBUVIJAYAJI, Gaekwad's Oriental Series No. 136, Baroda, 1961.

Śābarabhāṣya(F) = FRAUWALLNER 1968. (containing *Śabarabhāṣya* ad *Mīmāṃsāsūtras* I.1.1–5)

[ŚBh(Y)] *Ācārya-Śabarasvāmi-viracitam Jaiminīya-mīmāṃsā-bhāṣyam, ārṣamata-vimarśinyā hindī-vyākhyayā sahitam*, edited by Yudhiṣṭhira Mīmāṃsaka, vol. I., Bahālgaṛh, 1987.

The Śāṅkhāyana Śrauta Sūtra, together with the commentary of Varadattasuta Ānartīya, ed. Alfred Hillebrandt, vol. III, Calcutta, 1897.

[*Ślokavārtika* (with *Tātparyaṭīkā*)] *Ślokavārtikavyākhyā (Tātparyaṭīkā) of Umveka Bhaṭṭa*, edited by S. K. RAMANATHA SASTRI, revised by

K. KUNJUNNI RAJA and R. THANGASWAMY, Madras University Sanskrit Series, No. 13, 1971.

[*Ślokavārtika* (with *Kāśikā*)] *The Mīmāṃsāślokavārtika with the Commentary Kāśikā of Sucaritamiśra*, edited by K. SĀMBAŚIVA ŚĀSTRĪ, Part II, Trivandrum Sanskrit Series No. XCIX, Trivandrum, 1929.

[*Harṣacarita*] *The Harshacarita of Bāṇabhaṭṭa. Text of Uchchhvāsas I–VIII*, edited with an Introduction and Notes by Mahāmahopādhyāya P. V. KANE, Motilal Banarsidass, Delhi, 1997 (reprint of the first edition, 1918).

Hetubindu = STEINKELLNER 1967.

BHATTACHARYA, R. 'Cārvāka Fragments: a New Collection' in *Journal of Indian Philosophy* 30, 2002, pp. 597–640.

BÖHTLINGK, Otto. *Pâṇini's Grammatik herausgegeben, übersetzt, erläutert und mit verschiedenen Indices versehen*, Leipzig, 1887.

GNOLI, Raniero. *The Pramāṇavārttikam of Dharmakīrti. The first chapter with the autocommentary. Text and critical notes*. Serie Orientale Roma XXIII, Roma, 1960.

GRANOFF, Phyllis. 'Being in the Minority: Medieval Jain Reactions to Other Religious Groups' in N. N. Bhattacharya (ed.), *Essays for J. C. Jain*, New Delhi, 1994.

GRÖNBOLD, Günter. 'Blaugekleidet oder Schwarzgekleidet?' in P. Kieffer-Pülz and Jens-Uwe Hartmann (eds.), *Bauddhavidyāsudhākaraḥ. Studies in Honour of Heinz Bechert on the Occasion of His 65th Birthday*, Swisttal-Odendorf, 1997.

HACKER, Paul. 'Jayantabhaṭṭa und Vācaspatimiśra, ihre Zeit und ihre Bedeutung für die Chronologie des Vedānta' in *Alt- und Neu-Indische Studien* 7, 1951, pp. 160–169. (= *Kleine Schriften*, pp. 110–119.)

JAINI, Padmanabh. *The Jaina Path of Purification*. Motilal Banarsidass, Delhi, 1998 (reprint of 1979 edition).

KATAOKA, Kei. *What Really Protects the Vedas? Jayanta on Śāstra-prayojana*. Paper read at the Indological Research Seminar, All Souls College, Oxford, 1999.

Marui, Hiroshi. 'Some Remarks on Jayanta's Writings: Is *Nyāyakalikā* his Authentic Work?' in *The Way to Liberation. Indological Studies in Japan in two volumes, Japanese Studies on South Asia No. 3*, ed. Sengaku Mayeda, vol. I, Manohar, New Delhi, 2000, pp. 91–106.

Mimaki, Katsumi. *La réfutation bouddhique de la permanence des choses (sthirasiddhidūṣaṇa) et la preuve de la momentanéité des choses (kṣaṇabhaṅgasiddhi)*. Publications de l'Institute de Civilisation Indienne, série in-8, fascicule 41, Paris, 1976.

Mirashi, V. V. *Inscriptions of the Kalachuri-Chedi Era*, ed. by Vasudev Vishnu Mirashi, Corpus Inscriptionum Indicarum, vol. IV, Ootacamund, 1955.

Mylius, Klaus = *Āśvalāyana-Śrautasūtra*

Pollock, S. 'The <<Revelation>> of <<Tradition>>: *Śruti, Smṛti*, and the Sanskrit Discourse of Power' in *Lex et Litterae. Studies in Honour of Professor Oscar Botto*, eds. S. Lienhard - I. Piovano, Torino, 1997, pp. 395–417.

Raghavan and Thakur = *Āgamaḍambara (ed. pr.)*

Ray, Sunil Chandra. 'The Identity of the Yaśovarman of Some Mediaeval Coins' in *Journal of the Asiatic Society of Bengal, Letters*, vol. XVII, No. 1, 1951.

Sanderson, Alexis. 'Purity and Power among the Brahmans of Kashmir' in *The Category of the Person*, ed. Michael Carrithers, Steven Collins, and Steven Likes, Cambridge, 1985, pp. 191–216.

— 'Śaivism and the Tantric Traditions' in *The World's Religions / The Religions of Asia*, ed. Friedhelm Hardy, London: Routledge, 1988.

— 'Meaning in Tantric Ritual' in *Essais sur le rituel III. Colloque de centenaire de la section des sciences religieuses de l'Ecole Pratique des Hautes Etudes sous la direction de Anne-Marie Blondeau et Kristofer Schipper*, Louvain-Paris, 1995.

Steinkellner, Ernst. 'Die Literatur des älteren Nyāya' in *Wiener Zeitschrift für die Kunde Süd- und Ostasiens* V, 1961, pp. 149–162.

STEINKELLNER, Ernst. *Dharmakīrti's Hetubinduḥ. Teil I: Tibetischer Text und rekonstruierter Sanskrit-Text.* Veröffentlichungen der Kommission für Sprachen und Kulturen Süd- und Ostasiens (Österreichische Akademie der Wissenschaften), Heft 4, Wien, 1967. *Teil II: Übersetzung und Anmerkungen.* Veröffentlichungen der Kommission für Sprachen und Kulturen Süd- und Ostasiens (Österreichische Akademie der Wissenschaften) Heft 5, Wien, 1967.

UNO, Tomoyuki. 'Ontological Affinity Between the Jainas and the Mīmāṃsakas Viewed by Buddhist Logicians' in *Dharmakīrti's Thought and Its Impact on Indian and Tibetan Philosophy. Proceedings of the Third International Dharmakīrti Conference, Hiroshima, November 4–6, 1997*, edited by Shoryu Katsura, Österreichische Akademie der Wissenschaften, philosophisch-historische Klasse, Denkschriften, 281. Band, Wien, 1999.

WEZLER, Albrecht. 'Zur Identität der *"ācāryāḥ"* und *"vyākhyātāraḥ"* in Jayantabhaṭṭas Nyāyamañjarī' in *Wiener Zeitschrift für die Kunde Südasiens* XIX, 1975, pp. 135–146.

— 'Zur Proklamation religiös-weltanschaulicher Toleranz bei dem indischen Philosophen Jayantabhaṭṭa' in *Saeculum* 27, 1976, pp. 329–347.

WILLIAMS, R. *Jaina Yoga. A Survey of the Mediaeval Śrāvakācāras*, London, 1963.

INDEX

Sanskrit words are given according to the accented CSL pronuncuation aid in the English alphabetical order. They are followed by the conventional diacritics in brackets.

k	ṭ	t	p	ṅ	n	m	*(Except āḥ/aḥ)* ḥ/r	āḥ	aḥ	*Initial letters:*
k	ṭ	t	p	ṅ	n	ṃ	ḥ	āḥ	aḥ	k/kh
g	ḍ	d	b	ṅ	n	ṃ	r	ā	o	g/gh
k	ṭ	c	p	ṅ	ṃś	ṃ	ś	āś	aś	c/ch
g	ḍ	j	b	ṅ	ñ	ṃ	r	ā	o	j/jh
k	ṭ	ṭ	p	ṅ	ṃṣ	ṃ	ṣ	āṣ	aṣ	ṭ/ṭh
g	ḍ	ḍ	b	ṅ	ṇ	ṃ	r	ā	o	ḍ/ḍh
k	ṭ	t	p	ṅ	ṃs	ṃ	s	ās	as	t/th
g	ḍ	d	b	ṅ	n	ṃ	r	ā	o	d/dh
k	ṭ	t	p	ṅ	n	ṃ	ḥ	āḥ	aḥ	p/ph
g	ḍ	d	b	ṅ	n	ṃ	r	ā	o	b/bh
ṅ	ṇ	n	m	ṅ	n	ṃ	r	ā	o	*nasals* (n/m)
g	ḍ	d	b	ṅ	n	ṃ	r	ā	o	y/v
g	ḍ	d	b	ṅ	n	ṃ	*zero*[1]	ā	o	r
g	ḍ	l	b	ṅ	l̃[2]	ṃ	r	ā	o	l
k	ṭ	c ch	p	ṅ	ñ ś/ch	ṃ	ḥ	āḥ	aḥ	ś
k	ṭ	t	p	ṅ	n	ṃ	ḥ	āḥ	aḥ	ṣ/s
gg h	ḍḍ h	dd h	bb h	ṅ	n	ṃ	r	ā	o	h
g	ḍ	d	b	ṅ/ṅṅ[3]	n/nn[3]	m	r	ā	a[4]	*vowels*
k	ṭ	t	p	ṅ	n	m	ḥ	āḥ	aḥ	*zero*

[1] ḥ or r disappears, and if a/i/u precedes, this lengthens to ā/ī/ū. [2] e.g. tān+lokān=tāl̃ lokān. [3] The doubling occurs if the preceding vowel is short. [4] Except: aḥ+a=o '.